The Devil's Wind

By

Patricia Wentworth
(Mrs. G. F. Dillon)

Author of " A Marriage under the Terror," " A Little
More Than Kin," etc.

" When the Sepoys who were taken at Cawnpore were asked why
they had mutinied, they replied : ' Surely it was a madness ; a wind
from the Devil was abroad in Hindustan.' "

G. P. Putnam's Sons
New York and London
The Knickerbocker Press
1912

The Knickerbocker Press, New York

AN ADDRESS

MADAM CLIO:
      I have taken two liberties with the facts
which are your province, and after the modern
manner I hereby make the honourable amend
upon—not in—a white sheet.

That Sereek Dhundoo Punth, commonly known
as the Nana Sahib, had a nephew known as the
Rao Sahib, is a solid fact. I have given him a
half share of English blood, which is fiction.
Those of my readers who have been in India will
understand my motive.

This is the first liberty which I have taken.

I now pass to the second.

Your votaries are in the habit of stating that
the survivors of Cawnpore were four, and four
only—to wit, the four survivors of No. 1 boat,
Major Vibart's.

Some of the said votaries throw in a casual
reference to Mr. Shepherd, but omit to remark
that four and one make five.

May I be permitted to enumerate the persons

who actually did come alive through the siege and massacre?

They are as follows:

1. Captain Mowbray Thompson, Mr. Delafosse, Private Murphy, and Private Sullivan, usually alluded to as the four survivors of Cawnpore.

2. Mr. Shepherd, who left the Entrenchment a few days before the surrender, and was imprisoned by the Nana.

3. Elizabeth Spiers, her mother, brother, and little sister Isabella.

4. Mrs. Eliza Bradshaw and Mrs. Elizabeth Letts. These women, with the Spiers family, owed their escape from the massacre at the Suttee Chowra Ghaut chiefly to the fact that they were dark enough to pass as natives.

5. A native wet nurse.

6. Two European women whose names have always been suppressed.

7. Miss Wheeler, Sir Hugh's youngest daughter, a girl of nineteen. She was carried away by a Mohammedan trooper, and for a long time search was made for her.

The survivors were therefore thirteen in number, without counting the native wet nurse.

I need, therefore, make no apology for the escape of Adela, and in the matter of Richard and Helen I throw myself upon your indulgence.

The boat actually grounded as I have described, and the first great downpour of the rains came on. It might have happened. Next day the boat was captured and taken back to Cawnpore.

For the subsequent wanderings and adventures of Richard and Helen there is ample warrant.

This, Clio, is my apology, and I am,

Your very respectful servant,

PATRICIA WENTWORTH.

CONTENTS

Contents

The Devil's Wind

The Devil's Wind

CHAPTER I

HOW MRS. MIDDLETON DISAPPROVED

> Sometimes a marriage for love,
> Sometimes a marriage for gold,
> Sometimes a head too hot,
> Sometimes a heart too cold.
> Each one seeking his own
> Whether for money or pleasure,
> Leads to a marriage in haste,
> Leads to repentance at leisure.

IN the year 1854 Mrs. Lauriston's London drawing-room was as ugly as contemporary taste could make it. This is saying much, but not too much.

The June sunshine slanted in, and rested with unsparing candour upon a cabbage-coloured carpet patterned with monstrous magenta blooms of uncertain family. Gloomy oil-paintings in gorgeous, fog-dimmed frames covered the greater part of the wall space.

Helen Wilmot had never been able to decide whether she thought the wall-paper uglier than

the portraits, or the portraits more frightful than
the wall-paper. She found a certain fascination
in following the immense green curves and
spirals that wound and twisted between the pictures. She had a fancy that there in secret,
behind the unattractive presentments of great-
uncle James and great-aunt Maria, that ebullient
vegetable growth must burst into flower. She
had beguiled many a dull half-hour by speculat-
ing as to the sort of bloom it would produce,
and had decided ultimately on an orchidaceous
nightmare of orange and maroon. The stamens,
she thought, would be green—a very bright green
—and they would bear monstrous pollen sacs
of a pale, unwholesome pink.

In the middle of the room stood a large round
table. It was made of handsome polished wood,
very good and solid. Everything that stood on
it had its own little mat. The photograph
album with the gold initials on a ground of
crimson plush lay upon a miniature carpet of
emerald silk and wool. A daguerreotype in a
folding frame stood by itself on a little orange-
coloured island. It was a likeness of Mr. Lauriston, and his widow used to gaze tearfully at
it when her sister Harriet was more masterful
than usual, or her daughter Adela harder to
manage.

Mrs. Lauriston was a pretty, faded little woman
of uncertain health. All the strong colour in
the room annihilated her own delicate tints. It

accentuated the grey in the fair hair which she
wore dressed à l'Impératrice, and drew attention
to the fine, interlacing lines about her mouth
and eyes. She wore a beige-coloured dress, and
the sofa which she so seldom left was upholstered
in dark maroon to match the curtains. Only
Helen thought it ugly, but then Helen had spent
nearly all her twenty years of life with her
mother's people, and her grandmother, old Mrs.
Delamere, had possessed many beautiful things,
some brought from India, and some inherited
from her French relations.

Helen Wilmot looked at her aunt now, and
thought for the hundredth time that she was
like a water-colour drawing—an amateur water-
colour-drawing. There were the same pretty
tints, all faint and indeterminate, the same weak
lines, and absence of definition. She made up
her mind that she would like to see Mrs. Lauriston in a room full of soft old faded things, with
a little very pale gilding here and there. Helen
was very fond of making pictures in her own
mind. She would have liked to paint them, but
she lacked the skill, and had sense to know that
she lacked it.

If Mrs. Lauriston was like a water-colour,
Helen herself resembled an etching. Her pallor
had the same warm, living quality, and the
shadows on her hair and dress, the same deep
tone.

She sat by the window with her lap full of

embroidery silks, that shone like jewels against the black of her full skirt. The sunlight just glanced across one sloping shoulder and threw her head into strong relief. She was all black and white in the strong light—white skin, white hands, white neck, white collar; black dress, black hair, and eyes that looked black too until she raised them, and you saw that they were a very deep, soft grey.

She raised them now because Mrs. Lauriston made a little restless movement.

"Helen, my dear."

"Yes, Aunt Lucy."

"Did I hear a carriage?"

Helen took a fold of her dress in one hand, so as to keep her silks from slipping, and leaned sideways towards the window. One corner of her mouth twitched a little, and she caught it between her teeth.

"Well, my dear?" said Mrs. Lauriston, fidgeting, and Helen turned a perfectly grave face towards her.

"Dear Aunt Lucy, I was counting; I had just got up to ten——"

"Ten?"

"Ten carriages. I think the very fat lady at No. 12 must be giving a party."

"My dear, what has that to do with us? Oh, my love, you don't say the window is open! How exceedingly careless of Mary! Pray shut it. The least breath—and really to-day when I feel so unequal, and Harriet coming. Not, of course," she explained, collecting herself, " that I am not very pleased to see your Aunt Harriet —very pleased indeed."

" Oh, of course," murmured Helen, and bent her head over a tangled skein.

Mrs. Lauriston put her handkerchief to her lips for a moment.

" Yes, of course," she said nervously, " but at the same time, love, your Aunt Harriet—she is sure to talk so much about Hetty, and Hetty's marriage, and you know so much conversation —and then I think she was rather offended at my not coming to the wedding, and I have not seen her since, so altogether——"

" Yes," said Helen without a smile, " conversation about Hetty is rather tiring."

" And that she should have made such a match!" exclaimed Mrs. Lauriston with sudden energy; " Sir Henry Lavington, and all that money, and Hetty always *was* plain."

" Plain and sensible. I don't know which is worse, but I suppose he wanted a sensible wife," remarked Helen.

" My love, you should not disparage sense. I am sure you have plenty. Now if Sir Henry had fallen in love with you! But Hetty—it is more than I can understand. Hetty never attracted me, my dear, but of course her mother could not be expected to understand that, nor should I wish it."

Helen laid a blue and a green skein together, and wished that the bluebells were not over, and that she was not in London.

"Shall I leave you and Aunt Harriet for a little when she comes, Aunt Lucy?" she asked.

"Oh, no, my dear, not at first—oh, no. If I thought I should like a little private talk with her later on, I could let you know. It would be quite easy. I could ask you to fetch me a handkerchief, or my smelling salts, and you need not come back for a time; but at first—oh, I really think it will be a relief to have you here, my dear. Harriet is *all* that is excellent, but you know my nerves are not very strong, and if she is offended—no, no, my love, I had much rather you stayed."

Mrs. Lauriston's soft voice fluttered as she spoke. She patted a refractory cushion into position, and settled herself against it.

"I hope Adela will come in before your aunt leaves," she said, and sighed a little. "I am afraid Harriet will think she should have been at home; but really, just now, my dear child, one is so anxious, it does not seem as if one should interfere, and Mrs. Willoughby was so very eager to have her."

"Oh, she is sure to be home early because of Hetty's party this evening," said Helen, cheerfully.

Mrs. Lauriston clasped her hands.

"Helen, do you think—" she began, and then paused, panting a little.

"My dear, are you in Adela's confidence at all?"

Helen looked up with a shade on her brow.

"No, I don't think I am," she said.

"And I certainly am not," said Adela's mother; "and oh, my love, I feel so anxious, so very anxious. Young Manners now—do you suppose—do you imagine that Adela means to accept him?"

"I am sure I hope not," said Miss Wilmot with decision.

"Oh, but, my dear, why should you say that? Such a good-looking young man, such splendid dark eyes—I always think dark eyes are so romantic—and so devoted. I really never saw anything like his devotion! And then Manners Park, and such a satisfactory provision."

"Yes," said Helen. She stopped to thread a needle. "Yes, if he is able to establish his claim."

"Oh, my dear, surely there is no doubt about that. It would be most unfair. Why, his father was a cousin of Mr. Lauriston's great-grandmother, or was it his grandmother's step-mother was a Manners? He could never be passed over, and his mother a lady of such high rank, sister—or is it cousin?—to that wealthy Rajah of Bithoor, whose portrait Mr. Azimullah showed us, and who, he said, would be a sort

of Emperor, only we have taken away his kingdom, or stopped the revenues, but fortunately
he has plenty of money of his own besides. Oh,
no, Francis Manners is certain to succeed with
his claim, and his father's marriage so romantic
too."

"Dear Aunt Lucy," said Helen, half laughing.
Then she bit her lip. "He has to prove that
there was a marriage," she said.

She took a few delicate stitches and did not
look at her aunt.

"My love, you shock me," exclaimed Mrs.
Lauriston. A faint colour made her look younger.
"You shock me, indeed you do. Colonel Manners was married. To suppose otherwise—Helen,
my dear! I think, love, that you should struggle
with that unfortunate prejudice against persons
with dark blood in their veins. It is that which
puts such shocking ideas into your head. Mr.
Azimullah now, so handsome, such charming
manners, but I notice how you avoid him when
he comes here. You get it from your father, I
suppose. In fact I have observed that all Anglo-
Indians are the same. I fear going to India
and joining your father will not improve you.
It is an unchristian prejudice, love, not that of
course I would for a moment seek to imply that
dear Edward was unchristian. I do hope, my
dear, you would not imagine such a thing, or
your excellent grandmother, and after she had
brought you up so nicely, and to be such a good

girl, and now that she is dead and all. No, no, my dear, all I meant was that prejudices of this nature should be struggled against; and oh, Helen, my dear, you won't try to imbue Adela with such notions? I am so anxious, so very anxious about her future. You know, love, there will be so little, oh, so little when I am gone, and Adela is so beautiful."

Mrs. Lauriston's voice trembled very much, and became almost inaudible.

Helen dropped all her silks on the floor, and ran to her. "Dear Aunt Lucy, what is it? Why do you trouble yourself? Adela is beautiful, and there are much nicer people to fall in love with her than poor Mr. Manners."

"No, no. There's only Captain Morton, and he is poor, and Adela is not fit to be poor, and go to India,—and I want to see her married before I die."

"You are going to live to be a great-grand-mother like old aunt Maria," said Helen, kissing one of the trembling hands. "Only you'll make a much, much nicer one, and all the great-grand-children will love you."

"My dear, you shouldn't. Oh, Helen, love——"

"What is it, dearest?"

"My health," whispered Mrs. Lauriston.

Helen gave her a little pat.

"You are just delicate, and delicate people always live the longest. Yes, it is quite true.

Grandmamma always said so. And there's nothing really wrong with you, is there?"

"I don't know," said Mrs. Lauriston in a low, hurried tone. Her eyes looked past Helen as if she saw something that frightened her.

"Now, Aunt Lucy, dear," said Helen cheerfully, "don't upset yourself. Adela will make a splendid match, and live happy ever after, and you will spoil her children, and they will adore you, and—oh, that really is the carriage at last."

In a moment Mrs. Lauriston was all in a flutter. Death and marriage were uncertain, but Harriet was at the door. "Oh, my dear, my eyes. Do they look red? Give me my handkerchief, and then push it under the cushion in case I want to send you for one—and move that chair a little, no, not so close, yes, that will do. Oh, I wish Adela were in, but there, her aunt never was really fond of her, and —Helen, my vinaigrette—yes, it fell down, I think. Have you found it? Oh, thank you, my dear."

The door opened as she took the little cut glass bottle. The maid announced Mrs. Middleton, and Harriet Middleton came into the room with a great rustling of violet silk.

She wore a shawl of China crêpe and an immensely full skirt trimmed with seven rows of broad black velvet ribbon. On her head was a bonnet with an inner frill of blonde, showing the abundant black hair which always looked as if it had been freshly lacquered. She had a handsome, wooden face, with very smooth, dark eyebrows, and firm red cheeks. Her voice was as strong and deep as a man's.

One of the red cheeks just brushed her sister's pale one, and she settled herself into the chair which Helen proffered.

"Well, Lucy, you look poorly enough," she remarked, "but what else you can expect when you lie on a sofa all day, I don't know. How d'ye do, Helen. Come here, and let me have a look at you. How long is it since I saw you last?"

Helen appeared to be giving the matter her earnest attention. "About two years, I *think*, Aunt Harriet," she said.

Mrs. Middleton looked disapprovingly at her niece. The light caught her prominent brown eyes and gave them a shiny look. They reminded Helen of small bull's-eyes.

"You are as pale as a piece of plaster too, and less like Edward than ever. And where on earth you and Adela got that untidy frizzly hair from, I am sure I don't know. None of our family ever had such a thing. My girls have both got hair like mine, I am thankful to say, nice, smooth hair that can be kept tidy, and plenty of it. But a great deal can be done with pomatum. Wilkin's is the best. I will send you a pot to try. I gave one to Adela when she

came down for Hetty's wedding. Has she used
it?"

Helen looked interested, and Mrs. Lauriston
observed feebly:

"Adela wears her hair in ringlets."

"And very untidy she looked. That was why
I gave her the pomatum, Lucy; but, of course, if
you encourage her— By the way, where is
Adela?"

"Adela has—has gone out. She had an engagement, Harriet—she was so sorry——"

"An engagement—without you?"

"My health," faltered Mrs. Lauriston. "I
am unable to take Adela out myself, and Mrs.
Willoughby has been most kind."

Mrs. Middleton snorted.

"I always took my girls about myself. I felt
it a duty. But if you are really unable to go
out with Adela, I must say, Lucy, that I should
have thought Hetty, her own cousin, a more
suitable chaperon than Mrs. Willoughby."

"Hetty is so young," began Mrs. Lauriston,
flushing.

"Hetty is a married woman, and excep-
tionally discreet for her years. She would at
least have prevented Adela from getting herself talked about," said Mrs. Middleton with
emphasis.

"Harriet!"

Mrs. Middleton unfastened her shawl and
threw it back. She had come on purpose to

talk to Lucy about her daughter, but she had meant to lead up to the point more gradually.

"Your room is stifling," she observed. "Helen, won't that window open?"

"I think it will," said Helen, but she did not get up.

"Harriet, what do you mean?" cried Mrs. Lauriston.

"It is an extremely hot afternoon, and you have everything closed," began Mrs. Middleton, but for once her sister interrupted her.

"Harriet, what did you mean about Adela?"

"My dear Lucy, how you agitate yourself. What did I say?"

"You said—you implied that Adela was being talked about."

"Well, Lucy, and what can you expect when you let her go about with a flighty young woman like Mrs. Willoughby, and pick up with illegitimate, half-caste young men?"

"Harriet!"

"My dear Lucy, what is the use of taking that tone? Every one is talking about it. I wish I had come to town two months ago."

Mrs. Lauriston caught at her dignity with tremulous hands.

"Mr. Manners is an excellent young man, his father was a cousin of Mr. Lauriston's," she said. "He is devoted to Adela, and when he has established his claim to the Manners estates——"

"Really, Lucy! is it possible that you have encouraged him?"

"And why not, Harriet?"

"Lucy, are you crazy? Why not? Why not?"

"He is Colonel Manners's son."

"And his mother?"

"I don't understand you, Harriet. His mother was a native lady of rank, or so I understood."

"And the proofs of the marriage?"

"Mr. Manners certainly has ample proof."

"Mr. Manners certainly has no proof at all," said Mrs. Middleton, and saw her sister whiten.

"Oh, Harriet!"

"He has no proof at all," she repeated. "I felt it my duty to let you know at once. He consulted Mortimer James, and Mortimer told Hetty that there was no proof at all—absolutely none—that would justify any respectable firm of solicitors in taking up the case; I felt you could not know the truth too soon."

Mrs. Lauriston burst into tears.

"Now, Lucy, for mercy's sake don't cry. Adela has got herself into a mess, as I always foretold that she would, but we must do what we can. How far has it gone? They are not engaged?"

"Oh, no," sobbed Mrs. Lauriston. "Oh, Helen, dear love, where is my handkerchief? Oh, my dear, what a dreadful thing! Adela is so wilful——"

"Aunt Lucy, dear, please——"

"Adela is so wilful. She will make friends that I cannot approve of, Mrs. Willoughby now, and Mr. Manners. Of course being as it were a cousin—only now I come to think of it, it *was* Mr. Lauriston's grandmother's step-mother who was a Miss Manners, so one cannot say that there is any relationship, can one?"

Helen said, "No, one could n't," and Mrs. Lauriston went on talking and dabbing her eyes, from which flowed a constant effortless stream of tears.

"And not being a relation, even if he is legit-imate, only I should n't talk of such things to you, Helen, I can say now that there was always something I did not *quite* like about Mr. Man-ners. He never seemed to me to be quite— quite straightforward, and of course Adela thought those dark eyes of his so romantic, but to me dark eyes are a little unreliable. Now, blue eyes—so becoming with sunburn—a soldier should be sunburned—and don't you think, Harriet, that people with dark blood in them are never *quite* reliable and straightfor-ward?"

Mrs. Middleton tapped with her foot upon the cabbage-coloured carpet.

"Is Captain Morton sunburned, and has he blue eyes?" she inquired drily.

"He has, Aunt Harriet," said Helen with equal dryness.

" And so much in love with Adela, and really such a fine man, though I find him just a little trying to my nerves. I never seem to know whether he means quite what he says, or not, and he has a way of fixing his eyes on one that makes one feel as if he were reading all the secrets of one's past."

Mrs. Middleton gave an angry sniff.

" My dear Lucy, you never had a secret in your life," she ejaculated, but Mrs. Lauriston took no notice. She had stopped dabbing her eyes, and looked quite cheerful.

" Yes, really most piercing eyes," she murmured, " but when he looks at Adela, it is quite touching, they soften so—his devotion——"

" And his prospects?" inquired Mrs. Middleton in tones of sisterly contempt.

" Oh, my dear Harriet, he really has a brilliant future before him. He distinguished himself very greatly at the siege of—of—no, I have forgotten the name—Helen, love, what was the name?"

" Multan," said Helen Wilmot.

" Yes, yes—of course, when those two poor men were killed. Captain—oh, dear, it has gone again—Helen love, the names of those two poor fellows. Oh, of course, Mr. Anderson and Mr. Vans Agnew. They were murdered, you know, and that wonderful Major Edwardes collected an army, and Captain Morton was with him, and they did the most extraordinary things, and

Captain Morton was wounded in the head—such
an escape——"

"Yes—yes," said Mrs. Middleton impatiently.

"One can't be too thankful——"

"Well, Lucy, what I should like to know is
this—how much *is* there to be thankful for? He
is not dependent on his prospects in the future,
and his pay in the present, is he?"

"I think there was an uncle—I think he said
an uncle had died and left him something. I
know I did not really listen, because I felt so
uncomfortable at his telling me—so pointed—
and I never thought then——"

Mrs. Middleton opened her mouth, and then
shut it again firmly. She had a strong desire
to speak her mind, but a stronger desire to see
her niece Adela married; she controlled herself,
therefore, and talked at large about Hetty, and
Hetty's glory, only returning to Adela's affairs
in the calm of the tea-hour.

Finally, she resumed her shawl, pinned it
across her chest with a very large cameo brooch,
bordered with plaited hair, rose majestically,
and pecked at her sister's cheek.

"You are not going?"

"I must get back. I promised Hetty. Now,
Lucy, take my advice, get Adela safely married
to this Captain Morton. Once a girl has got
herself talked about, her chances are gone.
Especially if she is pretty. People always believe the worst of a pretty girl—get her mar-

ried. Goodness me, Lucy, what is the use of
looking at me like that? If no one else tells you
the truth, I do—I always did, and I always shall,
and perhaps some day you will be grateful to
me. Good-bye, Helen. When do you sail for
India? Has n't Edward sent the money for
your passage yet? Oh, he has. Well, it is time.
Your grandmother has been dead six months,
and really if Lucy had not been able to take
you in, I don't know what you would have
done. *I* could n't have invited you for the best
part of a year."

When Helen had taken her aunt downstairs,
she came back into the drawing-room and shut
the door. She was smiling a little.

"Poor Sir Henry," she said.

"Oh, my dear, why?" protested Mrs. Lauriston, a little shocked that any one should pity
a baronet with fifteen thousand a year.

"Hetty is going to be exactly like Aunt Harriet. That 's why," said Helen.

CHAPTER II

Serve seven years for Honour and seven years for Love.
The children of Honour are many, thou shalt 'stablish
    them, branch and root.
And what of the children of Love, shall Love then bear
    no fruit?
Sufficient unto the day is the good and the evil thereof.

AS Adela Lauriston crossed the ballroom at
Lavington House a good many people
watched her, and then turned to whisper with
their friends.

Adela was worth looking at. Even Hetty
Lavington admitted that, though her round,
prominent eyes were full of disapproval as she
observed her cousin, and noted that it was on
Francis Manners's arm that she was leaving the
room. "Really!" she said, in a low angry voice,
and Sir Henry Lavington, who knew very well
what she meant, tried to look as disapproving
as he was expected to. He did not really find
it very easy. A good many people had expected
Adela Lauriston to stand in her cousin Hetty's
place. Hetty Middleton's engagement had come
as a great surprise to these people. Rumour
even had it that it had come as a surprise to

Sir Henry himself. He looked away from Hetty in her diamonds, and her unbecoming dress, and his eyes followed Adela, as she went lightly and proudly down the long room; she was not tall, but how well she moved, and how all these lights flattered her!

Her hair, a dark chestnut in colour, fell all about her shoulders, in a shower of curls,—those curls to which Harriet Middleton objected so strongly. They shaded a face which Greuze might have painted, and were caught over the ear on either side by a scarlet geranium. Adela's colouring stood the test triumphantly, for her lips were as red as the flowers, and the tint in her cheeks, though much fainter, was just as pure and fine.

From under arched brows, her hazel eyes looked smilingly upon all this crowd of people who must be admiring her in her new dress. It was her last glance in the mirror that had waked the smile. She carried with her a pleasant memory of many white silk flounces, all veiled with blonde, and caught up here and there with vivid clusters of geranium flowers.

She smiled very sweetly under Francis Manners's admiring gaze, and her modestly dropped eyes caught a faint reflection of her white and scarlet bravery from the polished floor at her feet.

" By Jove, that 's a pretty girl! " said Freddy Carlton, half to himself, and then, being a communicative soul, he turned to his neighbour, and received a shock.

"What, you, Dick! Lord, what brings you to a dance?"

"Hullo, Ginger!" said Captain Richard Morton. He looked down at the top of Freddy's head with affection.

"And what brings you?" he said. "I did n't know you were home."

"Just come. Jolly glad to be out of the romantic East too. Lavington is my second cousin fourteen times removed. I say, fourteen times is n't too much for his wife, is it? But what on earth brings you here? You 've never been learning to dance?"

Captain Morton looked a little rueful.

"A cousin of mine tried to teach me once. You remember Floss Monteith—and she said it was n't any use. You see I 'm rather large to go about treading on people—at least that is what she said, and now with all these flounces and fallals that girls wear——"

Freddy had an inward spasm.

"Old Dick dancing—my stars! I wonder who she is," he said to himself, and then aloud:

"I say, who is that jolly pretty girl who is just going out? No, not the one in pink, the other one, with the fellow who looks as if he 'd been dipped in the ink over night and had n't got it all off?"

Captain Morton drew his brows together. A

moment before his eyes had been very blue and
gay.   Now they darkened.

"That is Miss Lauriston," he said, and Freddy
had another little spasm, and said to himself,
"The one and only!"

"And who's the man?   If it were n't England
I'd give him about eight annas in the rupee."

"Intelligent Frederick.   Do you remember old
Manners in the palmy days of our youth?"

"What, at Seetapore, when we were kids?
Retired in the year one, and settled down with
a native wife?"

"That's the man, and the dark boy is his
son."

"What's he doing?"

"Trying to get accepted as his father's heir.
Apparently a few odd cousins and people
dropped off, and old Manners would have come
in for a whole lot of property if he had lived."

"And the half-caste son succeeds?   Well,
some people have all the luck."

"Oh, I don't know about luck."   Richard
Morton's frown deepened.   "He's a poor creature, but one can't help feeling sorry for the
boy.   There's a screw loose somewhere, and
apparently he won't get anything."

"Stupid business marrying a native," was
Freddy's comment.   "Always leads to trouble.
Oh, Lord, Dick, who in the world is this?"

A very magnificent person had just come into
view.   His dark skin contrasted strongly with

the shirt of fine white muslin which he wore
buttoned to the throat with emerald studs. His
tall figure, not yet too full for shapeliness, was
set off by a long coat of green and gold brocade,
and his waist was confined by folds of crimson
kincob, against which there glittered the jewelled
hilt of a dagger. A long necklace of many rows
of pearls hung down upon the crimson and gold
of the sash, and a pearl and emerald aigrette
showed up bravely against his muslin turban.
Three ladies hung on his every word, and his
dark eyes roved from one to the other. Critics
might have detected a certain insolence in his
glance, but London vowed that his manners were
charming.

Captain Morton looked for a moment, and
shrugged his shoulders.

"Blatant beast," he observed.

"But who—what is it?"

"Used to be a *khitmutghar*, I believe. Picked
up English and got taken on to teach in a school
at Cawnpore. You know old Bajee Rao—last
of the Peishwas—disreputable old blackguard—
well, his adopted son Dhundoo Punth—the man
they call the Nana Sahib—took a fancy to this
Azimullah creature, and made him his *vakil*.
Now he has unlimited influence, and apparently unlimited cash."

"What is he doing here?" inquired Freddy,
wrinkling up his upper lip.

Dick Morton laughed a little grimly. "Was

it David, or Shakespeare, who said that all men were fools? "

" Original I think, dear boy," murmured Freddy.

" True, anyhow. Azimullah Khan is the idol of the season. Look at old Lady Mountjoy smiling away at him, and that pretty creature in blue. No party is a success without the ' Indian Prince,' and he dresses the part all right, does n't he? "

" Beast—oily beast," said Freddy Carlton with conviction. " What is he doing in England at all, though? "

" Trying to get a hard-hearted Company to continue Bajee Rao's pension to his beloved adopted son. It's been a grievance for a long time, and now Azimullah is trying to get things settled. Also, I believe, he is financing and generally looking after young Manners, whose mother was the Nana's sister, or cousin, or something of that sort."

" I met the Nana Sahib once—rather a sportsman. Well, I hope he 'll get his money, I like to hear of some one getting money out of the Company. By Jingo, Dick, I wish they 'd give me some! By the way, I saw George Blake on my way down country, and he said you were going into the Civil—cutting the regiment. It's not true? "

" Yes, it is."

" Why on earth? "

" A regimental officer has no chances."

Freddy burst out laughing.

" Why, you 've seen more service than any of us. I wish I 'd had your luck."

" Well, I was n't at Multan with the regiment, and it was n't regimental work that took me to Burmah, and the chances get less every day."

He paused. Freddy Carlton and he had been boys together. He had not many near relatives, and this coming home had been rather a lonely business. Looked forward to for ten years, it had resolved itself into a counting of empty places, a wandering to and fro amongst haunting memories, and a realisation of how dead, how absolutely dead, were the friendships and the interests which in anticipation had seemed warm and still alive.

He had an impulse towards confidence.

" There have been times when I could have thrown up the whole thing," he said. " Then Edwardes showed me a way out. I 'm not supposed to be going for good. I learned Pushtoo when I was up at Multan, you know, and I 'm to be lent for a year or two for special work, under Edwardes at Peshawur. Things are pleasantly fluid in the Punjab at present. I 'm pretty sick of a régime of red-tape and doddering inefficiency."

Freddy's little greenish eyes twinkled.

" Oh, insubordinate young man!" he exclaimed. He pulled at his sandy moustache.

"You 've still got old Crowther for a colonel, I see."

"Oh, Lord, yes. Crowther will die—or at least we 'll hope so—but he 'll never surrender. Heavens, Freddy, what sort of a system is it that never gives a man his chance till he 's past taking it? I dare say Crowther was all right once."

"I 'll swear he was n't," grinned Freddy.

"No, I don't suppose he could have been; but this hanged system of purchase does wear a lot of good fellows out. They have n't got the money, and their chances pass them by, and when they 've wasted the best years of their lives, and fretted their hearts out, and the chance does come,—why the rust has gone too deep, and they just crumble."

"That how you feel? Man to man now, Dick, how deep has it got with you? As for my humble self—well, I don't know that I feel so very rusty."

"Oh, you 've used it up on your hair," said Dick Morton, laughing, "and I——"

"Rolling stones gather no rust—eh? What 'll George Blake do without his *fidus Achates,* Dick?"

"I hope he 'll get the Adjutancy."

"So you are getting out of his way?"

Captain Dick could still blush in spite of the sunburn. The colour ran up to the roots of his black hair, and he looked cross.

"What rubbish!" he said, and Freddy permitted himself the merest ghost of a whistle.

"Oh, I won't let on," he said wickedly.

"How are you fellows?" asked Captain Morton in an abrupt voice.

"Oh, fairly gay, thanks. Willoughby's married, and Smith's going to be, and Renton's homesick, and I'm on the verge of bankruptcy, and the only really bright spot is, that we don't think the Colonel's liver will stand another hot weather. If it were n't for that, I declare we'd offer him to you, lock, stock, and barrel, and take old Crowther in exchange, hanged if we would n't."

"No, thanks, Freddy, we would n't deprive you for the world. And if Crowther went tomorrow they'd give the regiment to Marsh,—Marsh whose idea of Heaven is a place where we can all stand in rows for ever and ever, and never soil our pipe-clay with a profane touch. I tell you, Ginger, before I came away, I was hourly expecting to be told to keep the men in cotton-wool, once they were dressed."

"Well, I like 'em smart," protested Freddy with a grimace.

"Smart—oh, Lord, they're smart enough. They're a deuced sight too smart, Ginger, and they're getting to know it. They want taking down a peg or two, these stall-fed, caste-proud Brahmins. They'll be able to do without us soon; and they're beginning to know that too.

I'd like to see 'em in sensible clothes, and I'd like to see 'em think less of their pipe-clay and more of their discipline."

"Clothes, what sort of clothes? What's wrong with their clothes?"

"Everything. Too tight. Too hot. Too much pipe-clay. Damn pipe-clay!"

"All right—I don't mind. 'Damn it' all you like. But what's wrong with the discipline? I'd bet my boots your men were disciplined within an inch of their lives, whilst you were Adjutant."

"Rotten—that's what the discipline is," said Richard Morton, with his black eyebrows in a straight frowning line.

"Insubordinate, are they?"

"I'd like to see 'em." Captain Morton's eyes went very bright and hard. "No, but they'd like to be. Ginger, if I'd a free hand for six months—but with Marsh and Crowther over one's head, it's a sickening, heart-breaking job,—and besides, I don't want to be chucked out of the service for telling 'em what I think of 'em, and it's bound to come if I stay on."

"Then you'd better go, my son."

"That's what Edwardes says, so he's asked for me. I made friends with his horde of ruffians at Multan. Not much pipe-clay there. I tell you some of them would wake our Bengal regiments up a bit, only they wouldn't wear tight red jackets, and tight white pantaloons."

"No, no, I draw the line at the wild **Pathan**, Dick. He's all very well for Irregulars."

Richard Morton's eyes brightened.

"I tell you, Freddy, we are wasting our best material, absolutely wasting it. Look at the Sikhs. Every regiment is ordered to enlist two hundred of them. How many have you got?"

"Oh, I don't know. About fifty."

"And we've got sixty-two. Have you got a Sikh native officer? No. Nor have we, nor has any one else. Can't get recruits is the cry, but, Lord, we didn't kill the whole Sikh army at Moodkee and Ferozeshah."

Freddy shrugged his shoulders.

"Well, I'm not over partial to Sikhs myself," he said lazily. "Dirty beggars, and the other men don't like 'em."

"Have you seen them fight?"

"Oh, we don't all have your luck, Richard, my son."

The band struck up an air that was very popular that season,

> "Oh, shall I miss
> That earliest kiss——"

and Captain Morton pulled himself up and made a feint of looking at his programme.

"I've got a partner to look for," he said, and his eyes went towards the door by which Adela Lauriston had gone out.

"Going to dance with the poor girl?" inquired Freddy Carlton with malice, "because, if so, I'd better be hunting round for a doctor. Once those beetle-crushers of yours take the floor——"

"All right, Ginger. Wait till I pick you up by the collar, and carry you round the room. I'd do it now for twopence."

"Have n't got twopence," complained Mr. Carlton ruefully. "But do it just to oblige an old friend, won't you, Dick?"

"I would if I'd time. See you again, Ginger"; and Richard Morton went off, with his head in the air, and his big shoulders well above the crowd.

CHAPTER III

HOW TWO MEN PROPOSED TO ADELA

Oh! All the gold that the Fairies have is the gold of the
  Summer sheaf,
And all the gold that the Fairies give it fades with the
  fading leaf;
And he who would borrow a day of sorrow, and pledge the
  morrow to grief,
He shall sell his soul for the Fairy gold that turns to a
  withered leaf.

MISS LAURISTON and her partner passed
out of the brightly lighted ballroom into
the great conservatory that was Sir Henry Lavington's pride. His income was fortunately a
very ample one, for he spent an extravagant
amount upon his glass-houses, and kept this one
filled with strange exotics, whose scent hung
heavily on the moist warm air.

"How hot it is!" said Adela. She looked up
at her companion with a teasing glance. "I
expect you like it, Mr. Manners. It must remind
you of your home."

"My home?" said Francis Manners. The
words stung him, but it never crossed his mind
that Adela had uttered them with intention.

"Yes, India. India is your home, is it not?"

The young man's dark eyes dwelt on her.

"I do not think I have any home," he said, and the queer sing-song accent gave an added melancholy to the words. "Oh, no, I have not any home now; but when I was a boy in India, and my father was alive, we used to talk about home, and we meant England."

Adela was a little annoyed. Sentiment which was not directed towards herself always annoyed her. She exclaimed in admiration of a scarlet cactus, and moved deeper into the conservatory.

Beyond the cactus a bank of orchids threw out strange white and violet blooms, which were reflected in a brimming marble bowl. Adela moved slowly towards the flowers, and stood looking down into the clear water.

A tiny stream trickled into it and slid drop by drop into a second pool beyond. Thus the water moved continually, showing a ceaseless interplay of faint grey shadow and crystal light, broken here and there by gleams of reflected purple. As Adela bent above the basin she could see her own red lips, her own bright eyes, and the vivid jewel flash of the scarlet flowers in her hair.

With a little laugh she broke the head from one of the geraniums at her breast, and set it sailing. The current drew it slowly across the pool, and then, just as it touched the rim, young Manners put out his hand and snatched the flower—fiercely—as if he were afraid that some one would be before him.

"Oh, Mr. Manners!" said Adela, and turned a look of smiling reproof upon his agitated face.

Francis Manners was very young, and very much in love. The first hot passion of youth beat miserably at his sore heart, and mounted like fire into a brain that was none too strong. His father had died when he was fifteen, and from that time the half native life had merged into one from which English habits and English training had vanished. For a time there had been friends of his father's who had kept an eye upon the handsome, undisciplined lad; once there was even a summer spent in the hills with a Manners cousin and his wife. That was after he had been so ill, and the English doctor said he would die if he remained at Seetapore.

Then when he was seventeen had come his mother's sudden reconciliation with her own people, their removal to Cawnpore, and his uncle's influence. Sereek Dhundoo Punth, thirty years of age, and steeped in Oriental vice, but withal pleasant and affable, was willing enough to cement his alliance with the conquering English by exploiting a relative who had English blood in his veins. If his sister liked to spend the old Colonel's savings in propitiating the Brahmins, what was it to him? He himself took his advantage where he found it.

They called him the Nana Sahib now, grand-

son of the Peishwas by an adoption as sacred
as any tie of blood. Some day, perhaps, some
day there would be a Peishwa again, and he
would be father of a royal line, as well as son
of kings. Meanwhile he entertained royally at
Bithoor, and English officers came and went,
called him friend, dubbed him sportsman, and
partook of his lavish hospitality. Francis Manners shared this life for four years, and then,
learning of his father's inheritance, he accompanied his uncle's agent to England, and put
forward his claim to the Manners estates. A
claim—there was the sting. It was only a claim.
No evidence of marriage—nothing to found a
case on—nothing at all. That was what the
lawyers had said. He had gone from one to
another, and at each repetition of the verdict
he saw receding into the distance, not wealth
and independence, not Manners Park, but—
Adela Lauriston.

He looked at her now. There was a veil between them, a hazy veil that was like distance
made manifest. Then as her face laughed at
him from the water, and he snatched her flower,
his misery broke from him in a cry of
" Adela! "

" Mr. Manners, don't—how wet you 'll make
yourself."

" Adela! "

" Well, I supposed there would be a scene,"
said Miss Lauriston to herself with resignation.

What she said aloud was entirely the proper
thing.

"Mr. Manners, please don't."

"I cannot help it. Oh, no, I cannot. I love
you so much, so very much."

"Oh, please."

"But you do know that. Oh, yes, you must
know it. Have I hidden it? Has it not been
for all the world to see? Your mother saw, and
she was not angry. Only last week she called
me Francis, and said that we were cousins.
And you saw—oh, yes, you saw——"

"Indeed——"

"When we were in the boat together, two days
ago only—in the moonlight, and you let me hold
your hand, did you not see? And you were
kind, you were not angry at all."

Adela felt a passing sensation of anger. The
boat incident was one of those which had made
so much talk. She would never have risked it
had she dreamed of the turn that things were
going to take.

At the same time her heart beat not unpleas-
antly. She was perfectly mistress of herself.
She must be kind, but firm. It really was foolish
of him to harp so on a week ago, three days
ago—as if most important changes could not
take place in a far shorter time. After all, if
it were not for the talk she was not sure that
she would have cared to marry him, even if his
claim had proved as good as they had expected.

"Adela, speak to me—you are not angry now!" And now she was quite ready for him.

"Oh, no, Mr. Manners, not angry, why should I be angry? I am only sorry that you should have misunderstood."

"But I have not. You were kind."

"My mother and I were friendly, because your father was a connexion, but I never thought, never dreamed——"

"Never? Not when I held your hand? Not when I kissed it? Not when I looked at you? Oh, yes, you must have seen. My heart was full of my love, and my eyes were full of it, and you smiled, you smiled at me—only this evening you smiled."

Adela felt a little cross. Really this young man was very unreasonable. She withdrew herself a pace or two, and in a flash, there was the poor boy on his knees, catching at her dress, and stammering out some confused appeal to her, not to be angry, not to go, not to leave him.

"But, Mr. Manners——"

"You called me Frank. Only yesterday you called me Frank."

Adela was provoked.

"A week ago—what has a week ago to do with to-day?" she cried.

He turned a quivering face up to hers.

"What is it that you say? What is it that you mean?"

Adela's eyes flashed. Could the man not take his answer? Had he no perceptions?

"Oh, Mr. Manners, do be sensible," she exclaimed.

"What is it that you mean? Why do you say 'a week ago,' like that."

She set her lips firmly together, and he answered his own question with a sob.

"It is because of what the lawyers say. It is because you think that I have nothing to offer you now. But you said it yourself—India is my home. In India I am a prince. In India I can give you a home. If my father's people will not have me, there are my mother's people still. There is my uncle, the Nana Sahib. He would be a great king if the English had not taken the throne from his father. He is a rich man still—verree rich, and a Rajah. Oh, he has jewels, and elephants, and everything verree rich. He is the friend of the English. Lots of English officers are his friends, English ladies come to his parties. You would be like a princess—Adela, beautiful Adela."

The sing-song accent gave the sentences a broken, foreign ring; the words came haltingly because the boy's lips trembled so much. He was quite white, and the moisture stood in beads upon his forehead. He held Adela's dress in an anguished grasp, and as she shrank back and was afraid to free herself because it would be such a pity to tear her flounce, she wondered how she could ever have thought him handsome.

"Adela!" he repeated in a sort of whisper; and she spoke indignantly:

"Mr. Manners, please let me go. It is all quite impossible. You have no right——"

He cried out sharply, and she repeated her last words.

"You have no right at all to behave like this. Let me go at once."

"You say that too—you too. No right—I have no right. I have no right to my name, and so I have no right to love you. I have no right to be alive. Oh, I did not ask to be alive. I would rather be dead, oh, yes, much rather I would be dead."

He let go of Adela's skirt, and put his hands to his face. There was a long pause, and then Adela said quickly:

"Some one is coming. The next dance has begun. Mr. Manners, do get up."

He did not move.

"Some one is coming. For mercy's sake, get up. Mr. Manners! Francis!"

He got up stumblingly.

"Some one coming?" he said in a dazed fashion.

"Yes. We must go back. Don't you hear the music. Let me take your arm. That will be best."

She put out her hand, and he caught at it and kissed it, and kept on kissing it, until she snatched it from him. Then, as Richard Morton's tall figure came towards them through the palms, he walked away, swaying on his feet, like a man who has drunk too deeply.

Adela drew a breath of relief, and moved a little farther from the pool, and the shaded light that burned above it. Under a branching, dark-leaved tree there were a couple of chairs, and she sank into one of them, with a soft billowing of her pretty skirts.

Captain Morton came past the shining water, and sat down beside her.

"I ought to be penitent for keeping you from a partner who can dance," he said.

"And are you?" asked Miss Lauriston.

"Not a bit."

His eyes laughed at her, and she blushed a little, very prettily.

"Don't you ever dance, Captain Morton?"

"I did once."

"Only once? Why was that?"

"The casualty list was too heavy. You see I tread on people, and my feet are so large. Six young ladies cut me dead next day."

"Oh!" said Adela, in a soft vague voice. She never quite knew whether Captain Morton was in earnest or not.

He was frowning, and he looked grave, but his eyes twinkled.

"One bouquet, two flounces, three fans, one set of—what do you call 'ems—gathers—is that right? and four lost programmes, besides a girl who was lame for a week, because I stepped right on her foot. I said I could n't help it, and that seemed to make things worse. It really was a large foot, though. But you see how it was that I did n't persevere with my dancing."

"It is very pleasant sitting here," said Adela gently.

His remark about flounces had reminded her of her own. She bent her head and tried to see if there were a tear. How that foolish Francis Manners had crushed her skirt! And, oh, dear, how tiresome, how too tiresome, the blonde flounce was certainly torn! That was the worst of blonde; it tore so easily, and only looked well when it was quite fresh. She wondered if Helen would darn it—Helen darned so beautifully. Or perhaps it would be better to put another cluster of geraniums there, quite a small one. That would hide the place. Her face had a pensive expression which softened it. Richard Morton's blood stirred as he looked at her and thought how sweet she was. How sweet and dear, how young and gentle!

"Yes, it is very—pleasant," he said, and his eyes dwelt on her.

"Is India like this?" she asked idly.

"India is rather a big place, Miss Lauriston."

"My cousin, Helen Wilmot, is going to India this autumn. You know her father, my uncle Edward, don't you?"

" Yes, I know him."

There was no particular enthusiasm in Captain Morton's voice.

" It is five years—no, more—seven years since he was in England. I should think Helen would find it very strange, going out to a father she has not seen for so long. She would have gone out before, only her grandmother was ill for a long time. She died at Christmas. That is why Helen is not going about. We wanted her to come here to-night, but she would not. She was very fond of her grandmother—Mrs. Wilmot's mother you know, no relation of ours."

Captain Morton felt no special interest in Miss Wilmot's affairs, but he liked listening to Adela. He thought her solicitude for her cousin very pretty and womanly.

" Would you like to go out to India?" he asked abruptly, and Adela coloured.

" I? Oh, I am never likely to go there."

" Never is a very long day. Should you like to go?"

" I don't know. Do you like it?"

" Well enough, but I'm a poor homeless creature, you know."

" Do you mean that you live in a tent?"

" No, I didn't mean quite that." He paused a moment, and then went on lightly, " My friend George Blake and I share a great tomb of a house—a regular whited sepulchre—rooms about thirty feet high. Furniture chiefly matting."

" It sounds—cold," said Adela, feeling she was expected to say something.

" I wish it felt cold," said Captain Morton heartily, " I only wish it did. Most of the time it feels a great deal too hot to be pleasant. But I go out to Peshawur, in the North, and there it really is cold, for a couple of months or so, and when the spring comes the whole place is smothered in roses and peach blossom."

" How beautiful! "

" Would n't you like to see it? "

" Oh, yes, indeed."

" Come, and see it—with me," said Richard Morton.

His voice dropped on the last words, and something in it made Adela catch her breath.

She had thought it all over—planned it—told herself it was inevitable. She must accept him, oh, yes, she must certainly accept him. She knew very well that unless her engagement were given out promptly, her little world would turn the cold shoulder upon pretty Miss Lauriston. Aunt Harriet had made that very clear. Well, if she went to India, she need never see Aunt Harriet again. That would be one comfort. Nor Hetty—that odious Hetty, in the diamonds that would have been so very, very becoming to Hetty's cousin. It was balm to reflect that they accentuated every bad point which Hetty possessed. What a mess she had made of things—Sir Henry Lavington, and Francis Manners, and others.

'Adela Lauriston had never lacked admirers, and yet Hetty, plain Hetty, stood there to-night in diamonds, and Adela must marry a soldier, and go to India.

Indian jewelry was beautiful. Visions of all the gems of Golconda floated before her, all in a glittering mist. She bent her head and as the delicate colour came and went in her cheeks, Richard Morton could have kissed the damp pavement under her feet.

"Oh, you dearest, will you—will you come?" he said; and Adela looked up, and looked down, and breathed a faint assent.

"Oh, how he is crushing my flowers," was her next coherent thought. "They'll be sure to stain the silk, and it will be ruined. Oh, I *do* wish he would let me go. I do *wish* he would."

"Oh, please, please," she whispered, and he slackened his embrace, and laughed down at her blushes.

"Did I frighten you? What a great clumsy bear I am! You'll have to tame me. Only don't make me love you less. Could you, I wonder? Did you hate the bear's hug very much—did you, love?"

His eyes were radiant with a smiling tenderness. Under it there were depths. Any woman's eyes must have fallen. Some would have been full of tears.

Adela looked down at the bosom of her gown, at the crushed, scarlet blooms. The red from the bruised petals had stained her breast, and stained the silk and lace below. "Such a stain! It will never come out," ran her thought, and as the words went through her mind, Richard Morton kissed her soft flushed cheek, and she felt his hand tremble upon her arm.

"Adela," he said, and his voice shook too, "Adela, I've not much to offer you now, but I swear I'll make a name for you. I'm an ambitious man, but now it is all for you. Every bit of it is for you,—like my life—like my love. My God, Adela, how I love you!"

And he raised her head with a strong shaking hand, and kissed her on the lips.

CHAPTER IV

HOW ADELA DID NOT FORGET TO SAY HER PRAYERS

> If you go shod with dreams,
>   Your feet shall be
> On paths as soft as sleep
>   Where dreams are free.
> These are the ways of the World;
>   Dear Heart, take heed,
> If you go shod with dreams
>   Your feet shall bleed.

THE bedroom which Helen Wilmot shared with her cousin had two large windows which looked away over the houses to the east. It was at the top of the high, narrow London house, so the windows caught the first of the moonlight, and the first of the sunrise. The moon was gone now. An hour ago she had slid into a bank of clouds that folded the west in gloom, but light was coming back with the sun, and little silvery streaks of it began to outline the heavy green Venetian blinds in the bedroom.

Helen Wilmot, propped up in bed, with Adela's two pillows as well as her own, glanced at the window, drew her dwindling candle a little nearer, and turned a page of the book which she was reading, wearily, but with determination.

45

As she did so, there was a step on the stair, and in a moment the door opened, and Adela came in, with a candle in her hand. She went straight to the dressing-table, and as she went the white crêpe shawl slid from her shoulders, and left them bare.

Adela let it lie, tilted the glass, and for a long moment she stood and looked at her own reflection. Then she stretched out her hand, and pulling one of the green blinds sharply aside, let in the first grey light, that was scarcely daylight yet. It struck full upon her face, but glow and colour, warmth of hair and skin, were proof against its disillusioning touch, and Adela, smiling, let the blind swing back, and turned to pick up her shawl. She met Helen's half-sarcastic look.

" I wanted to see if I looked as dreadful as all the other women did, when they came out into this odious light," she said, and gave a little yawn. " You should have seen Bella Wilson. She looked forty! "

" Perhaps she is forty," said Helen lazily.

" If she could hear you! But I don't look bad, do I? "

" My *dear* Adela, do you imagine I am going to pay you compliments at four in the morning. That, my child, is not what I kept awake for."

" Well, I 'm sure no one asked you to keep awake," retorted Adela.

She unclasped the string of pearls which was

her only ornament, and said coaxingly, "You
might say I look nice. Really you might,
Nellie."

"Don't call me 'Nellie' then," said Helen,
laughing. Her heart was full of something like
worship for her beautiful cousin; some of it came
into her eyes, but her voice was cool and teasing
as she added,

"You look quite—nice—Adie."

Adela turned away pettishly, and laid her
necklet down on the dressing-table.

"These wretched pearls seem to get smaller
and smaller," she said, and Helen laughed again.

"That is because you have been looking at
Hetty's jewels. You were n't here when Aunt
Harriet gave us the whole list of them. Aunt
Lucy and I took turns to say 'How lovely,' till
I felt as if I were repeating the responses in
church. Some day, if I am very good, Hetty
will ask me to tea, and show me some of them.
Do you think I can live up to it? What did
she wear to-night? And how did she look?"

"How does Hetty always look?" said Adela
scornfully.

She came across to the bedside, and knelt
down.

"Undo me, will you? And it's all pins, so
be careful, or the blonde will tear. Oh, Helen!"
she pursued with energy, "do you remember a
dress I had last year? No, I don't believe you
ever saw it, for that idiot Emma hung it too close

to the fire, and it caught, and was ruined. I
had only worn it twice, and I was so angry.
Emma had no thought for any one but herself.
She said her mother was ill, or something. She
was a stupid creature. Well, it was a very
pretty dress, white illusion and forget-me-nots,
you know the sort of thing. Would you believe
it—Hetty must have copied it! Hetty!"

"Adela, do keep still."

"She had it on to-night. Imagine my fury.
I must say Aunt Harriet or some one might
tell Hetty how perfectly hideous she looks in
white. And she had got forget-me-nots all the
wrong colour—like cornflowers, and nearly as
big. Oh, Helen, you are pricking me! There's
another pin on the shoulder."

"All right, I've got it. Yes, Hetty *is*
lumpy."

"And her nose," said Adela in an animated
tone. "It always *was* flat, but I never knew
how flat a snub nose could look, till I saw Hetty
with a tiara."

Helen burst out laughing.

"Did Hetty wear her tiara on her nose? Is
that the latest fashion? And how did she keep
it on? Now, Adela, if anything tore then, it was
your fault, and not mine. There, that's done,
and don't let us talk about Hetty any more. It
is really too dull. Whom did you see?"

Adela got up, and hung her bodice over the
back of a chair. Then she slipped out of the

full skirt, and stood up small and slim in a much be-flounced white petticoat.

"I saw Frank Manners," she said, and turned to lay her skirt full length upon the ottoman at the foot of her bed.

"Oh," said Helen. Her voice was cold. "I thought Aunt Harriet gave him a hint to stay away; and Aunt Harriet's hints!" she broke off with an exclamation— "Oh, Adela, how did you tear that flounce? I never noticed it before, but the light is right on it now."

Adela turned her head away, to hide a curious little smile. In retrospect there was something rather agreeable and flattering about that scene with young Manners.

"Frank Manners tore it," she said, and went on with her undressing, folding each garment carefully and neatly.

"Did he step on it? No, it's too high up. How did he tear it?"

"He clutched at it," said Adela, still with that satisfied little smile.

"My dear Adela!"

"Men are so silly," said Miss Lauriston, lifting her chin. "He behaved like a great baby. I declare, Helen, he cried—actually cried!"

Helen shut her book with a snap and pushed it under the pillow. "He proposed to you then. I rather admire his courage—after seeing Aunt Harriet."

4

"If you call it proposing to ask me to go to India and live with a lot of heathen natives."

"Don't!" said Helen sharply.

Adela stared. She was brushing out her hair now, and the loose curls were very becoming.

"I haven't the least intention—" she began, but Helen stopped her.

"Of course not—I didn't mean that, and quite well you know it."

"It's what you said," observed Miss Lauriston innocently.

Helen's head went up.

"I think you are dreadful, Adela!" she said. "I think you ought to be ashamed of yourself!"

"Thank you, my dear. It was he who was dreadful. Such a scene! I can't think how men can be so foolish. If they only knew how much more attractive and agreeable they are when they don't make scenes—why, he didn't even look handsome to-night."

"Why did you lead the wretched boy on?" she said.

Adela came and sat on the foot of the bed.

"I didn't lead him on," she said. "Really, Helen, you *do* say things. I wouldn't stand it from any one else. And you who always hated Frank Manners! How can I marry him when he hasn't got anything to marry me on? It's not my fault. He is—well, you know—I couldn't possibly marry any one who had n't even got a right to the name he was called by "; and Adela blushed deeply.

Helen looked at her.

" I don't want you to marry Mr. Manners," she said.

" Well," said Adela, looking down. " I should n't have minded if things had turned out differently. But then they have n't, and what is the use of fighting against Providence? I think it is very irreligious not to—to accept things. If I had been *meant* to marry Francis——"

" Providence would have arranged for his father and mother to have been properly married," interrupted Miss Wilmot.

Adela blushed again.

" Helen, you are odd," she said.

" And you are—no, I sha'n't tell you what you are. Go on, Adie."

" Go on—with what? "

" Tell me the rest."

" Helen, what do you mean? The rest? "

" Yes, my child. Exit Francis Manners, dust to dust, ashes to ashes, and all the rest of it, and enter—who? "

Adela looked first blank, and then shocked.

" Helen, you should n't. That 's in the Prayer Book," she exclaimed.

" So is the Marriage Service, Adie. How does it go?—I, Adela Frances, take thee—Richard, is n't it?—do you know his second name? "

" Helen, don't—what an odd way you have of putting things! "

" Have I? " Her voice softened. " Well, Adie, are n't you going to tell me? "

" Why, Helen, how do you know? "

" Because I am very clever," said Miss Wilmot. " You don't imagine that I burn the midnight candle-end for nothing? "

" You 'll never get married if you are so clever," said Adela seriously.

" No, but you will. Are you engaged, Adie? "

Adela gave a little conscious laugh.

" Yes, I am."

" To? "

" To Captain Morton, of course."

" Adie——"

Helen put out her arms, and the girls kissed. Helen's lips were soft and a little tremulous. It was she who kissed, and Adela who turned her smooth cool cheek to the caress.

" Oh, Adie," Helen whispered. " What does it feel like? Are you happy? "

And Adela shivered a little, her triumph grown suddenly cold. India was so far away. From the stretches of land and sea that lay between her and the country she must go to, there rose as it were a faint, chilly mist. It made the future look grey—nebulous—uncertain.

Adela caught at herself, and drew away from Helen. She spoke, and the sound of her own voice reassured her.

"I think it will do very well," she said, "and really you know, Helen, he is rather distinguished. Don't you think so?—though of course he is n't handsome. Now Francis Manners is handsome. I do admire a man with dark eyes, don't you?"

"No, I don't," said Miss Wilmot shortly.

Adela made herself comfortable on the floor. She leaned against the bed, close to Helen, and went on talking, chin in hand.

"Of course," she said thoughtfully, "Henry Lavington would really have suited me best of all. He would have been comfortable to live with. He would n't have made scenes like Frank Manners, and he would n't have been jealous. Now Captain Morton is jealous, I am sure. Henry Lavington would have let me do just as I liked, and I might have married him, you know."

Helen exclaimed, and Adela nodded.

"Yes, I might. I should have been Lady Lavington now, if I had n't been so foolish as to let him go and stay with Aunt Harriet without me, just when we had had a quarrel. I made up an excuse and would n't go, and the next thing I heard, he was engaged to Hetty. It was such a silly quarrel too—all about nothing—and when I saw Hetty in those diamonds to-night, I could have pinched her."

"I see," said Helen Wilmot. "Henry Lavington first, Francis Manners second, and Richard Morton—third. Is that it?"

'Adela took no notice.

" We sha'n't be so badly off," she said. " I
really could n't marry a poor man, but mamma
was right about the uncle. He left quite a nice
little sum, and I dare say if I did n't like India,
that Richard would sell out and settle down at
home. Yes, I think I shall make him do that."

" I thought he was ambitious," said Helen.
" They say he has a career before him."

" Oh, yes, he told me how ambitious he was.
And then he spoke so oddly about his ambition,
and about me—I thought he was quite profane.
It was quite like swearing. I could n't repeat
it "; and Adela's colour deepened.

" Swearing that he loved you? " said Helen
Wilmot in a curious voice.

" Of course, my dear." Adela's tone was a
little superior. " I expect we shall be married
pretty soon," she went on. " He has to go back
to India in September. Why, Helen, you will
be able to come out with us; I never thought
of that."

" So I shall."

Adela got up, yawning.

" Well, I must get into bed. Give me my
pillows. No, that one is n't mine. You can put
out the candle."

Helen dropped her book on the floor, blew out
the light—and lay down, with her face to the
windows, where a little tinge of gold was warm-
ing the streaks of light, which half an hour ago

had been cold and grey enough. The day would
be fine. She closed her eyes and called up a
picture of the sunrise, the air very clear, and
the colours in it faint yellow, ethereal green and
grey, with just one little rosy cloud, high up
where the grey was changing into blue. With
the unconscious plagiarism of youth she made
serious comparison in her own mind between
this dawn of day, and the dawn of Adela's new
life.

First the frail exquisite colours, then the
rhythmic mystery of flowing light, the glow, the
mounting glory, and afterwards full day, blue
sky, the happy work-a-day world and love's companionship. Helen did not blush, but a warmth
ran through her. She had a passionately romantic
nature, which she shielded under a somewhat
sarcastic mode of speech, and this contrast between what she felt, and what she expressed,
often caused her to give Adela credit for feelings which matched her own. She saw her
cousin's faults, but above them, transfiguring
where it did not hide, hovered the rainbow
breath of Adela's beauty, and the weakness of
Adela's character made strong appeal to her own
strength. All her romantic imaginings were for
Adela, none for herself. Her own path in life
was clear. Poor papa had his weaknesses,—so
much her grandmother had hinted,—and Helen's
imagination had immediately supplied her with
a picture of herself as the devoted daughter,

soothing, helping, companioning. As long as
poor papa lived, Helen would never leave him.
There would be a devoted lover, of course, but
she would dismiss him in a scene of the purest
poetry, and pursue a path brightened only by
such light as may be supposed to radiate from
ideals of the loftiest, the most fervent character.

Adela was different. For Adela she desired
all the blessings which she herself renounced.
She loved her cousin with the whole-heartedness
of an ardent young woman, who had had no one
younger than a grandmother upon whom to ex-
pend her affection. And then again and always,
there was Adela's beauty, and Helen responded
to beauty as a sunflower turns to the sun. *Il
y a toujours l'un qui baise et l'autre qui tend
la joue,* and Adela, nothing loath, submitted with
a good grace to being adored. She herself was
perhaps fonder of Helen than of any one else
in the world.

Helen lay looking into the daylight and watching it brighten until she grew drowsy, and slid
into a dream.

Suddenly there was a little rustle in the quiet
room, and she raised a sleepy head; dreamland
was pleasant, and she was tired.

"What *are* you doing, Adela?"

"I forgot to say my prayers," said Miss
Lauriston's soft voice with a shocked note in it.

She went down on her knees as she spoke, and
Helen blinked at her.

" And shall you say morning or evening ones? " she murmured.

Adela raised her head and looked puzzled.

" I always say my evening prayers when I come to bed," she said.

" And shall you say just the same as usual? "

" Yes.   Do hush, Helen," and Adela's head with the loose chestnut curls was buried in her hands.

Helen snuggled down and drifted comfortably back along the impalpable ways of sleep, but as Adela rose from her devotions she was again disturbed.

" Helen, would you have the wedding-dress satin, or a really good thick silk? "

This time Miss Wilmot was roused to anger.

" I don't care if you are married in your chemise," she declared, and Adela was too much shocked and offended to pursue the conversation.

CHAPTER V

Man is as old as his burden, but when will he understand
That a wayward woman is bridled, when a rope has been
made from the sand?

ADELA LAURISTON was married in the
beginning of September. She wore white
satin, and a wreath, and was not in the least
agitated.

"I must say I think a bride should be *pale*,"
said her Aunt Harriet with a disapproving eye
on Adela's soft, steady colour. "Either pale, or
blushing. But there, I always did say that
Adela had no heart."

"Helen is pale enough," said Hetty Lavington.

"Helen is always pale," returned Mrs. Middleton with severity. "It is perfectly absurd for a
healthy girl to have so little colour. However,
there is one thing, India cannot possibly make
her any paler, whereas Adela will probably lose
her complexion entirely within a year. Good
gracious me, Lucy will require a second pocket-
handkerchief if she is going to cry like that all
through the service. I hope Helen has seen that
she is provided."

After a brief honeymoon, Captain and Mrs.

58

Morton sailed for India, and Helen Wilmot went
with them, poor papa having managed at last to
send the money for her passage.

Azimullah Khan and Mr. Francis Manners
were also on their way to the East, at a not
very much later date, but they halted for a while
in Constantinople, where they acquired an ex-
haustive knowledge of the current rumours as
to British reverses and British incompetence in
the Crimea. And if some of the rumours were
exaggerated, others, it is to be feared, were only
too true. By the time Azimullah brought his
master the account of an unsuccessful mission,
he could bring him also flattering hopes of such
decay of the British power as should one day
place the Peishwa's representative upon the
Peishwa's throne, and meanwhile there was
pleasure enough.

An Oriental prince may be vicious at his will.
There are none to check, and many to pander
to him.

Dhundoo Punth's vices became a byword
amongst his own people. He drank deeply.
Francis Manners drank with him, and when his
unstrung nerves played him false, he drugged
them with opium, and followed his uncle deeper
and deeper into the morass of vice.

Captain and Mrs. Morton reached Peshawur
at the barest and ugliest time of the year. It
was quite cold too, and Adela wrote pettishly
to Helen Wilmot at Mian Mir:

" MY DEAR HELEN : This place is frightful. I can't think how Richard could have drawn such glowing pictures of it. I would never have come to India if I had known what it was like. And the houses! Tumble-down mud heaps, and you never in your life saw such frumps and frights as all the women are. I shall make Richard sell out."

Richard laughed consumedly when his wife repeated her remarks to him.

" And how are we to live, my child? "

" Why, you have some money," said Adela, colouring.

" Yes, goose, and I have some ambition. You know I told you so before you married me. Come, madam, I did n't deceive you with false pretences, did I?   I told you I was an ambitious devil, and you took him, and now you must make the best of him."

" *Richard,* I do wish you would n't——"

" Would n't what? "

" Use such language.   It 's not *nice.*" And Adela held up her head and looked so pretty that Richard kissed her, and told her she was a dear little saint, which she quite believed.

Presently, however, she returned to the charge.

" Richard, how can we live in a house like this? The floor is all soft mud, under that horrid, untidy matting, and the walls are all soft too, and Ayah says thieves sometimes get in by just scraping a hole in the wall. Ayah says the people here are dreadful. They are all thieves."

"Well, my dear, when one pays us a visit, I 'll shoot him for you. Will that do? He shall make his hole in the wall, and as sure as ever his head comes through, I shall shoot, and then we will dig another hole in the nice soft floor, and bury him, and no one will be a penny the wiser."

"Richard, how horrid! But really that floor——"

"I 'll give you a Persian carpet for a Christmas present. You shall come down into the city and choose it, if you like. Does that make things any better? "

Adela smiled a little, but her soft voice was still complaining.

"I wish Helen were here. She is clever about houses, and curtains, and things like that. I never was. If she were here she would be such a help. I 'm sure Uncle Edward did without her very well for all those years, and by all accounts he is n't a very proper person for Helen to be with. Now, Richard, you said so yourself. I do wish Helen had come on with us."

"I don't know that I do."

"Why, I thought you liked Helen. She likes you. She always did."

"I want my wife to myself," said Richard Morton, putting his arm about the said wife's waist.

" But don't you like Helen? "

" Of course I do, we are great friends. You
may send her my love when you write—and a
kiss, too—for the matter of that."

" Richard! "

" Shocked again? "

" I don't call it a very nice way to speak.
Well, Richard, I'm sure I've said nothing to
laugh at."

Captain Morton laughed all the same.

" Well, I'll kiss you instead. I don't know,
on the whole—on the whole, you know—that I
would n't rather. One, two, three—there I give
up the kiss, but I insist on your sending my
love."

Adela pursed her lips.

" Richard, I do think you are foolish, and I
wish you would be serious. No, you are not to
kiss me again. Oh, Richard, this dress crushes
—I sha'n't be writing to Helen for a whole week.
I do wish she would come and stay. She'd be
some one to talk to when you are out all day.
I am sure I shall never care for any of the ladies
here. They are such dowds! "

Captain Morton laughed.

" Well, my dear, you are a bride and a beauty,
and you would n't like it if they were better
dressed than you, or better looking, would you?
But there are some nice people here, and one
great friend of mine—Mrs. Lister; you have n't
seen Mrs. Lister yet."

" Yes, I have; she called to-day.   Richard, she 's plain—and she must be quite thirty.   You can't admire her? "

Richard Morton frowned.

" She 's a dear," he declared.

" That plain woman! "

He looked at Adela in surprise.

" Good Lord, child, one does n't choose one's friends for their looks! "

" I thought men did—when the friends were women," said Adela, flushing.

She slipped off her husband's knee, and he let her go, with half a sigh.

" Mrs. Lister is a real trump," he said.   " I wish you would make a friend of her.   They took me in when I had fever once, and she nursed me as if I were a brother."

" Oh—a brother! " said Adela.   Her tone was peculiar, and Richard Morton looked at her sharply.

" What do you mean, Adela? " he said in a voice that matched his look.

Adela was frightened into further imprudence. With a little toss of the head that was half temper and half nervousness, she exclaimed:

" Mean—oh, nothing.   Brother, or cousin— it 's all the same, and very convenient when people want to flirt."

Richard turned white with anger; his brows made a straight line, and beneath them his eyes blazed.

Adela burst into tears.

"Richard! Don't look at me like that! What did I say? I am sure I don't know why it should make you so angry. Did you never flirt with any one? I thought all men did—especially in India. And as to her—I am sure any one might want you to—to admire them—you can't expect *me* to think that strange, or an impossible sort of thing to happen. No, you really can't." And Richard called himself a brute, and petted her, and tried to forget what she had said, and the sharp revulsion of feeling which had seized him when she said it. All the same, the scene, and others like it, left a little sting, a little soreness, and on the whole, it was just as well that Captain Morton was kept very busy over the much-discussed Afghan Treaty and the impending visit of Hyder Khan, son and heir-apparent of the Amir.

In March Adela's letters became more cheerful.

"This place is getting rather pretty now," she wrote to Miss Wilmot, "and it's warm, and we have been quite gay. The peach blossom was out a little while ago. We gave a dinner-party, and I wore my peach-coloured silk, and a wreath of real peach blossoms in my hair. Captain Bannister of the 150th said some rather pretty things. And I have n't lost my complexion and if you write to Aunt Harriet, or to Hetty, you might say so. You could say I was 'much admired.' It would really be quite true, and I

don't see why some one should n't tell them.
Mamma seems very poorly. I expect it is a
great deal fancy, but she writes such depressed
letters. It is rather selfish of her. I get quite
moped after reading one."

A week later it was:

" I saw Hyder Khan, the Amir's son, yesterday. He is a big fat man, with a black beard,
and black eyes, but his skin is quite fair. He
wore a sort of dressing-gown, and bundles and
bundles of clothes underneath it. I am sure he
asked who I was. He did stare, and then he
turned and spoke to Major Edwardes, and Captain Bannister who was with me got quite red,
and said something I could n't catch, and when
I told Richard about it in the evening, he was
just as ridiculous. I believe they were both
jealous! "

Helen Wilmot laid down the rustling sheets,
and frowned at them.

She was trying very hard to live amongst her
dreams. She was trying very hard to keep them
intact and beautiful.

Papa's little weakness had proved to be an
inability ever to say " No " to a brandy peg. On
the infrequent occasions upon which he was
quite sober he was a mournful person, with a
manner of impenetrable gloom. When he was
drunk, he was either jovial or violent. When
jovial, Helen was called upon to listen to songs
and anecdotes of a broadly convivial nature.

When violent, she went in terror, for once already he had struck her. The bruise ached for a long time under the thin muslin of her bodice. Her bruised ideals ached longer still. Under such stress as this, the stuff of which dreams are made wears very thin indeed. The grey star-bordered robe of self-sacrifice, the golden garment of romance, she drew them tightly about her, denying the rents and the worn places in them—dreading to find them fall away and leave her naked and ashamed—oh, how ashamed.

Adela, and Adela's happiness, belonged to the dream life. Surely with Richard Morton, Adela would be happy and safe. Helen and he had made great friends during the long sea-voyage. They had enjoyed many a battle of wits, and had come to a pleasant sense of comradeship, and understanding. And how he loved Adela! His very voice changed when he spoke of her. His every look proclaimed the tender pride with which he regarded her. Helen had felt so happy for them both, but now— She frowned again as she took up another letter and looked through it.

" Captain Bannister thinks my new muslin dress a great success. It is made with five flounces."

" Captain Bannister is teaching me to ride."

" Captain Bannister valses divinely. His step suits mine in the most delightful manner."

" Now I wonder what Richard thinks of so

much Captain Bannister," reflected Miss Wilmot, frowning so deeply that poor papa, who
came in very irritable, remarked, with much
vehemence and profanity, that it was enough
to make any man cut his throat, when he came
home to find his daughter looking like a mute
at a funeral.

"I like a lively woman," he observed, and
Helen took her thoughts to her own room.

Richard had thought, too. One day he spoke
them out very plainly. He had been up to his
eyes in work, but at last there came a breathing
space.

On the 30th of March, Hyder Khan and Mr.
John Lawrence, representing those high con-
tracting parties, the Amir of Afghanistan, on the
one side, and on the other the British Government, signed the Treaty which bound Dost
Mohammed Khan, his heirs, and his successors
to perpetual peace and friendship with the
Honourable East India Company. Three years
later the Treaty was to save India for us, when
mutiny, fanned by a tempest, ran through all
the length and breadth of the land.

On the frontier, all the wild tribes stirred.
The whisper went round that a Mohammedan
Emperor sat on the Peacock Throne at Delhi,
and that there was much loot to be had. But
Delhi was far—Cabul nearer—and on the throne
of Cabul the Amir, whose word was as the word
of the Prophet. And the word that came from

Dost Mohammed was a word of peace. All along the frontier it passed. The Amir says, " sit still "—and Eusufzai, and Utmankhel, Orakzai, and Malikdin Khel Afridi, stayed in their villages in peace, whilst their sons went down to Peshawur and took service with the hard-pressed British Raj.

Herbert Edwardes reaped his reward then, but now he stood aside and let another take the praise for what was his own achievement.

He had worked for it against heavy odds, fought for it against official coldness and discouragement in his quarters. Now it was accomplished and he was content.

John Lawrence signed the Treaty, and then tents were struck, presents exchanged, elaborate farewells taken, and Hyder Khan and his retinue moved off through the Khyber Pass.

Peshawur settled into quiet, and Captain Morton had leisure to contemplate his own private affairs. What he saw was very far from pleasing him.

" Bannister comes to the house too often," he said with the abrupt directness which Adela had learned to dread. She fluttered a little.

" May n't I have *any* friends? It is *rather* hard, I think, and when I have scarcely *seen* you for six weeks. What did you wish me to do? Sit indoors and do plain sewing, like your Mrs. Lister? "

She looked so pretty—her spurt of temper was so like a child's that Richard softened.

"Now, Adela," he said, and she repeated:

"May n't I have even one friend?"

"You are a silly baby," he said, putting his arm round her. "Yes, you are. Why don't you make friends with some of the other ladies?"

"Oh, Richard, I told you I never could, you must remember that I told you so. You might be fair, even if you are cross. Now Captain Bannister——"

Richard's arm dropped.

"My dear child, not to put too fine a point upon it, Captain Bannister has completely lost what little head he ever had. He always was an ass."

"Richard!"

"The man's in love with you, Adela," said Richard in his most annoyed tones. "That is why I won't have him here."

Adela looked down, modest but complacent.

"I don't see why," she said.

Richard Morton's face hardened. Adela said afterwards that he glared at her.

"I do," he observed, and there was a disagreeable silence.

After a moment Adela stole a glance at him.

"Really, of all the fusses—" she thought, and aloud she murmured:

"How jealous you are, Dick!"

"It's not a question of jealousy, it's a question of common decency. I won't have a man in my house, when he makes no secret of being in love with my wife."

He looked hard at Adela as he spoke, and then began to walk up and down the room, a proceeding which always got upon her nerves.

"Oh, Richard, don't!" she said sharply. "It's exactly like having a wild beast in the room. And you are too ridiculous about poor Captain Bannister, who is *most* nice and respectful—a great deal more respectful than you are, sir"; and she ventured a little coquettish glance which sent the blood to Richard Morton's head.

He came across to her with a couple of great strides, and took her by the shoulders.

"Adela, do you put us on the same footing?"

"Oh, you are hurting me!"

"Answer me. Do you?"

"Dick, how ridiculous! As if one could have two husbands, or wanted to! I am sure one is enough. *More* than enough."

"Are you sorry that you married me?" asked Richard Morton.

There was something in his tone that would have gone to the heart of a woman who loved him. Adela welcomed it.

"Not when you are nice. When you are jealous, and unreasonable, and horrid—well, I don't know," and she threw him a teasing glance.

A few months ago it would have brought him

to her feet. Now he let go of her, and said with rather a heavy sigh:

"My dear, you took me with your eyes open. I suppose some one else might have made you happier, but I am your husband, and you mustn't forget it. You mustn't forget it, Adela."

He went out of the room without kissing her, and Adela sat down pouting, to tell Captain Bannister that she was afraid she could not ride with him as she had promised.

This was the first of many like scenes. Captain Bannister went his way, and next it was Mr. Burnet, the young civilian, whose name occurred in every letter. Dick was very un-reasonable about him too, "and really, my dear Helen," wrote Adela, "it is too hot to have fusses."

In May Mrs. Morton went up to Murree, and held quite a little court there.

"There is a Mr. Duncan who is quite *devoted* to me," she wrote to Helen Wilmot, who was still at Mian Mir. "He is so handsome, and a charming partner."

But a little later on it was—"Mr. Duncan is getting rather tiresome. He has begun to make scenes," and so it went on, until Captain Morton came up on leave, and at the end of it carried his wife back to Peshawur, where she had perforce to spend a very quiet winter, for her mother died suddenly after so many ailing

years, and she herself was nervous, and out of
sorts.

In the spring a baby boy was born to Richard
and Adela Morton—born only to die.

Adela recovered very quickly. Helen looked
out anxiously for letters, and when they came
they were full of Adela's delight at being, as she
phrased it, " presentable " again; and of Adela's
apprehensions lest her looks should have suffered from her illness.

" I really believe," she wrote to Helen in
April, " I really do believe I look all the better
for the *rest*, though I did hate it at the time.
What with being in mourning, and not being
fit to be seen, it was a *dreadful* winter. It is
so nice to have a waist again. I can wear my
last year's muslin dresses already, and I have n't
had to let them out, as Mrs. Carruthers said I
should. I have made great friends with her.
She is the only woman here with an idea of how
to dress. I am going to share a house with her
in Murree this year. I wish you could come up.
I think Uncle Edward very *selfish* to keep you
down. Men *are* selfish. Imagine Richard expecting me to stay here with him, and after all
I have been through, too—I said no, not unless
he wanted to kill me, and I told him what I
thought about his selfishness. Only I believe it
is more *jealousy* with him. As if I could help
people admiring me! Richard is very dull and
mopy just now. He is really absurd about the

poor baby's death. As if a father's feelings
could possibly be as deep as a mother's. Every
one knows that men don't really care for children when they are so small, and as I tell him,
if I can think about other things, and be resigned, he ought to be able to. If the poor little
thing had been *meant* to live, it would have lived.
I am afraid Richard is not at all religious. He
has quite given up going to church, and goes
out shooting instead. So Major Morrison calls
for me, and we go for a drive afterwards. That
odious Mrs. Lister told Richard, and made out
that people were talking, and he made a scene,
and last Sunday he *did* come to church, and sat
there looking—well, stiff was n't the word, and
a most shocking sort of sarcastic look on his
face. He really is too unreasonable. I shall be
delighted to get away from here."

In the early autumn of 1856, Colonel Wilmot
died, and Richard Morton wrote to Helen and
asked her to make her home with Adela. Between the short sentences, Helen divined an
appeal.

That summer in the hills with Mrs. Carruthers
had proved a most disastrous one; Mr. Duncan
—who made scenes—had put in an appearance
once more, and Adela had allowed him to make
her the talk of the place. Finally, when Captain Morton came up to Murree in August, there
was a scene beyond all other scenes. Mr. Duncan, repulsed by the now terrified Adela, went

away and made an unsuccessful attempt to cut
his throat. The scandal may be imagined, and
its effect on Richard Morton. Adela thought it
all very hard.

"Richard talked as if I were a *murderess*,"
she wrote to Helen. "I believe he would like to
see me *hung!* As if it were my fault that
Charlie Duncan tried to do such a wicked thing.
I have *always* said I thought it *very* wicked of
people to commit suicide. It shows that they
haven't been well brought up, and that they
haven't proper religious principles. I said this
to Richard, and I said it only showed how necessary it was to have religious principles, and
you've no idea, Helen, how *unkind* he was, or
what things he said. And after all it is all a
great fuss about nothing, for Mr. Duncan is all
right again, and he has taken furlough and is
going home immediately. When he is gone,
people will stop talking."

But when Helen Wilmot came up to Peshawur
in October, she found that people had by no
means stopped talking. Adela was desperately
aggrieved.

"Richard has gone and got himself trans-
ferred," she complained. "I am sure I don't
really mind, for this place is simply *too* hateful,
now, but I did hope if we were going down
into Oude, that we should go to some nice big
station, but of course no one considers me,
Richard least of all, and the place we are going

to is a horrid poky little hole, called Urzeepore. Richard is to officiate as Deputy Commissioner, and of course he is pleased because his old regiment is stationed there. I told him I could n't think why that should please him, for he always said that Colonel Crowther was a cross between a monomaniac and a sick baby, whatever that may be. And Mrs. Crowther must be a dreadful person. But of course Richard is *immense* friends with Captain Blake, who is Adjutant now, and Richard is a person who is very fond of his friends, though he won't let me have any!"

"Adela!"

"Well, he *won't!* If you knew the fusses there have been!"

"My dear Adie, how can you expect——"

Adela stamped her foot.

"I won't have it, Helen! Not from you—I declare I won't. When you said that, you looked the exact image of Richard. He is most unreasonable, and it is n't as if I were not *particular*. Why even Charlie Duncan never so much as kissed me. Bella Carruthers would n't believe me when I told her so. She lets men kiss her, but I *never* do. I should n't think it right, and it is n't only men Richard objects to, so you need n't look at me like that. He was as nasty as he could be about Bella Carruthers!"

"I don't wonder. She sounds odious," said Helen shortly.

"Well, she *is* rather fast," admitted Adela.

"And I'm not nearly as fond of her as I was. I'd much rather have you, Helen. Do you know I think you have improved a lot—in looks I mean—I like your hair in that big plait all round your head. Richard likes it, too. He said he thought you were very nice-looking, and he hardly ever notices people's looks. If it were any one but you, I should be jealous, though of course Dick isn't like that. He really doesn't even look at another woman. Sometimes I wish he would."

"Adie! How silly you are."

"Well, it's because he watches me. It's too horrid. You remember what poor mamma used to say about the way he looked at me? Well, it's quite true, and if he would only look at some one else for a change, it would give me a rest. Of course, I don't mean anything serious. Just a flirtation, but Richard doesn't flirt."

"And you are not going to either. Adie, you have been a goose, but now you are going to be good, aren't you?"

"Oh, I suppose so," said Adela, and she went away, humming a tune.

Helen sat down and cried. In the two years since she and Adela parted, Helen had learned many things.

Now the dreams were all gone.

CHAPTER VI

> Yesterday's fire is clean gone out,
>   Yesterday's hearth is cold.
> No one can either bargain or buy
>   With last year's gold.
> Greet the new as it passes on,
>   Bid Good-bye to the old,
> Yesterday's Song is sung to the end,
>   Yesterday's Tale is told.

THE Mortons had been in Urzeepore for a fortnight when Mrs. Crowther gave a dinner-party, to which they and all official Urzeepore were bidden. It was a warm March night, and the dinner was rather a tremendous affair, Mrs. Crowther desiring to make it quite plain that, Deputy Commissioner or no Deputy Commissioner, she herself was the leading lady of Urzeepore society, and intended to remain so.

She wore a fateful air, and a garment which was believed to have been her wedding-dress. It was now dyed grass green, and was adorned with seven little flounces of green tulle, edged with yellow tinsel trimming. Above all the expanse of green, Mrs. Crowther's brick-red countenance looked several shades redder than usual. Her masses of brilliantly golden hair hung low

77

on a sunburned neck. Her features were as harsh as the voice in which she was addressing much rapid conversation to faded, white-faced Mrs. Marsh, who sat on the sofa beside her.

On either side of the couch stood Carrie and Milly Crowther, and when their mother wished to make a remark unsuited to their youthful ears, she dropped into what she believed to be the French language. It had a most respectably British ring. It was many years since she had acquired this habit, and it had become second nature.

She rose in the middle of a sentence to shake hands with Mrs. Monson and Mrs. Elliot. The latter put her head on one side and said languidly:

"We are to meet the Mortons, are we not? I hear she is quite lovely, and dresses so well. Have you seen her yet?"

"No," said Mrs. Crowther. She dropped Mrs. Elliot's hand and sat down again.

"No," she repeated, "I have not seen her; I don't believe any one has seen her. I called. She has singularly ill-trained servants. The man I saw had been asleep. He actually yawned in my face. Insolence *incroyable!* And he said —he said "—Mrs. Crowther glanced to right and left, searched in her memory for a recalcitrant French word and decided upon her native tongue —"he said the Memsahib is in her bath. Dong song bang!'" she repeated in tones of returning confidence.

Mrs. Elliot fixed her with an admiring gaze. "One always bows to courage," she murmured in Mrs. Monson's ear, to which that little lady responded with a severe "Do be good, Grace."

"One never does know what they say," complained Mrs. Marsh. She was fidgeting with the lace at her elbows, and had conceived a panic lest the hole she had discovered should be visible to Mrs. Crowther's searching eye.

"I wonder if Mrs. Morton is as pretty as they say," she said hastily.

Mrs. Crowther sniffed aloud.

"I never liked Captain Morton," she said in virtuous tones. "I never liked him, but if all that one hears is true, I am sorry for him. He was a most interfering person as Adjutant. I am sure he used to make my poor Colonel quite ill. Always fussing about, and wanting to manage everything and everybody. But if half one hears is true, he can't manage his wife. *Elle est très vite*," she added in a thrilling undertone, and felt happily convinced that she had informed Mrs. Marsh of the scandalous fact that Adela Morton was fast.

"Oh, really!"

"Yes, I fear it is too true. *Trop vrai.* My friend, Mrs. Blacker, who was in Murree last year, wrote me *des histoires très,—très—*er— shocking, I do assure you. Had it not been for

Captain Morton's former connection with the regiment, I really do not know that I should have called. *Je ne peux pas dire. Il faut considérer mes filles.* As it is I shall *not* encourage any intimacy with Milly and Carrie, and I shall keep my distance. Mrs. Elliot, how is your baby?"

"I believe it is quite well," said Mrs. Elliot indifferently. "The ayah would have told me if anything were wrong."

"The ayah!"

"Yes—don't you think it is so much better for one person to manage a child? I don't interfere."

"Grace!" murmured Mrs. Monson.

She turned to her hostess with a quick, birdlike movement.

"How curious that the Mortons should have been sent here!" she exclaimed.

"Very *tactless,* I call it," said Mrs. Crowther. She drew herself up, and the green silk bodice, made in slimmer days, receded dangerously.

"Tactless?" inquired Mrs. Elliot. "Oh—of course—I see. Yes, it really *is* when you come to think of it. Of course he takes precedence of Colonel Crowther."

"Oh, no," protested Mrs. Marsh.

Mrs. Crowther inclined her head—just in time.

"But he is only *officiating.*"

"That makes no difference."

" How *wrong!* And she? "

Mrs. Crowther once more imperilled her shoulder-straps.

" If any one imagines that I am going to walk out of any dining-room but my own behind my own Adjutant's wife, well—*je ne veux pas, c'est tout!*" and Mrs. Crowther rose with majesty to greet a further instalment of guests.

" How do you *do,* Captain Blake. You are to take Miss Wilmot in to dinner; you have not met her, of course. Oh—you have—I should scarcely have thought it possible, since you only returned from Cawnpore yesterday. You must have called this morning—really you were most prompt. Mrs. Morton should be *flattered.* How do you do, Mr. Purslake; you will take my daughter Carrie. Carrie, show Mr. Purslake the last drawing you made. Milly, go and tell your papa that it is getting very late. Oh, here *are* the Mortons. How do you do, Captain Morton. And which of these two ladies is your wife? Oh, *not* this one. Really, Miss Wilmot, I should have taken *you* for the married lady; you look so much graver than your cousin."

" A bad compliment to me," said Richard Morton, laughing. " Why should I be expected to have a depressing effect upon my wife, Mrs. Crowther? "

" I alluded to the cares and responsibilities of the married state," said the lady, in her most tremendous tones, and Captain Morton discov-

6

ered some intention in the glance with which she favoured Adela.

He hastened to greet his old Colonel, who had just wandered into the room, convoyed by his daughter Milly. Colonel Crowther was small, and wore the worried air of a man whose digestion is not at peace within. He gave Richard two chilly fingers, and an absent glance, and was drifting in the direction of Dr. Darcy whom he wished to consult about a new symptom, when he encountered his wife, who despatched him to the dining-room with Adela.

Helen Wilmot, after admitting to Dr. Darcy that she liked India, and had been out nearly three years, applied herself to her dinner, and to making friends with Captain Blake. She found him hard to talk to, but she liked his shy ways, his deep-set eyes, and his obvious devotion to Richard Morton.

" Richard must find it curious, being here with his old regiment," she said, after a while.

" He 's a deserter, and ought to be court-martialled," said Captain Blake abruptly. Then he looked rather alarmed, and tried to cut through the bone of a cutlet. " Oh, you know, I don't really mean that, Miss Wilmot," and Helen laughed.

" I 'll tell him," she said, and George Blake began to think her a charming person. In a vague, absent-minded manner he admired the way in which she screwed up her eyes when she laughed. He thought it made her look much younger. Suddenly he became aware that he was staring, and he blushed and made haste to say:

"We've all told him. It's no good. And now he is the high and mighty Civil official, and much too grand for the poor old regiment."

"And you don't really mean that either, do you?" said Miss Wilmot, and after that they talked about Richard, and Richard's doings, until Dr. Darcy insisted on his share of Helen's attention.

After dinner she found herself next to a pretty little dark-eyed woman, with smoothly banded hair.

"I am Mrs. Monson; my husband commands the 11th Irregulars," said this little lady. She had a very friendly smile. "It seems rather odd we should meet here," she went on; "I mean it's odd because we live next door to each other, and this is a mile away."

"Oh, is yours the house with the roses?" exclaimed Helen.

"Yes," said the little lady, dimpling. "Aren't they nice? I am so fond of them. We have been here for two years, and I have begged, borrowed, and stolen cuttings from every compound in the place. We all love flowers."

"I think I have seen your little girl in the distance," said Helen.

Mrs. Monson laughed—a funny little laugh, with a gurgle in it.

"Oh! She won't remain in the distance, I am afraid. We *can't* keep her in our own garden. She will go off and pay calls! I only hope she won't bother you, Mrs. Morton."

Helen started.

"But I 'm Miss Wilmot," she said quickly, and Mrs. Monson blushed scarlet.

"My dear Miss Wilmot, what a stupid mistake! I am so short-sighted, you know, and I never noticed who went in to dinner with whom, and you are so much taller than your cousin, and —and——"

Afterwards she confided in Captain Monson:

"James, was n't it foolish? You can't think how silly I felt, but she sat there looking so handsome and composed, and the other little creature had just fluttered out on to the verandah with Mr. Purslake, all smiles and blushes, and mauve and white ribbons, so of course I thought *she* was the unmarried one."

"Which shows you don't listen to gossip, Lizzie," said Captain Monson, and his wife blushed and said:

"And why should I, sir?"

Mrs. Crowther had also watched Adela disappear into the soft dusk of the verandah. This was exactly the sort of behaviour that she had been led to expect. Mr. Purslake too—who had obviously joined the ladies early, in order to have a word with Carrie. Adela had intercepted him, in the most brazen way, and was

walking away with her prize in a manner which
bespoke considerable practice.

"I am sure your garden looks perfectly *sweet*
by moonlight," she murmured as she passed her
hostess, and Mrs. Crowther became crimson.

"Worse than I expected," she said in an awful
undertone to Mrs. Marsh. "Worse, much worse.
I regret having called. Levity I was prepared
for, heartlessness I anticipated. It did not for
an instant surprise me that she should be in
colours so soon after Colonel Wilmot's death, no
—but some slight respect for me—*pour la femme
du Colonel*—I did look for—I had a right to
look for. Did you notice how she walked out
of the dining-room, without so much as turning
her head to see if I were coming? It was just
as if *je n'existais pas!*"

"No, no, don't say so."

Mrs. Crowther turned to her daughters, and
raised her voice.

"Carrie and Milly, you may join Mrs. Morton
and Mr. Purslake upon the verandah. The night
is extremely warm."

"Well, did you have a pleasant evening?"
inquired Captain Morton, as they all drove
home.

"*Pleasant!*" Adela's voice was distinctly
cross.

"You did n't, then?"

"My *dear* Richard—such dreadful people!
Following one about! Interrupting one's con-

versations! You and Helen may have been amused, but I 'm sure I had n't a chance, stuck between Colonel Crowther and that stiff Major Marsh at dinner, and then interminable ages of that dreadful woman, who kept explaining to me that it would be quite absurd for me to go in to dinner before she did."

" Oho, I had n't thought of that! Lord, what a joke! Of course you do."

" Do what? I never can understand what you mean."

" Why, go in to dinner before our Lady Crowther. Must n't she be wild? Was that why she looked at you so affectionately when you said good-night? "

" I don't know which is worse, she or her husband," said Adela.

" What did he enliven the dinner-hour with? He has only two subjects of conversation, you know—temperance and his own health—sometimes he blends the two."

" He was perfectly disgusting," said Adela, with a toss of her head.

" Oh, then you had the action of alcohol upon the human stomach. That 's a great favourite; he loves talking about alcohol, and always starts when Mrs. C. is safely out of hearing. She will have wine on state occasions, but it is so bad that it really does more to advance the cause of temperance than all old Crowther's dissertations. He can't call his soul his own, so she gets her own way, and he bears testimony on the sly, when she is n't listening."

" He was dreadful," said Adela, quite shocked.

Richard laughed, and touched the pony with the whip.

" You should have heard him after dinner," he said. " First he talked to Darcy, until Darcy went to sleep. Then he came over to me, and told me all about his malaria, and how he felt when he had a cold fit, and what Darcy said when he had a hot fit, and all about his liver."

" Richard ! "

" Well, he did, and finished up by asking me to feel his pulse."

" I don't think this is at all a *nice* conversation," said Adela with decision.

" Quite right, my dear; we 'll talk about something else. How did you get on with Blake, Helen? "

Miss Wilmot turned from the moonlit landscape. There was a queer little smile on her face.

" Oh, I liked him," she said.

" He 's a very good fellow. Not a lady's man, of course."

" I liked him very much. All of a sudden, you know, the queer way one does, sometimes. At least I do. One minute you don't care in the least, and the next you like the person so much that you feel as if you had known him for years."

"My dear Helen, are you trying to break it to us that you have suddenly formed an unrequited attachment?"

"Yes, that's it," said Helen, laughing. "Suddenly you know, in the middle of the pudding course, I felt as if he were quite an old friend. I wondered so much what he would do if I were to murmur: 'A sudden thought strikes me, let us swear an eternal friendship!'"

"Really, Helen!" protested Adela.

"He'd probably have been delighted. You try him, and if he doesn't respond, I'll call him out. Under that shy manner of his, he's the soul of romance."

"What would he be likely to do?" inquired Miss Wilmot.

"Well, he might seize the nearest menu card, and suggest that you should immediately subscribe the most tremendous vows, with a pen dipped in your mutual gore, or he might drop his eyeglass into the finger bowl, and fly, taking the earliest opportunity of hinting to me that he feared you were not—not quite, er—right—in the—er—head—you know, Dick"; and Captain Morton imitated the shy, hesitating drawl which was Captain Blake's medium when embarrassed.

"Well, I think you are both mad," said Adela.

"What, poor George too? Well, you can tell him so, for he's coming on to have a talk and a smoke."

" To-night? "

" Yes, to-night. I 've not seen him—to speak to—since he got back. So if you want to tell him he is mad, and if Helen wants him to swear eternal friendship, now 's your chance."

" Thank you," said Miss Wilmot; " I can wait."

The trap drew up, and Adela spoke in a vexed tone as her husband helped her down.

" You are going to sit up and smoke? "

" We are. Imam Bux," to the sleepy bearer who stumbled to his feet as they came up the verandah steps, " Blake Sahib is coming. Bring pegs."

" That horrid tobacco! The house will be full of it next day."

" Oh, I don't think so."

" Well, I do. Really, Richard, if I had only thought of it, I would have made you promise to give up smoking before I married you."

" Would you? " said Richard, lifting the split bamboo screen for the ladies to pass into the house.

Helen went silently to her own door, but Adela hung back. " You would have done it to please me *then*," she said. She was pouting a little, and inclined to flirt with her husband, since there was no one else available.

" I don't think so, my dear."

" You *would*. You were in love with me then, Dick——"

Captain Morton raised his eyebrows, and looked round to discover that they were alone.

"My dear Adela, suppose you follow Helen to bed."

"You *were*—madly. You would have done anything that I asked."

"I might have reflected that a woman who could make so unreasonable a request—" Richard Morton paused, and turned to the table. He took up the heavy cut-glass decanter which stood there, and measured out a peg.

"You would have done *any*thing," repeated Adela.

Richard looked at her, half absently. Perhaps he was trying to recall the memory of those hot days of passion. Perhaps he was trying to forget them. A proud man, whose feelings are at once deep and sensitive, may well shrink from recalling a passion which has humiliated him, and has failed to satisfy a single one of the cravings of his nature. Things were settling down now. Helen Wilmot was a comfortable third person in the household. Her presence made for safety and domesticity. Her influence with Adela was decidedly a success. Richard Morton valued peace in the domestic circle. Since his wife's cousin had been an inmate of his house, there had been no more scenes.

Adela spent a good deal of money on clothes, but she was not always riding with some infatuated young man. She no longer passed whole mornings gossiping with Mrs. Carruthers, a person to whom Richard had the greatest objection.

He traced all these improvements to Helen Wilmot, and was duly grateful. But, whilst anxious for peace, he was very far from desiring to renew the old service of adoration. Of late he had thought that Adela resented this attitude. His temper stirred as he suspected a desire to employ some otherwise idle moments in bringing him once again under the yoke. He did not look at Adela now, and there was a little frown between his eyes as he crossed to the fireplace, reached for his pipe, and said rather shortly:

"Blake will be here in a moment. You had better go to bed, Adela."

She went as far as the door and came back again.

"You *are* cross," she said, "and you've never said a word about my new dress. I don't believe you even *noticed* it. And it is so pretty. I designed it, and Helen stood over the dirzee whilst he made it. I am sure it looks just as if I had had it out from home. Don't you think so? Don't you like it?"

"Yes, it is very pretty."

"And becoming, too, don't you think? That pale mauve is a very trying colour, you know, but Helen said she was sure I could stand it, and it goes so well with my amethyst necklace. Do you remember when you gave it to me?"

Yes, he remembered. It was when the world
seemed too little to give. Eighteen months ago
in Murree, and she had just told him about the
child. He could see the blue hills now, and the
blue mist across the plains. Intimate memories
which had been hushed away into silence woke
a little, and whispered in him. There was only
one lamp in the room, and it threw a hazy
golden light over Adela in her soft white dress.

" Dick, don't you ever remember? "

Adela was quite close now, her hand on the
mantelpiece beside his arm, her bare arm brushing his shoulder. If he were to turn his head,
and bend it ever so little more, he might kiss
the dimpled hollow beneath her upraised chin.

Yes, he remembered—and with remembrance
came a sharp stab of anger. That she should
be capable of stirring such a memory for the
sake of furthering an idle flirtation, would have
served, had it been necessary, to divest Richard
Morton of his last illusion with regard to his
wife. But it was not necessary. During the
two and a half years of their married life he
had come to realise, at first dimly and with great
pain, but later on with a certain hard clarity
of vision, that Adela neither responded, nor desired to respond, to anything but admiration.
For this she lived. For this she had an appe-
tite so insatiable, that deprived of it she pined,
and could be driven to seek it even from the
husband whose prodigality in this respect had

once awakened the tyrant in her. But any answer of the heart, any response of the intelligence, any home affection, Adela had not to give. That her beauty still had power to move him was a fact of which Richard Morton was aware —a fact for which he despised himself.

He had no desire that Adela should share either the knowledge or the contempt. He had given of his best, and it had not been received. He would not offer his worst upon the altar once held sacred. She had been the mother of his child—his son.

That bitter disappointment ached in him still.

" Dick, you might—look—at me," said Adela's soft voice, very softly.

Through the open doorway came the sound of wheels. Richard Morton straightened himself, with a breath of relief.

" There 's Blake," he said ; and as Adela turned pettishly away he moved to the table, and took a long drink before going to meet his friend.

CHAPTER VII

HOW CAPTAIN MORTON TALKED ABOUT CHUPATTIS

Borrow of Life as you please,
What has it got to lend?
What that is better than these—
A sword, and a horse, and a friend?

Love is but dangerous stuff,
Heavy at heart in the end.
These three things are enough—
A sword, and a horse, and a friend.

"COME along into the office, George," said Richard Morton, leading the way. "Imam Bux, give the Sahib a peg, a large peg, and the chair that does n't break when you sit on it. Son of owls, that *is* the broken chair. Take it away and have it burnt. Do you wish to kill Blake Sahib?"

"Blake Sahib is my father and my mother," said Imam Bux with much gravity. He set a lamp upon the office table as he spoke and the light struck upwards, and gave his long grey beard a golden tinge.

"Much obliged to you, I 'm sure, Imam Bux,"

said Captain Blake. "You look very well. You didn't get your throat cut in Peshawur after all, you see. Last time I saw you, you were quite sure that a wild Pathan was going to slit that villainous old gizzard of yours, eh?"

"By the favour of the Sahib I am returned alive," said Imam Bux. "Peshawur is a bad place. All those who are not thieves there, are murderers."

He salaamed and waddled ponderously to the verandah door, where he disappeared into the darkness. After a moment or two a sound of muffled snoring announced the resumption of his slumbers.

"Light up, George," said Captain Morton.

"Sure it's allowed?"

Richard gave a short laugh.

"You are a heathen, George. You don't know your prayer-book. It is the lady who says 'obey' in the marriage service, not the man."

"Saying isn't doing," observed Captain Blake, with some wisdom. "Same old service five-and-twenty years ago, I take it, so the Crowther must have said she'd obey the poor old Colonel. Nobody has ever noticed her doing it, but perhaps the Colonel got muddled up and said her bits by mistake. If he was the same five-and-twenty years ago as he is now, it's more than likely."

"You've hit on an isolated case."

"I've hit on an awful warning," said Captain

Blake solemnly. All the time he was talking,
his eyes were upon his friend's face, with the
gentle absent expression which was one of his
characteristics. His voice was very slow and
inexpressive. He was n't quite sure about the
solitariness of that awful warning. Dick looked
as if he had had some pretty bad times since
they had met. There was a deep vertical line
between his eyes that used not to show like that.
H'm, marriage was certainly the deuce, and
Captain Blake thanked fate and his own caution
that he was a lonely bachelor.

"How are you settling down, Dick?" he inquired, after a moment or two. "Adamson left
you something to do, did n't he? I hope to goodness it 's true that he does n't mean coming back.
He was the laziest man in Oude when he had n't
got fever, and the limpest rag in Asia when he
had."

"I should think he was about as much good
at his job as Imam Bux would be. Young Jelland seems a nice boy, but inclined to take things
easy. Fatehshah Khan seems to have done more
work than the other two, but, Lord, George,
fancy leaving land cases to be settled by a native
extra Assistant Commissioner! Talk of muddles. It 's a year since we annexed Oude.
Goodness knows things must have been mixed
up enough to start with, but Adamson seems to
have managed to give 'em just that extra amount
of tangling that makes it perfectly certain

they 'll never come straight. I wish I had come here at once, when we took things over. One would n't have been bound by the muddles of the Oude Government, but Adamson's muddles are a different story."

" Oh, you 'll get it straight in time."

" A combination of Solomon, Manu, and Socrates could n't get it straight," said Captain Morton with emphasis. " As far as I can make out, no matter in whose favour a suit is settled, there will always be at least two other claimants, quite as likely to be in the right. And that 's what we call pacifying the country districts. It 's this blessed chuckladaree system that 's the very devil and all."

" Can't say I 've ever grasped it," said Blake.

" Happy George! You have n't had to. I 've been struggling for a fortnight, and as far as I 've got, it 's like this. Oude was split into twenty-two chuckladarees or districts under the late King. Each chuckladaree had its own chuckladar, who paid a fixed sum to the Government, and then collected as much more as he could from his unfortunate district. The more he could squeeze out, the better for him, of course. Then we get the zemindars. There are any amount of them round here—large landowners—and a lot of them have done the same thing on a small scale as the King of Oude has done on a big one. They were too grand or too lazy to collect their own rents, so they set up

agents who paid them a fixed amount, and made
what they could on the transaction. Son would
succeed father as agent, and things would go
on very comfortably for every one, except the
wretched peasant, until the King's chuckladar
appeared on the scenes, and demanded more than
the zemindar would pay. The chuckladar would
back up his demand with troops—who were also
on the lookout for a chance of making money
—and discretion being the better part of valour
the zemindar would either pay or run away.
In the latter case, the muddle becomes most com-
plicated, for in many cases the agent seems to
have taken the opportunity of making a bid for
the possession of the land. If the chuckladar
thought he could make money out of a change
of ownership he was quite willing, and after a
hundred years of this sort of thing, I ask you
how is a wretched Deputy Commissioner to discover which of all the gentlemen who are swearing by their fathers' beards, and their children's
heads, and Mother Ganges, and all the rest of
it—which of 'em, I say, is the least deeply dipped
in perjury? "

" Why ask me? " murmured Blake.

" I don't. Fatehshah Khan would like me to
ask him, but I don't do that either. Now there
was a queer thing happened yesterday. A case
came up—it had been dragging on from Adamson's time—just the sort of thing I have been
describing. Every one swearing themselves

black in the face. Adamson, guided by Fatehshah Khan, had apparently more or less com-
mitted himself to a gentleman called Madho
Missa, who had a whole pile of documents which
at any rate proved conclusively that he had always collected the revenue. Jelland informed
me that the betting in the bazaar was upon
Madho Missa. Jelland apparently has sporting
tastes. Then Aunut Singh, the rival claimant,
came along and declared with oaths and tears
that Madho Missa's family were only agents
of his family. He wept profusely. When he
stopped, I had a good look at him. He was a
plump person with only one eye, and a very
crooked front tooth that showed every time he
opened his mouth. George, my friend, I recognised him."

"You what?"

"Recognised him. It is—it is my long-lost
uncle, and all the rest of it. What it is to have
a good memory! Ages ago, in the prehistoric
past, my old governor raised a regiment for the
King of Oude, and Aunut Singh's brother was
one of the native officers. Aunut Singh came to
visit him, and I remember him very well. I was
eight, and his crooked tooth and rolling eye
remained fixed in my memory."

"What did you do? Fall on his neck?"

"No, I restrained my ardent feelings, but I
directed a few questions to Mr. Madho Missa
that brought what novels call 'tears of sensibil-

ity' to his eyes. You see I had had the advantage of hearing the matter threshed out in detail between Aunut Singh and his brothers, and at eight years old one takes a passionate interest in other people's affairs. I am now trying to get hold of an impartial witness or two, if there is one to be had, and I should n't wonder if Aunut Singh went to his grave calling down blessings on my head."

" I don't see how you remembered."

" I don't see how, but I did. D'ye know, George, we were camped here for a time, and every now and then when I am out riding the queerest recollections come over me. A bridge, a temple, or a turn of the road is as familiar as can be. For perhaps a dozen yards or so I could go blindfold, and when I look over my shoulder I expect to see my father on his great black horse that the natives called 'Shaitan' because he killed a man who attacked him when he was riding home in the dark one night."

" Killed him, did he? "

" Yes, got him by the shoulder, shook the breath out of him, and then trampled him to death. The governor got off with a scratch, and there was n't a native in the district who did n't believe the horse was possessed by the Colonel Sahib's own private and particular devil."

Richard Morton filled another pipe, pushed his tobacco pouch across to his friend, and asked :

" How 're things with the regiment, George? "

There was a little bit of a pause. Then Captain Blake said in his usual half-hesitating manner:

" Have the native officers been up to see you, Dick? "

" Some of them have."

" Not all of them? "

" No, not all of them."

" Which of them did n't come? "

" It 's more a case of which of them did come," said Richard Morton with no expression in his voice. His face was in shadow, and he did not look at his friend.

" Er—yes. Which of them did come? "

" Amanut Khan, Jowahir Lal, Dewan Ali, and Durga Ram."

" Not the Subadar Major? "

" He had a bad foot."

" No one else? "

" Issuree Singh, my old orderly."

" Is that all? "

" That is all."

There was another short silence.

Then Richard Morton took his pipe out of his mouth and said, " What does it mean, George? "

" What should you say it meant? "

" That they were up to something, and not too anxious to meet me."

Captain Blake emitted a dense cloud of smoke, and stared through it at the rafters. They looked immensely high up, and black, and far away, and the smoke rose towards them in thin wreaths that lessened and vanished.

"Just so—not too anxious to meet you," he said. "I suppose you know they have always believed you have the power of reading a man's thoughts."

"Nonsense."

"Fact. Ever since that business of Mir Ali's eight years ago. And here is proof. I 'd no sooner got back yesterday evening than my bearer came to me with the bazaar version of that very yarn you 've just been spinning. It appears he comes from Koti, Aunut Singh's village, or his brother's second cousin's grandmother lives there, or something—you know what natives are. Well, he says of course every soul in the place knew that Aunut Singh was in the right, but the other man had the papers, and the favour of the extra Commissioner Sahib—your friend Fatehshah Khan—and no one was going to make unpleasantness by offering an unsolicited opinion. Adamson was bamboozled, and did n't care; as old Purun remarked, ' Adamson Sahib is like a child. When a man swears, he believes him. He says, " Has he not sworn? " But God reads the heart, and so does Morton Sahib.' "

"A little difficult to live up to—that," said Richard Morton.

His voice was rather hard. Perhaps he was

thinking that this quality of his had served him
but poorly in his private occasions.

He pulled at his pipe for a moment, and then
said:

"What are they up to, George?"

Captain Blake remained silent.

When the silence had lasted a long time he
said:

"The Colonel is quite satisfied. So is Marsh."

"And you?"

"Do a bit of your mind-reading," said Captain
Blake, with a curious laugh.

"Well, George, you are not a brick wall.
If you want me to say it, you're damned
unsatisfied."

"Quite so, Dick"; and another little pause
ensued.

The night was warm and still. The screens
of split bamboo which usually meshed the two
long windows had been rolled up to admit the
air, and a strip of dark, star-sown sky could be
seen between the line of the verandah roof and
the tangle of rose and oleander which made an
impenetrable thicket on this side of the neglected
garden. In the distance there was a faint rustling sound that might be the first whisper of a
coming breeze. It was far away on the extreme
limit of consciousness, but it was there.

"Well, what is it, George?" said Richard
Morton at last; and Captain Blake stared at the
ceiling and said:

"You can call it the new cartridge, if you like. They are all playing the fool about that."

"But you 've never got 'em here so soon? The world must be coming to an end if you have."

"No, of course we 've not got them here, but d' you think a little thing like that is going to stop them? We had half a dozen men at Umballa to learn the new drill, and since they came back at Christmas——"

"Well?"

Captain Blake crossed his legs.

"Of course I had them up and talked to them like a father, and they agreed with every word I said."

"Beshak Sahib!" interjected Captain Morton with half a laugh.

"Damn their Beshak," said Captain Blake, with the hesitation gone clean out of his voice. "I believe the wildest tales have been going round. Pig's lard, cow's fat, anything you please, all mixed up to grease this infernal cartridge with."

"If they really believe that there will be big trouble," said Richard Morton quickly.

"Who 's to say what they really believe!"

"Well—" Richard considered. "What about the men who went to Umballa—any of them Brahmins?"

"Yes, four of them."

"How did the others receive them? Will they eat with them, and so forth?"

"Oh, yes, that's all right."

"H'm. If they really believed the new drill obliged men to bite cartridges greased with beef fat, they'd have outcasted them."

"Well, I hear that has happened in other places."

"That a fact?"

"Enough of a fact to make the authorities give a whole batch of the Umballa men a month's leave, and orders to rejoin at the depot—at the depot—afterwards."

Captain Morton whistled.

"That's bad."

"Damn bad," said George Blake, his pensive gaze still fixed on the rafters.

After a time he looked down, and observed:

"Ever seen chupattis passed round, Dick?"

"Passed round?"

"Passed from hand to hand, and from village to village, all over the country."

"I've heard the talk, of course. Has it been going on here?"

Captain Blake nodded.

"And at Cawnpore," he said, "and round Agra. Everywhere else for all I know."

"When?"

"Just before you came."

"What do the natives say?"

"They don't say anything. There have been lotus leaves passed round in the lines too."

Captain Morton put down his pipe.

"Lotus leaves?"

"Yes."

"That's queer. I never heard of them."

"Did you ever hear of chupattis going round —before this, I mean?"

"Yes, I did, when I was a child. We were at Mahumdee at the time, and there was a lot of talk. The servants all talked, and of course I took it all in."

"What did they say?"

"They wondered what was going to happen. Apparently they at once expected something to happen—something calamitous. But they did n't know what."

"Did anything happen?"

"Yes, a very bad smallpox epidemic."

"But how, in Heaven's name?"

"Yes, I know, but it did happen, and every one believed the chupatti had been a warning."

Captain Blake looked at his watch.

"We had better get vaccinated in the morning," he observed, "and meanwhile we had better go to bed; I 've got an early parade."

CHAPTER VIII

HOW MISS MONSON PAID A CALL

Have you heard the Piper calling?
Have you heard the echoes falling?
Have you heard the Piper calling,
  The Piper on the hill?
For if you have heard the Piper play
You must follow by night, you must follow by day,
Though it 's over the hills and far away,
  You must follow the Piper still.

HELEN WILMOT lay in bed and watched
the light creep lower and lower upon the
whitewashed wall. The verandah shaded the
doors which opened upon it, but a dusty shaft
of sunshine slanted through a small oblong window set high up under the rafters. As the light
shifted slowly downwards it was reflected in
faint rose and violet tints upon the white expanse above the long glass doors. The doors
themselves stood wide, and a delicious freshness
came through the screens of split bamboo which
filled the open spaces.

A chattering of birds, a murmur of voices
from the servants' houses—little mud huts

clustering at the edge of the compound,—and
the far-away droning of a Persian wheel made
up a most soothing, drowsy noise, and Helen,
though she had been awake for an hour, felt
lazy, and by no means inclined to get up.
She closed her eyes, and listened to the sparrows
fighting under the eaves. Perhaps she even
dozed.

Suddenly she was roused by a little fidgeting
sound, and in a moment she turned and was
aware of a small person, who was standing just
inside the nearer of the two long windows. It
was a quaint small person in a white frock and
starched white pantalets. In one hand she held
a broad-brimmed grey felt hat that obviously
belonged to some one several sizes larger than
herself. The other hand rested on the chick behind her, as if to secure her line of retreat.
When she saw Helen's eyes open, she stared into
them with a pair of very round brown ones, and
then said in a particularly clear and emphatic
manner:

"I have come to pay a call."

"Dear me," said Miss Wilmot. "How rude
of me not to be up!"

"I like you in bed. I like paying calls. I
did forget to bring a card, but my name is Miss
Margaret Elizabeth Monson."

"Oh," said Helen, much impressed. "Must
I call you all that?"

"It would be polite."

Miss Monson advanced into the room with a slow and stately step. With her left hand she retained her hold of the hat, and held up an already sufficiently abbreviated skirt. Her right hand she offered to Helen, who had an instant recollection of Mrs. Elliot's languid manner of shaking hands.

"How do you do, Miss Wilmot?" she said in the accents of polite society. "I hope you are well. I hope you are quite well."

"Yes, thank you." ·

The conversation languished a little. Miss Monson suddenly dropped the grey felt hat, and put her hand on Helen's arm.

"I am bored of being polite. Are you bored of being polite? I am very bored of it. I am bored of calling you Miss Wilmot. I would much rather call you Helen lady. You are the Helen one, are n't you? And I am bored of being Miss Margaret Elizabeth Monson. If you like you can call me Megsie Lizzie, like my papa does."

Helen received the permission with gravity.

"And what does your mamma call you?" she inquired.

Megsie Lizzie was climbing on to the foot of the bed.

"'My lamb,'" she answered in matter-of-fact tones. "She calls me 'my lamb' and 'my precious,' and 'my own lovey darling,' but you could n't call me all those things."

"No, of course not."

"I'm five. It's rather old for India, is n't it?" Again there was a reminiscence of some older person. "But if I went away from my mamma, her heart would break—right across in two pieces."

"Oh, dear!"

"Yes, *indeed*," said Megsie Lizzie, screwing up her button of a mouth, and nodding with an uncanny air of wisdom.

A distant, unhappy cry of "Missee Baba!" became audible. After a moment it was repeated. Megsie Lizzie frowned.

"Is that some one calling you?" asked Helen.

Megsie Lizzie's frown deepened.

"It is Mooniah. She is a most iggerant woman. I suppose I have told her three million times that I will not be called 'Missee Baba.'"

"Missee Baba—a—a!" wailed the voice, shrilly nasal on the high note at the end.

Mooniah was a good deal nearer.

"Megsie Lizzie," said Helen, "I'm afraid you've run away."

Megsie Lizzie tossed her head; seven brown ringlets tossed too.

"She is a stupid thing. Let us talk 'bout something else."

"Very well, what shall we talk about?"

"Shall I tell you a story?"

"That would be very nice."

" Well, once upon a time there was a man, and his name was Gideon and——"

Megsie Lizzie stopped abruptly.

" I forgot—it's a Sunday story," she explained.

" Never mind—do go on."

" But this is a Wednesday. You can't tell Sunday stories on a Wednesday day."

" Why not? "

Megsie Lizzie looked doubtful. Then she said firmly :

" Because Sunday days is different from Wednesday days. They are quite different. They are a different colour."

Helen looked at the earnestly frowning little face, and did not smile. Instead she said in a soft, lazy voice:

" What colour is Sunday? "

" White," said Megsie Lizzie, screwing up her eyes as if she were trying to see something. " A very shiny white, and up at the top there are some little goldy speckles. And Wednesday is green, so of course you could n't mix them, without getting the Sunday colour all spoilt."

Helen thought for a moment.

" Supposing we were to pretend it was Sunday," she suggested.

" Are you a good pretender? " inquired the child.

" Very good, and I am sure you are. Let us both pretend very hard."

Megsie Lizzie put both hands over the damp little forehead, and pressed them so tightly that the knuckles stood up white on her plump, brown hands.

There was a pause.   Then she sat up very straight.

"Have you pretended? I have. Now it is Sunday, and I have said my prayers, and had my breakfast, and so have you, and you are my fifth daughter, and I am going to tell you a Sunday story. A real proper one, so you must attend."

" Missee Baba—a—a—a! " called the afflicted Mooniah in tones of despair.

Helen could see her now, standing at the edge of the verandah where an abandoned doll betrayed its mistress's passage.

Megsie Lizzie turned her head, and saw too.

" Mooniah—chup—be silent," she cried, and Moniah fidgeted from one bare foot to the other, and called again:

" Ai Missee Baba! Very narty Missee Baba."

" There is n't *any* Missee Baba here 't all," retorted Miss Monson hotly. " There is only a Miss Sahib, a big Miss Sahib. I am paying a call. I am with Wilmot Miss Sahib. I also am a Miss Sahib. Mooniah, daughter of an owl, am I a Miss Sahib, or am I not? "

" God knows," snuffled Mooniah.

" I know," said Miss Monson with decision. " Thou also knowest. Sit down and wait till I come, and be silent. The Miss Sahib and I are talking."

Mooniah collapsed into a despondent heap, and Megsie Lizzie abandoned the vernacular.

"Now I will begin," she said. "That is a most inrupting woman—inrupting and iggerant. Well, there was a man called Gideon, and he rolled a cake into a tent. No, that's not the beginning. First of all he made a lot of soldiers come, and they did n't want to come, and they lapped water out of their hands, and God was angry with them. And do you know why He was angry with them?" she demanded impressively.

Helen experienced a slight confusion of mind in face of this rapid presentment of the Scriptural tale.

"Do *you* know why?" she inquired.

"Because they had n't *any* faith, not even the mustard-seed sort," said Megsie Lizzie. Then she relaxed the intensity of her expression, and said calmly:

"Of course it would have been all right if there *had n't* been any God."

Helen gasped.

"Megsie Lizzie, what do you mean?"

"Well, it would, because if there was n't any God they would n't have been wicked about not having faith. But of course there *is*, so they were."

"Yes, of course," murmured Helen, feeling a little incoherent.

8

"Yes," said Megsie Lizzie, nodding wisely.
"And what I think about it is this. If there
was n't any God, where do the trees come from,
and the flowers, and the little weeny teeny tiny
seeds what the trees come out of, because there
was seeds before there was any trees, was n't
there, and if God did n't make them, who did?"

Helen was speechless. When she came to
know Megsie Lizzie a little better, she recognised
the fact that argument with that young lady
invariably reduced the grown-up participant to
speechlessness.

Miss Monson now gave a little sigh, and arose.
"I s'pose I must go," she said, with regret.
"Mooniah! Mooniah! Get up. I am coming.
Do you like tea-parties, Helen lady?"

"Sometimes."

"Would you like a tea-party with me?"

"I should love it."

Helen smiled as she spoke, but the round,
brown eyes which were fixed on hers remained
preternaturally grave.

"Oh," said Megsie Lizzie. Then briskly:
"Shall we have a tea-party to-day? Shall we
have it here, in your house, in the verandah? It
is a nicer verandah than our verandah. And
I pour out the tea? And you pretend I'm a
lady what has come all the way from England
to pay a call?"

"How tired you will be!"

"Yes, I shall want lots of tea. My name will

be Mrs. Brown Jones. Yes, Mooniah, I am coming. It's very rude to inrupt ladies what is saying good-bye in a polite way."

Megsie Lizzie picked up the felt hat as she spoke, and crammed it upon her head. It came well down over her eyes, and was tilted at an extremely rakish angle, which went oddly with the prim starched skirts and crackling pantalets. When she was ready she kissed Helen gravely, and walked to the door, where she paused and turned, one hand on the chick.

" Thank you very much for my *kind* call," she said with great dignity, and departed, just in time to preserve Helen from the dangerous effects of laughter too long repressed.

" Whom on earth were you talking to? " said Adela, half an hour later, when Helen and the early tea arrived simultaneously upon the verandah outside her room.

" I have had the honour of a call from Miss Margaret Elizabeth Monson," said Helen gravely.

" Miss? Oh, that Monson child. I should say she was horribly spoiled. Mrs. Crowther said so last night."

Helen's lips twitched.

" I wonder what she says about us? " she said lazily.

" Why should she say anything? "

" My child, I should say she was a lady who had a great deal to say about every one. I should n't wonder, I really should n't wonder, Adie, if she said that you were spoiled too."

Adela tossed her head.

"As if I should care what she said! And as to being spoiled, I am sure I don't see who there is to spoil me—with Richard as cross as cross."

"Adie!"

"Well, he is, and if you were married to him, you 'd know he was. Why, he would n't even kiss me last night!"

Helen changed the subject.

"I am going to have a tea-party this afternoon," she announced.

"I suppose you mean you are going out to tea?"

"No, I don't. I am going to have a tea-party. Here. On this very spot. No, I suppose it will have to be the other side—outside the office—on account of the sun. Mrs. Brown Jones is coming to tea."

Adela looked cross.

"It 's some nonsense, I suppose," she said. "How can you be so silly, Helen, and at your age! I 'm sure I don't see anything to laugh at. Is it that child?"

"It is."

"Well, if you like to be bothered with her! Personally I can't imagine anything more tiresome. Children are so *wearing*."

Helen laughed.

"That's what I feel about young men," she said, with a spice of malice in her voice. "It does n't bother you to have adoring sticks of creatures trailing about after you all day, but I really could n't stand it. I should want to slap them, or scream, or something, after an hour or two. That is what I call wearing."

"You 've never tried it," said Adela, her eyes narrowing a little.

"I 've never had the chance, you mean, my dear!"

Helen's laugh was so good-tempered that Adela's irritation subsided.

"Well, it is your own fault if you have n't," she said graciously, "for really you know, Helen, you are quite good-looking. Of course you have no colour, but really some people think you quite handsome. I believe Richard does. I think you have improved too, or perhaps it is that no one has any colour here, so one does n't notice your being pale. If only you did n't look so—so clever—and forbidding, only you know you *will* look like a Roman Empress, or something of that sort, whenever a man looks at you, or pays you a compliment, or anything."

"A great many of the Roman Empresses were anything but repressive," said Helen pensively. "Some of them were n't even respectable—I think it 's rather hard."

Adela looked shocked.

"Helen—as if—I meant anything like that—

you do say things! You know quite well I meant that you looked haughty—and proud."

"I feel shy," said Miss Wilmot with the utmost composure.

"Then you should blush. That is becoming, and it does n't frighten a man."

Helen began to laugh.

"Oh, Adela—don't! I've laughed more than is good for any one already this morning. Will you teach me to change colour becomingly? Blushing in six easy lessons! My dear, it's a shameful confession, but I really could n't blush if I tried. I don't know how it's done. Perhaps I take after the Roman Empresses in that too. There was a lady called Messalina who could n't blush either. I really think you had better begin the lessons this afternoon. Megsie Lizzie could have them too."

"I sha'n't be at home this afternoon."

Adela was pouring herself out some more tea, and she did not look at her cousin.

"Why, where are you going?"

"I am going to ride with Mr. Purslake."

Helen passed her own cup.

"What are you going to ride, my dear?" she asked in an indifferent manner.

"He has a very nice horse which will carry a lady perfectly," said Adela, but she did not meet Helen's eyes.

"I wonder what lady it has carried," said Helen. "Miss Crowther, I suppose."

Adela put her chin in the air.

"What any one can see in that straw-coloured wisp!" she began, but Helen interrupted her:

"Adie, I would n't," she said in a soft, hesitating voice.

"Well, I am going to."

Adela flushed.

"Why? Really, Helen, do you suppose I am going to sit indoors all day long with my hands folded, and nothing to think of except how hot it is? I have said all along that it was perfectly odious of Richard to expect us to stay down in this heat. Inhuman I call it. I dare say Dick would *like* me to die, but I don't intend to oblige him, and riding is very good for me—and if Richard won't take the trouble to buy me a horse of my own, he cannot be surprised if I allow a friend to lend me one."

"A friend?"

"Yes! And an old friend too."

"Now, Adela!"

"It is quite true. I met Mr. Purslake at a dance quite five years ago."

"And you had completely forgotten that he existed, until you met him here last week."

"I suppose you are jealous," said Adela, her colour rising. "It is all very well to talk, but if you are n't jealous, why should you object to any one admiring *me?* And you do. I must n't speak to any one or have a friend, or go for a ride, or do a single thing. If you don't take care

you 'll be an old maid, Helen.   Men simply hate
a jealous woman! "

Helen's eyes grew vague.   She looked over the
tree-tops, and appeared to be thinking of something else.

Suddenly she looked at Adela, and laughed.

" Adie, how many feathers has a pink parrot
got in his tail? " she said.

Adela stared, and Helen's eyes danced.

" Oh, Adela, don't; it is n't kind of you; it
really is n't."

To which Mrs. Morton responded with dignity:

" Well, of course I don't want to hurt your
feelings, but it is true, and if I were not fond
of you, I should n't take the trouble to give you
a warning."

" But you have n't."

" I have n't done what? "

" Warned me.   What will happen when I find
out how many feathers—no, I really must not
laugh any more—a pink parrot—has in its tail?
Oh, dear! "

" Helen, are you quite mad? "

" No, my child."

" Is there such a thing as a pink parrot? "

" I expect not."

" Then what on earth——"

Mrs. Morton paused for enlightenment.

" Just a little mental slide," said Helen
gravely.   " If I had been capable of blushing,
I should have blushed just now.   It is quite

easy. Blushes—red—pink—a parrot on the peepul tree, a conviction that it was too hot to quarrel, a strong desire to change the subject, natural result the evolution of a creature hitherto unknown to history. Mrs. Morton, allow me to introduce to your esteemed notice that rare and curious bird—the pink parrot— only still I don't know how many feathers it has in its tail!"

"Sometimes I think you *are* mad," said Adela resignedly.

"So do I, but it is ever so much better than being cross. We will now do another mental slide. Shut your eyes and hold on. Pink is the starting-point. Slide from there to pink muslin. Now let go of the pink, steady yourself on the muslin, and catch hold of the next shade that comes. Rose—rose and grey—a combination common to cockatoos and your new muslin dress. And I've got a perfectly splendid idea for the trimming. So you had better come and see the dirzee with me at once, before it evaporates. He could fit you this afternoon."

"This afternoon I shall be out riding," said Adela in a small obstinate voice.

CHAPTER IX

HOW HELEN GAVE A TEA-PARTY

Oh! to hear the Piper calling,
Oh! to hear the echoes falling,
They are rising, falling, calling,
    At the wayward Piper's will.
And he who has heard the Piper play
Has the moon, and the stars, and the sun, and the day,
And the path to the hills of the Far-a-way,
    Where the Piper is calling still.

MRS. BROWN JONES was unfashionably punctual. All her garments appeared to have been freshly starched for the occasion. For a time it seemed as if some of the surplus starch had affected her manners, and the etiquette observed would have put the Austrian Court to shame.

"I have brought my daughter," said Mrs. Brown Jones, after many preliminary bows and compliments had passed, and the daughter, a very limp, dishevelled doll, was encouraged to extend a battered hand.

"Her name is Miss Anna Maria Matilda Jenkins Sweet Pea," said the fond mamma, in the

accents of lofty pride. Then with an abrupt
transition she became Megsie Lizzie, and entered
upon a rapid explanation.

"It isn't really, you know, Helen lady, because mamma called her Caroline, after Aunt
Caroline, who sent her to me when I was only
four, but now Aunt Caroline is dead, so we call
her something else."

"I think Anna Maria Matilda Jenkins Sweet
Pea is a beautiful name," said Helen.

"Yes, isn't it? It is prettier than Caroline,
only I must not say so because of Aunt Caroline
being dead. People who are dead are always
better than other people, aren't they?"

Helen had noticed this phenomenon herself,
but she did not say so. Fortunately Mrs. Brown
Jones did not wait for an answer. Experience
had taught her that grown-up people scarcely
ever answered questions about really interesting
things.

"She has a terrible lot of relations," she
sighed.

"Your aunt has?"

"No. We was her relations. She hadn't
any others. We hadn't got any relations to
speak of, because of both my grandmothers being only children," explained Megsie Lizzie at
her most grown-up. "But Anna Maria Matilda
has got lots and lots of relations. She has got
all the ones what we haven't got. They are
her relations. They are not my relations."

"Oh, dear," said Helen, "that does n't sound as if they were very nice."

"Some of them are nice, and some of them are n't," said Megsie Lizzie in a resigned sort of way. "There is Uncle Henry Albert."

"Is he nice?"

"Would you call a person nice, if they broke their leg—all to bits?"

"Did he do that?"

"Yes. Anna Maria did think it was tiresome of him."

"Oh!"

"Yes. She went to see them, and there he was, lying in bed, and screaming like twenty parrots, and like forty hundred mynas. I have got a myna; mamma says they are like the English starlings."

"Have you? But Uncle Henry Albert—how distressing!"

"Yes. Was n't it? He screamed and screamed, and Aunt Henry Albert cried, and cried, and he got so dreadfully wet with her crying that he got immonia!"

"Immonia? Goodness!"

"Yes, like Mooniah's little boy got, and he died, and I expect Uncle Henry Albert will die if it is immonia."

Perhaps it was just as well that tea should make its appearance at this harrowing juncture. Even mourners must eat.

Megsie Lizzie sprang up with great alacrity.

"I'm to pour out! I'm to pour out! You *said* I was to pour out," she cried, discarding Mrs. Brown Jones and the conventions. "Put the table here, Ali Bux. I am a burra Miss Sahib to-day. Put it in front of me. Helen lady, do you take three pieces of sugar? I do. May Ali Bux put the cakes close beside me?— because then I need n't get up. I don't think it is proper to get up when you are pouring out the tea. Asides, I might knock something down. The dhobi has put such an astravagan' lot of starch in this dress." The teapot wobbled alarmingly as she spoke, and Helen drew a breath of relief as it was set down again.

"Here. This is your tea, but you did n't say about the sugar."

"I was waiting for a chance," said Helen gravely. "And I am so very sweet myself that I think one piece will be enough. If I got too sweet, I don't know what might happen. The bees might want to make me into honey, and I should n't like that at all."

"Oh!"

Megsie Lizzie made round eyes of wonder. Then she helped herself to a flat round cake, and changed the subject.

"Perhaps Gideon's cake was like this," she observed, and Helen answered idly:

"No, I expect it was more like a chupatti."

"A chupatti would n't roll," said Megsie

Lizzie, severely practical. " I shall ask Ram Chand."

" And who is Ram Chand? "

" He is our bearer. I don't like him much. He is a rude man. But he knows all about chupattis."

Helen's curiosity was faintly stirred. Like every one else she had heard some idle gossip about the mysterious passing from hand to hand of the flat unleavened cakes which take the place of bread all over Upper India.

" What do you mean? " she asked.

Megsie Lizzie put her head on one side and considered.

" Mooniah, and Anna Maria, and I were in the garden, under the big peepul tree, and Mooniah was asleep, and Ram Chand was on the other side of my mamma's rose hedge, and he was talking to his brother, who is in Captain Blake's regiment, and he said, ' The chupattis have gone everywhere now, and the word has gone with them.' Then he said, ' Sub lal hojaega '—everything will be red. And his brother said, ' And our hands too '; and then they went away. So you see he knows all about chupattis. I shall ask him."

Helen felt a little crisping of the short hair at the nape of her neck. She was not consciously aware of matter for alarm. It was all part of some foolish superstition, some sacrifice perhaps. The word passed through her mind

and left, as it were, a little seed of dread behind it. Sacrifice—sacrifice. The confused
memories of her childhood gave up one sudden,
definite picture. She saw Aunt Lucy's room,
and the big illustrated Bible lying open on Aunt
Lucy's knee. Quite clearly she heard Aunt
Lucy's voice saying, " No, my dears, we will
pass over that picture "; and it was a picture
of the slaughter of Amalek. Helen had stolen
down in the night and looked at it, holding the
big book close to the window in the moonlight.
It was a dreadful picture, and there were dreadful words written under it, words which made
her child's soul shudder for years afterwards.

" Thou shalt slay man and woman, infant and
suckling."

For a moment the page seemed to be before
her eyes. Then it was gone, and Helen heard
herself saying:

" I don't think I should ask Ram Chand."

" Well, I won't," said Megsie Lizzie graciously.
" Not if you say not." And just then Richard
Morton rode up in a cloud of dust, and seeing
the tea-table, made for it, and demanded a large
cup, and much tea.

" I thought gentlemen drank pegs," said Megsie Lizzie.

" Does that mean that you and Helen want
all the tea for yourselves? " inquired Captain
Morton.

Megsie Lizzie was much shocked.

"We are not so *rude*," she declared. "We have got proper nice manners. It is n't at all proper nice manners to snatch, and to say, ' I want it *all* for myself.' Jackie Hill does that. I don't."

Richard's eyes looked very blue.

" I don't know that I can behave well enough for this tea-party," he said, as Megsie Lizzie handed him his cup with her grandest air.

Next minute she was back again with cake, apparently forgetting the impropriety of getting up. Having performed the duties of her sex by ministering to man's hunger, she now proceeded to gaze upon him with an admiration too open to be overlooked.

"I am afraid it is my manners that want mending," said Helen. " I never introduced you. How dreadful of me! Mrs. Brown Jones, let me present——"

" No," said Megsie Lizzie with decision. She edged nearer to the object of her admiration.

" No, I 've finished being Mrs. Brown Jones. Now I 'm Megsie Lizzie again, and I know quite well who he is, because I 've seen him riding by our house every day for two weeks."

" Well, and who am I? "

" You are Captain Morton."

Megsie Lizzie sighed.

" It 's a very polite name."

" Is it? Would you rather call me Richard? "

" That 's very polite too."

"My friends call me Dick. Is that rude
enough, or do you wish to proceed to actual
abuse? "

Megsie Lizzie's eyes grew rounder.

"Dick will do," she said. "Captain Dick.
It sounds lovely, it is n't at all polite. Captain
Dick and Helen lady. These are two quite nice
names "; and she turned a smile of royal con-
descension upon Miss Wilmot, who felt absurdly
gratified.

It was whilst she was smiling at Helen that
Captain Morton took a base advantage of a lady's
back being turned. With a strong brown hand
on either side of her waist, he tossed Megsie
Lizzie into the air. She shrieked with joy, and
came down on his knee, screaming, "Do it again,
do it again! Go on doing it! "

"It is too hot," groaned Richard, after
complying with the lady's request once or
twice.

"No, it is n't; it really is n't. Not for me.
Do it, do it, Captain Dick."

"Megsie Lizzie, would you like me to turn all
purple, and cockle up, and be a crumpled heap,
and melt, and nothing be left of me at last but
a pile of clothes, and a moist, moist pool? "

"Can you? Is that what would happen? "

Megsie Lizzie's eyes were like saucers.

"Dick! " protested Helen.

"Most probably," sighed Captain Morton,
mopping his brow.

9

"Oh, then *do!*" and Megsie Lizzie clasped beseeching hands whilst Richard and Helen broke into unmannerly laughter.

"Cruel person! And I've had such a day already. Don't you think it would do if I melted some other time, when I am not quite so busy?"

Megsie Lizzie gave the question some earnest thought.

"You are very busy?"

"Yes, dreadfully."

"Oh!"

A pause, during which Helen opened her work-bag, and took out a strip of embroidery.

Then Megsie Lizzie delivered her ultimatum.

"Very well. You may tell me a story instead."

"Good Lord, I don't know any!"

"About a little boy and a girl. You have n't got any little girl, have you?"

"No."

"Nor any little boy?"

"No," said Richard Morton.

A little mist came between Helen and her work. Through the mist she saw her needle tremble. Something in Dick's voice hurt her dreadfully, she did not feel as if she could bear to look up and see him with the child on his knees. She wondered if Adela felt so. Perhaps that was why she had spoken so sharply of the child. Oh, poor Adela!

Helen's foolish, soft heart was stirred with

compunction, but the next moment Helen's clear brain told her truly enough that Adela had never been fond of children, and had made scarcely a pretence of regretting her baby's death.

Helen's affection for her cousin had ceased to be the old blind, adoring love. It was more maternal now. Adela's faults were clear—her weakness manifest. And Helen gave of her strength, and gave, and kept on giving. The time when she expected any return was quite gone by.

These thoughts passed in her like a flash, and as she bent her head she heard Megsie Lizzie say calmly:

"I thought you had n't any little boy or girl. When I am grown up, I am going to have eighteen children and six of them will be boys, and seven of them will be girls, and three of them will be grown-ups, so as to help look after the others."

"Very thoughtful arrangement," murmured Richard.

"Yes—and I must have plenty of stories to tell them. So now, please, will you tell me about when you was a little boy?"

"You are a very dexterous person, Madam."

"What is dexerous?"

"It means right-handed," said Richard, with the utmost gravity.

Megsie Lizzie looked at both her hands. They might have been cleaner.

"Oh!" she said, in her solemn way. "And now will you please tell me about when you was a little boy."

"No escape!" groaned Captain Morton; he looked at Helen, and she smiled and shook her head.

In spite of quickly lowered lids he had caught the dazzle of tears in her eyes when Megsie Lizzie had asked the question a few minutes before. An instant's resentment had given place to a strange feeling of sympathy and companionship, oddly coupled with a quick memory of having seen Adela push away a child who was trying to climb on her lap. That was when they were just married. He had felt a little chill then. He felt it again now. He made haste to speak.

"It is such a long time since I was a little boy that I have forgotten all about it."

"Is it a hundred years?" asked Megsie Lizzie with interest.

"No, not quite."

"Then I 'spect you could amember it if you tried; I don't forget things even if they happened a hundred and fifty years ago."

"What can you remember that happened a hundred and fifty years ago? That would be much more interesting than my story."

"Lots of things," said Megsie Lizzie shortly. "Heaps and heaps, and heaps, an' jungles, an' tigers, an' snakes, an' hippomuses—an' now will you please tell me about when you was a little boy?"

Richard capitulated.

"When I was a little boy, I lived in a tent with my father and mother."

"Really?"

"Yes, really. I thought it great fun. And my father used to go out and shoot leopards, and all sorts of wild beasts."

"Hippomuses?"

"No—not—er—hippomuses."

Megsie Lizzie looked suspicious and he went on hastily:

"One day my father was out for a ride in the morning, and a man ran out of a village and said that a leopard had clawed his little boy, and was lying up in some long grass not far away."

"Was the little boy all clawed up dead?"

Captain Morton threw a despairing glance at Helen, who did not quite see how she could assist him.

"Er—yes, I am afraid he was. But my father did n't know that, and if he had, it would n't have made any difference, so he rode into the long grass with nothing in his hand but a hog-spear, which he always took with him when he went out riding."

"Why did he take it?"

"To prick the pariah dogs with when they got in his way."

"Oh!" said Megsie Lizzie, "it's very inresting. What did your father do?"

"He always rode very fast. The natives called him the Lightning Sahib, and he rode right into the leopard, and speared it, and the spear broke off short in the leopard's chest, and my father's horse reared up, and fell over backwards with him."

"Was he killed dead?"

"No, not that time, but he did n't know what was happening until he opened his eyes and found the leopard lying dead, and the village shikari talking very fast to the man whose son had been clawed, and three or four women crying very loud indeed, and he sat up and said——"

"What did he say?"

"Er—I don't exactly know. I was n't there, you see, but I rather fancy he was very angry with the shikari, because he had spoiled the leopard's skin."

"Then what happened?"

"Well, he got up and he rode home, and slipped in by the back door."

"Of a tent?"

Megsie Lizzie was down on him in a flash.

"No, this was when we were living in a house. We did have a house. Well, he slipped in by the back door, and he put on another coat—a dark coat."

"Why?"

"Because the leopard had clawed his arm be-

fore the shikari shot it. And he went in and
sat down to breakfast with my mother."

"And with you?"

"Yes. And now comes the part that I can
remember for myself. My mother poured out
the tea, and said how late he was, and helped
him to a chop, and he took the plate, and said
it was a very hot day, and then all of a sudden,
down he went on to the floor, like a ninepin,
when you knock it over. And when my poor
mother got round to him, she was frightened
to death, for his coat was all wet, and when
she touched it, it came off red on her fingers,
and she very nearly fainted herself."

"And what did you do?"

"I ran and called the servants, and they took
off my father's coat, and found the sleeve of it
all full of blood, and his arm and shoulder all
clawed."

"And was he *melting?*" asked Megsie Lizzie
in tones of passionate interest.

Helen's head went down, almost into her lap,
only this time it was to hide a laugh.

Richard Morton made no struggle, he roared,
and Megsie Lizzie looked much shocked.

"I should n't laugh if my papa was clawed.
Nor if he was melting. I should n't," she observed; and Helen, at least, felt rebuked. There
was an impressive pause. Then Megsie Lizzie
asked:

"Is that all?"

"Nearly all. My father was very angry indeed, and he would n't go to bed, but he had to let the doctor tie up his arm. The doctor said all sorts of dreadful things would happen, but they did n't. The arm healed up all right."

"And then you all lived happily ever afterwards," said Megsie Lizzie, in the perfunctory tone of one who makes an accustomed response.

She slipped off Captain Morton's knee, put on her hat, and jumped down from the highest part of the verandah, just at the corner.

"And now I will get you a buttonhole," she announced, and disappeared from view in a little cloud of dust.

Richard looked after her with a grim smile.

"No, there was n't much 'happy ever afterwards' about it," he said. "The poor old governor was killed out pig sticking a year later, and my mother, whom he had spoiled, and adored, and treated like a queen, had to go home, and live on the charity of relations, who never ceased girding at her because she was left so badly provided for. No," as Helen looked up in surprise, "there was no pension. My father left the Army as an ensign. He never could keep out of debt. He was a regular free-lance, you know. The natives adored him, and the old King of Oude swore by him, and I suppose he made a lot of money one way and another, but he never could keep a penny of it—he could n't say no to a friend, and in the end it was my mother who paid."

Helen looked up, her face very soft.

" I never heard you speak of her before. Did she die long ago, Dick? "

" Ten years. She made a very unhappy second marriage. A wretched business. We are an unlucky lot."

Captain Morton pulled himself up. His eyes were sombre. There was a moment's silence. Then with an abrupt change of tone he asked:

" Where is Adela? "

Helen looked fixedly at her embroidery. The light had begun to fail, and the fine work required attention.

" She has gone out riding," she said in cheerful commonplace tones.

Richard's brow darkened.

" Riding? She has n't anything to ride. I 've been so busy, but I saw a little mare to-day that might do. With whom is she riding? "

" With Mr. Purslake."

" Purslake? Is she riding one of his horses? "

" I believe so."

Richard lay back in his chair, and put up one hand to cover his mouth and chin.

" Purslake is not a man I care for," he said in a studiously quiet tone. " Also, he is a very new acquaintance, and I don't care about Adela being under any obligation. Do you think, Helen, that you could give her a hint that I would rather she did n't make a friend of Purslake? "

Helen hesitated. She guessed the effort with which Richard Morton spoke to her of his wife. Her heart began to throb painfully, she was so much afraid of saying the wrong thing—of making matters worse. That they were bad enough already she was well aware. On her arrival in Peshawur she had found a degree of estrangement which appalled her, and she had begun by thinking Richard hard. In the months that passed since then she had found it easier to comprehend his attitude. Her own relations with Adela had undergone a change. There had been scenes and quarrels. Helen hated quarrels, and was clever at avoiding them, but once and again Adela had hurt her very deeply. Such hurts heal, but in healing they harden too.

"I think Adela knew him before," she said quickly, when the silence had lasted so long that she felt she must say something. Captain Morton offered no comment, but there was a sarcastic expression about his eyes that increased Helen's discomfort and made her say:

"I don't care for him either. He is silly, but quite harmless, I should say "; and she tried to laugh.

"He is a cad," said Richard Morton shortly.

He rose, and walked to the edge of the verandah, just as Megsie Lizzie appeared with a handful of drooping flowers, which she pressed upon him.

"An' I must go," she explained, "I must go at once, or I shall be late for saying Good-night to my mamma, because she is going out to dinner, and if she did n't have time to hug me and God bless me first she would cry all into her soup, and that would n't be at all polite. Good-night, Captain Dick. Good-night, Helen lady," and she slipped away, humming a queer little tuneless song.

"Is n't she funny?" said Helen in tones of relief. When Richard did not answer she went on more from a desire to turn the conversation than from any other motive.

"Dick, she told me such an odd thing. You know all the talk there has been about those chupattis, and how every one said they meant something different?"

"Yes."

Captain Morton was listening now.

"Dick, I noticed you did n't talk, when every one else did. Was that because you thought it all too silly—or—or——"

"A most expressive ' or,'" said Richard Morton, with half a laugh.

The light had fallen so much now that Helen could not see his face, but she had the feeling that his eyes were intent upon her.

"Well, that child said she heard their bearer talking to a brother of his who is a Sepoy in the 114th, and he said the message had gone everywhere."

" The message? "

" Sub lal hojaega."

Helen shivered ever so little as she spoke. There was quite a breeze springing up, and the evening air struck chill, after the heat of the day.

" What does it mean, Dick? "

Richard Morton did not move.

" Does n't your Hindustani take you as far as that, Helen? " he said lightly. " It is n't very abstruse, ' Sub lal hojaega '—Everything will become red."

" Yes, I know. I did n't mean that. Why did Ram Chand say that everything would become red, and why did his brother answer: ' And our hands too? ' "

There was a pause.

Then Captain Morton moved a little, and said in his usual voice:

" My dear girl, one can never fathom these native superstitions."

Helen got up.

" Dick, did you ever know a woman who was n't inquisitive? "

" My dear girl, never."

" Well? "

Helen was standing beside him on the edge of the verandah, her chin lifted, and her brows arched, but Richard looked past her at the sun-

set. The sun was gone, and a line of dark ferash
trees stood out as black as cypresses against
the western sky. Behind their gloomy foliage
shone a belt of clear blood-red. It glowed, and
changed, passing from rose to scarlet, and from
scarlet to a hot and dusky orange. With every
change of colour the trees darkened, the light
failed, and the breeze increased.

" Well, Dick? "

" Well, Helen."

Helen came a step nearer. She spoke in a
hesitating manner. " Dick, I 'm not a child."

" You are not. You are positively elderly.
Only don't harp on the fact, because I am ten
years older than you are, you know."

Helen turned with a swish of her full skirts,
gathered up her work, and swept to the door.

" Lift the chick for me, Dick, will you," she
said in her usual voice, and as she passed into
the lighted room she turned her head rather
suddenly and looked Richard Morton full in the
face. As soon as she looked at him, he smiled,
but she had seen his eyes first. They were very
grave, and there was a deep vertical line between them. Helen looked away again at once,
and moved farther into the room. The freshen-
ing breeze followed her, and stirred her dress.
Outside, the trees rustled.

" How the wind is rising," she said.

CHAPTER X

THE RISING OF THE WIND

We broke the power of the Kings, we took the sword away,
And beat it into a ploughshare, for ever and a day.
Mussulman and Mahratta, Sikh and wild Pathan,
They should live together in peace, neighbourly man by
    man.
No more raiding for loot, no more justice by favour;
Life was a sorry affair, woefully lacking in savour.
And the King of Oude, his captains, their sons and heirs,
    instead
Must learn the English drill, and wear the English red.
Sepoys, not captains they, their fathers' greatness gone,
What wonder if under the English red a pulse of hate
    beat on.

MARCH went out, and India lay under the heat of April. Between the hazy sky and the parched earth, no breath stirred save that impalpable breath of approaching dread. Unheard, unfelt, the wind was rising, the wind which the natives called the " Devil's breath." The air was full of the dust of rumour, and the dust fell, silently, unheeded. No one knew where the rumours came from. They were not, and then they were. They came as the dust comes, and no one knew how.

A district, peaceful and contented one week, would be full of buzzing talk the next. Was it true that the new water-mills which the Company had set up were accursed things? Ai, brothers, who could tell? But why should they grind so cheaply? Could that be answered? A cousin at Koti had said that his uncle at Cawnpore had said that there was bone dust mingled with the flour—dust of pigs' bones! The man whose cousin's uncle lived in Cawnpore tore his hair, and wept, and praised all the gods that *he* had taken no grain to be ground in the Company's mills. Those who had done so, slunk away, or held their heads very high, and praised their gods louder still. And the district seethed like water that is going to boil.

In the lines the Sepoys talked. Always they sat, or stood in groups, and talked volubly. When an officer passed they stopped talking. Here and there one would look away. If he failed to salute his officer he had his excuse. He had not seen him. What did they talk about? Perhaps about Mungul Pandy of the 34th who had cut down his adjutant and the quarter-master-sergeant, in front of the quarter-guard at Barrackpore, no man putting out a hand to stay him.

Perhaps they debated whether to call him mutineer—or martyr.

For Mungul Pandy was hanged, and his regiment saw it done. Afterwards they put flowers

on his grave—secretly, as for many years they
had put flowers and flags on the grave of an
earlier mutineer. Then the regiment was dis-
banded, and the men went all over India telling the story of Mungul Pandy who had died
rather than break his caste by biting the accursed
cartridge.

There was a great deal to talk about in the
year 1857 and the month of April.

There was the court-martial upon two Sepoys
who made treasonable overtures to the native
officer on duty at the Mint, in Calcutta. There
was the disbanding of the 19th regiment at
Berhampore for mutinous conduct on parade.

They were to go to their homes. Such was
the clement sentence of the Government. And
they too went all over India, and there was more
talk, and more, and more, and at the beginning,
and in the end, the over-word was still the same
—the cartridge.

The Queen of England had said to Lord Gough
that all the native soldiers in India must become
Christians. Was that true? Undoubtedly it was
true. Here was a holy fakir who could tell them
the whole tale, ai, brothers, hear the tale then !
What did Lord Gough say? He said it would
take time, but it should be done. Then the
Queen was very angry, and said, " Let it be
done at once. Let it be done without fail."

For this reason the cartridges were devised.
They were sent out greased with the fat of cows

and with the fat of swine. If a Hindoo touched
them, his caste was gone. If a Mussulman
touched them, he had touched the accursed
thing forbidden by Allah, and by the prophet
of Allah.

Would it not be better to serve the King of
Oude, and have the plundering of the zemindars
again? Would it not be better to serve the Emperor of Delhi and draw the magnificent pay
of ten rupees a day? Would he give ten rupees
a day? Undoubtedly. Here was one who had
just come from Delhi, and there it was the
common gossip of the bazaars.

So the talk went, and April passed.

Richard Morton spent the greater part of
the month in camp, learning his district by
heart, establishing friendly relations with the
zemindars, cultivating the acquaintance of
the local Rajah, and absorbing information
generally.

He returned to Urzeepore with his mind a
good deal lightened. Some discontent there
undoubtedly was, but the greater part of the
district appeared to be peaceful, or at least indifferent. The crops promised well. It would
be a good season, and any distrust of the Government's motives would pass with time, and
their experience of an equitable rule.

He found his cousin Floss Monteith on her
way through Urzeepore with her silent husband
and her small son of six. They were bound for

Simla, where Colonel Monteith was going to settle them, returning himself to Mian Mir, where he had just been given an appointment on the Staff.

"Floss, will you take Adela and Helen up with you?" said Captain Morton, an hour after he rode in from camp.

Mrs. Monteith made a face behind his back, and then hastened to say all that was hospitable and cousinly.

But Adela refused to go.

"Is n't it just *like* Richard?" she said angrily to Helen. "He sees I am enjoying myself, and of course he wants to send me away."

"But the heat, Adie——"

"I am not feeling it at all. This is a very cool house. I am very well, and you know I *did* feel the height last year in Murree. The doctor said I was not at all strong. Of course, if Richard wants to kill me—and I simply can't *bear* Mrs. Monteith. I call her a very frivolous person."

The feeling was mutual.

"I like you. I like you immensely," Mrs. Monteith told Helen. "I can't think why Dick did n't marry you. You would have suited him ever so much better than that Adela creature. Mercy! what have I said? My dear, I beg your pardon, I really did forget she was your cousin. Now don't be vexed with me. I'm dreadful, you know. I always say just what comes into my

head. Fortunately my John has *very* strong
nerves."

The Monteiths went off the same evening, and
with them went Megsie Lizzie, who had begun
to droop with the heat.

Floss Monteith had discovered an old school-
fellow in Mrs. Monson, and her son Jack conceived a silent adoration for Megsie Lizzie. The
children's despair at the thought of being
parted led to an impulsive offer from Mrs. Monteith, which, after a few hours' hesitation, was
accepted.

"An' Miss Anna Maria Matilda Jenkins Sweet
Pea will love to write you ever so long letters,"
said Megsie Lizzie, leaning out of the window of
the dakgharri, waving brightly to her mother,
who stood by her husband's side, very pale,
and with hands that clasped each other very
tightly.

Next day there was bad news from Lucknow.
A despatch spoke of mutinous conduct on the
part of the 7th Irregulars. They had refused the
cartridge, threatened to murder their officers,
and had been with difficulty coerced into a
condition of sullen submission.

Richard Morton interviewed Captain Monson,
of the 11th Irregulars, and inquired into the
disposition of his men. Later he saw and talked
with Colonel Crowther of the 114th, Captain
Elliot of the Native Police, and Captain Lamington, who commanded the detachment of Native

Cavalry. His face was tolerably grave as he wrote his official despatch.

Captain Blake looked in about sunset, and they talked for an hour or more.

"I don't know what they'll do," said George Blake. "That's the truth, Dick."

"Have you begun ball-cartridge practice?"

"A fortnight ago."

"H'm! Any trouble?"

"No. I thought they would jib, but they did n't. Come to think of it, they had n't the ghost of an excuse, for the cartridges are some of the old lot. Our own make."

"But you are not satisfied?"

"No. It's an odd thing to say, Dick, but I believe I'd rather they had made a fuss. They 're too damned quiet. I don't like it——"

"Anything else you don't like?"

"Well, I don't know that I care about the sort of carelessness that results in getting ball cartridge mixed up with blank."

"That been happening?"

"Yes. Pure mistake, of course."

"Oh, of course."

There was a pause, and then Captain Morton said:

"Have you ever realised that there are only two British regiments in the whole of Oude? They 'd spread out pretty thin, if we had to spread 'em out, George."

"That is so."

"Please God, we sha'n't have to spread them out."

And George Blake said "Amen."

After a moment he spoke again.

"Some one told me Mrs. Morton and Miss Wilmot were going to Simla with the Monteiths."

"I wanted them to. My wife would n't go."

Richard paused, then he added:

"George, I wish to Heaven we had had this despatch yesterday. It's too late now. There's no escort. I can't get away. It's no good thinking of it."

That evening Adela grumbled at the heat.

"After all, I wish we had gone to Simla," she said, and Richard Morton lost his temper, and lost it badly. He echoed his wife's wish in language which she characterised as profane. Then he went back to his office, and worked till midnight, and Helen Wilmot listened to Adela's strictures with a curiously blank expression.

A week later came the news of the Meerut Mutiny. The mine had been years a-digging, the fuse had been months in the laying, but now the spark was set, and the wind fanned it, and fanned it still. Men began to catch their breath, and brace themselves against some vast upheaval. They watched the travelling spark, and set their teeth.

Delhi fell

"Delhi is far," quoted Captain Morton cheerfully. Again he held conference with the commanding officers.

"The Mohammedans won't move till their fast is over," he said. "And the Eed falls on the 20th. I think we should be prepared for trouble then. Fasting all day, and gorging at night, is n't too good for the temper, and when it is over——"

He broke off abruptly.

"Colonel Crowther, how many Sikhs have you in your regiment now?"

Colonel Crowther's wizened little face contracted.

"About fifty, I believe, and from what I hear, Captain Morton, I have grave reason to fear that they are a drunken and dissolute body of men. Drunkenness is a terrible thing, a very terrible thing. A man who is found drunk should be cashiered. It is an outrage, a simple outrage that a Christian Government should order us to enlist men who are well known to be intemperate in their habits!"

"You might convert them, Colonel," suggested young Lamington with a perfectly guileless expression.

Richard Morton put his hand up to his chin.

"Fifty," he said. "I remember you never liked the Sikhs, sir. You thought that they might have a deteriorating influence."

"And I maintain it now—the spectacle of open drunkenness——"

"Very shocking"—Captain Morton was extremely grave—"very shocking indeed. I would suggest, sir, that it would be possible to minimise the effect by drafting all the men into one Company; a strict watch could then be kept over their morals."

Colonel Crowther appeared to be struck by this idea, and Richard enlarged upon it later on to Captain Blake.

"Keep him up to it, George. Harp on the temperance string. If the old man had obeyed orders, and enlisted his full 200 Sikhs, they might be worth their weight in gold to us at present. But fifty staunch men, if we can only get 'em together——"

George Blake looked vaguely into the dark corners of the room.

"A Sikh came to me last night," he said. "His father was an officer of Runjeet Singh's, and he is a fine lad. He said, 'Sahib, there is much bad talk. Make us Sikhs into a Company, and make me Jemadar, and we will show these budzats that the Sikhs can fight.' How did you know that, Dick? I'll swear you were n't behind the door."

"No, I was n't behind the door, and I did n't know it. By Heaven, George, I'd like to make the Sikh Company."

"So should I. So would not old Crowther."

"Do what you can, George; get the Sikhs together, and let occasion make the Jemadar.
What is your friend's name?"

"Hira Singh."

"We are in a pretty bad position, you know,"
said Richard Morton after a moment. "Even
Monson admits that the Irregulars are not to
be depended upon. That was why he jumped
at the chance of getting his child away. Lamington won't hear a word against the Cavalry,
but is doubtful of the Police; Elliot believes in
the Police, but thinks that the Cavalry are very
shaky. Personally, I think he is right. Cavalry
are always the first to give trouble. They are
head over ears in debt to the bunniahs, and stand
to gain by change and lawlessness. I think
Elliot's Police might stand, but, George—I feel
doubtful, very doubtful about the old regiment."

"So do I," said George Blake.

The words were bitter in his mouth.

"If you had stayed on, Dick."

"Don't be a fool," said Richard Morton
roughly.

"All right. I say, Dick, the bazaar chowdri
reports this morning that the men won't take
their rations of flour."

"Why?"

"You've been mixing bone dust with it, it
appears, Richard."

"Necessity is the mother of invention. It
looks as if they were hard put to it for a pretext

—or as if there were faint hearts among them. Things are pretty rotten when one has to put one's trust in the faint-hearted." He spoke slowly. " I wonder whether Mr. Fatehshah Khan is n't one of the faint-hearted. He has been having a good many letters from Cawn-pore lately. They kept cropping up in the official mail. I remarked on it. They stopped. I don't feel sure about Fatehshah Khan —Extra Assistant Commissioner though he is."

At the Club the ladies talked. Mrs. Crowther, of course, had her word to say about the man-ner in which things were being managed, or mismanaged.

" Really Captain Morton seemed to think he had nothing to do but enjoy himself in camp," she remarked. " I should say he would be better employed in looking after his wife. If ever I saw a young woman who required it more— well, *montrez me la*—that is all. And after idling in a tent for a month, he comes back and makes the most outrageous insinuations with regard to his old regiment, and makes them to its Colonel. I had hard work to restrain the Colonel—hard work, I assure you."

She spoke to meek Mrs. Marsh, and to Miss Darcy, the doctor's elderly sister.

" Oh, Mrs. Crowther! " breathed the former.

" And what did he say? " asked Miss Darcy in her sensible voice.

The secrets of the Council chamber were evidently no secrets from Colonel Crowther's better half.

"He asked—he actually dared to ask—if Colonel Crowther had full confidence in his men."

Miss Darcy had no tact. "And has he?" she inquired bluntly.

Mrs. Marsh's exclamation this time was, "Oh, Miss Darcy!"

"He has. We both have. The most perfect confidence."

"Such a comfort," said Mrs. Marsh, "and my husband has too."

She raised her head a little, displaying a shade of very modest pride.

Mrs. Elliot came languidly out of the library. She and Helen Wilmot had been choosing books together. She stood a moment by Mrs. Marsh's chair, and inquired:

"What has your husband got? Not fever, I hope?"

Her clear voice always seemed to have a tinge of mockery in it.

Mrs. Marsh bridled perceptibly.

"My husband has confidence in his men," she repeated.

"Reciprocal, I hope."

Mrs. Elliot threw a sideways glance at Miss Wilmot, but Helen looked away. She did not consider Mrs. Marsh fair game.

"Oh, yes," murmured that poor lady, and Mrs. Crowther took up her parable again.

"My husband says that the rumours from Delhi and Meerut are probably grossly exaggerated."

Mrs. Elliot sank into a chair and fanned herself.

"Of course, if Colonel Crowther says so," she murmured.

"Of course. If half a dozen women and children were killed, it is the outside of what happened. It is absurd to talk of massacre. Most exaggerated."

"H'm!" observed Miss Darcy. "When I am killed I shall expect it to be called a massacre, even if I am the only one."

"A mere half-dozen casualties," said Mrs. Crowther, with a spark in her light eyes, "a mere half-dozen, scarcely merits that designation. I entirely discredit the extremely unlikely reports that are being circulated. I do not believe there was torture. I decline to admit the probability of mutilation."

"Oh, Mrs. Crowther!" said pale Mrs. Marsh.

Confidence, or no confidence, her nightly dreams were full of horrors, and her thoughts flew to the two limp, unattractive children, whom Mrs. Elliot had first dubbed the "Marsh Mallows."

"Some of the tales are pretty circumstantial,"

said Miss Darcy. "Now, that one of the sergeant's wife at Meerut——"

Miss Darcy had stout nerves. She told the story in a brisk and matter-of-fact way.

After a moment Helen Wilmot got up and walked away. At the farther end of the long Club verandah she found Mrs. Monson sitting by herself, and dropped into a chair beside her.

"What is it, my dear?" asked Lizzie Monson.

"Those women. They are enough to make one swear—yes, they are. There they sit, all pretending not to be frightened, and telling one another the most perfectly horrible tales—too horrible to be repeated."

"I wonder if they are too horrible to be true," said Lizzie Monson.

There was a gentle distance in her look, and her voice had an absent tone. Then without any warning she put her head down on her knees, and began to sob, very quietly, but in a tired-out hopeless way.

"I have pretended too," she said very low. "Oh, Helen, it's all we can do for the men— pretend, pretend, so that they sha'n't know that we know; but I can't go on, I can't go on. She's so far away, my little Meg, and I can't go to her, and I could n't leave James."

Helen squeezed the poor mother's shaking hand in both of hers.

"Oh, she must be safe—she will be safe," she said. "God won't let her be hurt—not Megsie

Lizzie. She is so dear"; and the two women kissed, and leaned together.

The sound of a tinkling instrument startled them. Helen went to the corner of the verandah and looked round it. What she saw did not please her very much.

Adela, in her long grey riding-dress and broad grey hat, was sitting in a cane chair, with young Jelland fanning her. Her cheeks were flushed, and her chestnut curls hung down over the white collar of her habit.

At her feet sat Mr. Purslake, pulling at the strings of a banjo. He had been home the year before and had caught the prevailing American craze. He twanged out a catchy tune, and sang:

> "In South Car'lina de darkies go—
> Sing song Kitty can't you ki me oh!
> Dat's whar de white folk plant de tow,
> Sing song Kitty can't you ki me oh!"

Adela's soft laugh rang out, and she shook back her curls, and looked over Mr. Jelland's shoulder to where Carrie Crowther sat at a little distance, with her large china blue eyes fixed upon the group.

" Now the chorus, Mr. Purslake," she said, and Mr. Purslake wagged his head, and sang:

> "Keemo, kimo, dar oh whar,
> Wid my hi, my ho, an' in come Sally singing,
> Some time pennywinkle, ling tum nip cat,
> Sing song Kitty can't you ki me oh!"

Helen came forward, and Adela turned to her.

" Mr. Purslake is so amusing to-day," she said. " Oh, and, Helen, what do you think Mr. Jelland has been telling me? You remember Frank Manners? Well, I always did say he was odd, and so did poor mamma."

" Did you? " said Miss Wilmot rather coldly.

" You know I did, and it shows how right I was. Why, he has become quite a native, Mr. Jelland says. And he takes opium dreadfully. Mr. Jelland says he will kill himself if he goes on. They call him the Rao Sahib now, just fancy, and he lives with his uncle at Cawnpore —no, that place near it—but he won't be friends with any of the English, though the Nana Sahib is. He pretends to hate English people, and if that is n't odd! "

Young Jelland coloured a little. He was rather afraid of Miss Wilmot.

Mr. Purslake twanged the strings of his banjo again.

" Sing song Kitty can't you ki me oh! "

he sang.

CHAPTER XI

HOW MAY WENT OUT

The wind of the East came out of the East
  And brought a bane,
It blew a madness into the blood,
  And a madness into the brain.

It blew a curse between race and race,
  Between man and man.
The wind of the East came out of the East
  And blew upon Hindustan.

MAY drew to a close.

In Lucknow, Sir Henry Lawrence, the Chief Commissioner of Oude, was fortifying the Muchee Bhowan, and laying in stores.

In Cawnpore, Sir Hugh Wheeler had finished his fatal entrenchment, and the women and children were ordered into it.

In all the smaller stations, commissioners and deputy commissioners followed these two examples to the best of their ability.

Christian at Seetapore collected all the non-combatants into his own house; others did what they thought best.

Richard Morton wrote to headquarters that

in event of trouble he had arranged with Maun
Singh, the local Rajah, to receive the ladies and
children into his fort.

"I have thought it wisest," he added, "to base
this request upon my apprehensions of a riot
during the festivities connected with the Eed.
We want all our prestige at present."

Contrary to expectation, however, the Mohammedan festival of the Eed passed off quietly on
May 20th.

Once again Richard Morton agreed with Captain Blake that things were too quiet. There
was, for instance, no friction between Hindus
and Mohammedans, such as is apt to arise on
a day of festival.

Captain Morton would have been decidedly
better pleased if there had been a moderate riot
—a few Hindu heads cracked by Mohammedan
sticks, a few Mohammedan turbans knocked off
by angry Hindus.

But now all was peace. Even the local bone
of contention, a Hindu temple said to have been
built over the tomb of a Moslem saint, evoked
on this occasion no angry recriminations, no
controversy of rival religions. All was peace.
It is very quiet when men are holding their
breath.

May went out and June came in. On the
morning of the second of June, Fatehshah Khan,
Extra Assistant Commissioner, rode out very
early. He was by way of copying English man-

ners. Captain Morton rode out early. Mr. Jelland rode out early. Fatehshah Khan therefore did the same.

He rode alone, having dispensed with the attendance of his sais, and presently leaving the dusty, grass-bordered Mall, he came out upon the Cawnpore road.

Early though it was, the road was full enough. Those who journey through Oude in June make what speed they may before the sun is high.

Grass cutters were coming in, with bundles of parched-looking grass upon their heads. A bullock cart lumbered slowly along, raising clouds of the choking dust, or an ekka jingled briskly past, drawn by a dried-up pony, whose projecting bones and sore flanks were scarcely atoned for by an elaborate adornment of blue and white beads.

The mails went by at a gallop, leaving a dense cloud behind. Fatehshah Khan covered his mouth with his hand, and rode through the cloud. Beyond it, under a big tamarisk tree, a blind man with horrible white eyeballs sat swaying to and fro. He wore dirty white clothes, and his beard was dyed a flaming red with henna. As he rocked, he sang in a high and nasal voice that quavered from one false note to another.

" Who goes to Salon? " he chanted, beating the dusty ground with the palms of his hands.

" Who goes to Karra or Hilsa?

" Who goes to Bihar or Bukhara?

11

"Pir Mohammed is in Salon.

"Shaikh Karrak is in Karra.

"And at Hilsa is the tomb of Jaman Shah Madari!

"Who cares for Muner or Ajmere,

"When a greater saint is here?

"For the Zinda Shah Madar—

"He is buried in Makanpore,

"A shining light, and a holy delight,

"And he whom the Maker will hold in favour,

"He comes to the shrine of Madar."

Fatehshah Khan drew rein as he heard the first words of the blind man's song. He rode very slowly towards him, and when the final quaver had died away, and the devotee, with a kind of inward groan, was drawing breath for a fresh effort, he interposed.

"Ai Madari," he said, "salaam"; and the blind man gave the greeting back again.

"I too have been at Makanpore," said Fatehshah Khan.

The blind man rocked in the dust.

"Who goes to Salon?" he began.

"Who goes to Karra or Hilsa?"

Fatehshah Khan stopped him.

"The road is empty, brother," he said, and the madari ceased his song, and spoke in a rapid, hissing whisper.

"Who comes to the shrine of Madar?"

"Brother, I have been there."

"Brother, what did you seek?"

" I sought the living saint."

" For him who sought the living saint, I have a message."

Fatehshah Khan bent from his saddle.

" From whom is the message, Madari? " he asked.

The blind man rocked in the dust. As he rocked he spoke:

" The message is from Azimullah Khan. The message is from the Nana Sahib's vakil."

" And what is the message, O Madari? "

" This is the message. Thus says Azimullah Khan, ' When the house burns, what does the wise man do? ' "

Fatehshah Khan looked up and down the long white road. There was a little cloud of dust very far away. He looked at it, and smoothed his close black beard.

" Does the house burn? " he asked.

And the blind man answered, rocking still:

" It burns. On Sunday the burning began. Yesterday it continued. To-morrow there will be much flame—much flame and the burning ash that carries the flame abroad. What then does the wise man do? "

" He leaves the burning house," said Fatehshah Khan, and he threw silver into the blind man's lap, and rode back along the way that he had come.

A little later, on that same morning, Captain Morton sat in his office, writing.

What he wrote was his daily bulletin to headquarters, and he had nothing very cheerful to say.

The air was very hot, and Richard had taken off his light coat, and flung it down upon the matted floor.

At a second table Mr. Jelland was occupied over some papers, and in the outer office sat Fatehshah Khan. He did not appear to be very busy, for he sat and stared out of the window. Presently a chuprassi came in, and stood salaaming.

Fatehshah Khan got up, spoke to the man, and then went into the inner office, where he addressed the Deputy Commissioner in his stiff correct English.

" Sir, there is a kossid from Rajah Maun Singh."

" Who has come? His agent? "

" No, sir. A servant—a runner. He has brought a letter."

Richard frowned. His pen travelled mechanically. He was expecting the Rajah's agent. A burden of defenceless lives weighed on him day and night. The red and dreadful streets of Meerut rose in his dreams. The tale of the Delhi murders rang in his ears. He had made up his mind to place all the women and children under Maun Singh's protection. The obligations of Oriental hospitality are inviolable. With the women and children safe, he could face and meet any development, however grave.

He took the Rajah's letter, opened it, and pencil in hand, followed the lines of flowery compliment with which it began.

Suddenly he looked up, his jaw rigid.

"Wait outside," he said sharply to the chuprassi who had brought the letter in. "Wait outside, and shut the door. Is all the heat to come in?"

When the man had obeyed, Captain Morton looked down again at the flimsy sheet of paper, with its strange twisted writing, and read it from beginning to end.

When he had finished he looked up.

"Jelland," he said.

"Yes, sir."

"Rajah Maun Singh writes that a most unlucky accident has befallen him. Part of the wall of his fort has fallen in. He will therefore be unable to receive the ladies, as arranged."

Richard Morton had addressed young Jelland, but he looked at his native assistant, and it was Fatehshah Khan who answered him.

"Oh, sir, this is a great misfortune," he observed, and Captain Morton's face hardened.

"Do you know what it means?"

"I, sir? Oh, certainly not, sir!"

"It is an excuse, of course. But why? There has been no fresh development—or has there? Have you heard anything?"

"Sir, there are always rumours."

"Ah—and what is the latest rumour, Fateh-shah Khan?"

"I have no knowledge, sir. Rumours are beneath notice of the educated. Only the common people believe them."

"And Rajah Maun Singh," said Richard sharply.

"Oh, sir!" Fatehshah Khan's contempt for the Hindu landowner was admirable.

"These Rajahs are very ignorant men—quite uncultivated. They have no education. Every bazaar rumour is the truth to them. Maun Singh is quite illiterate person, sir. That without doubt is why he says the wall of his fort has fallen down."

Fatehshah Khan went back to the outer office, and Captain Morton sat very still for perhaps ten minutes. Then he finished his official despatch and pushed it across the table.

"Send that off, Jelland. The man is waiting. Oh—and by the way, just ask Fatehshah Khan to go over to Elliot's house and see him about that fire in the Police lines last night. I thought he would have been round, but I suppose he is busy."

Mr. Jelland mopped a pink, perspiring brow, and did his errands.

When he returned, Captain Morton inquired without raising his head:

"Fatehshah Khan gone?"

"Yes, sir."

"Then just close the door into the outer office, Jelland."

Mr. Jelland did so, and then sat down on the edge of the office table.

"I say, sir, this is bad," he said in an uneasy undertone.

"It's not good," said Richard, still writing.

"What will you do now? Imagine Maun Singh playing us such a trick!"

"It is an accomplished fact, my dear boy. Imagination is not needed."

"Now I wonder why he did it," said young Jelland.

"I am afraid I know why."

"What?"

Captain Morton looked up. His face was very set.

"I've had my bearer fifteen years. This morning he told me that there was a bazaar rumour that the troops at Shahjehanpore had mutinied and killed every soul in the place."

"Good Lord! Do you think it's true?"

"I think something has happened."

"But when——"

"Sunday, they say, when every one was at church." ·

"But it's not possible that the news could have travelled so fast; it's a hundred miles as the crow flies."

"Ill news travels apace. I've known it come faster than that."

Mr. Jelland sank his voice to a whisper.

"D' you think Fatehshah Khan——"

Richard Morton gave a short laugh.

"Oh, yes. He knew. Can't you see when a man's lying, my dear boy?"

"Oh, Lord!" said young Jelland.

Richard laid down his pen.

"I'm afraid I sent him off on rather a flimsy pretext, but it was all I could think of. I wanted to talk to you. Will you go round at once to Colonel Crowther, Major Marsh, and all the other married men?—here's the full list —and say I think all women and children should remove to my house. I propose putting on a guard composed half of Sikhs—the other half to consist partly of Mohammedans and partly of low-caste Hindus—no Brahmins. A Police picket in Monson's compound. Then in case of a mutinous outbreak on the part of the troops, the ladies can fall back upon the ravine behind my house, and get across it into the jungle. Should the worst come to the worst they could strike the road three-quarters of a mile up, by the old bridge, and get away to Cawnpore."

"D' you think it is going to come to that, Morton?"

Young Jelland's pink face was very much sobered.

"Let us hope not," said Captain Morton at his curtest, and he returned to his writing.

Mr. Jelland came back very hot indeed. He was also very angry.

"They won't budge," he declared.

He threw down his hat, and mopped himself.

"Lord, it is hot! They won't move a yard. They've all got absolute confidence in dear John's, or dear Charles's, or dear something or other's men, and would n't show any distrust for the world. It might hurt somebody's tender feelings."

"Good Lord, man, I did n't tell you to see the women!"

"Well,"—Mr. Jelland got some shades pinker —"well, sir, I saw Colonel Crowther, and he seemed to think he would n't be able to remember to take his liver tonic, if Mrs. Crowther were n't there to give it to him, and then Mrs. Crowther came in, and wanted to know if you were aiming a deliberate insult at your old corps, and all the rest of it, so I came away, and went and saw Major Marsh."

"Well?"

"Very stuffy. Very huffy. All in his stiff polite way. Felt quite equal to protecting his own wife in his own house, by the aid of his own men in whom he had the completest, etc. You 'd have thought I was asking the lady to elope. Give you my word you would. I felt a dashed fool, so I came away from there, and dropped in on the old Sergeant-Major, and he said his wife had just had a baby. Yesterday,

it appears. Nice, pretty little thing she is too
—Mrs. Jones, I mean, not the infant. I used
to dance with her at the Sergeants' dances at
Cawnpore. Little Lou Canning she was, and
why she married old Jones—well, anyhow, she
can't move, and old Jones said in his most
apoplectic manner, 'The Colonel's lady would
have my life, sir, if I let her go. She would
indeed, sir.'"

Richard Morton drummed on the table.

"Fewer reminiscences if you don't mind, Jelland. This is serious."

"Yes, sir, I know. Well, the upshot is that
Mrs. Elliot will come round to-morrow, and perhaps Mrs. Hill too. Her husband has got fever
—badly—and she does n't know if he can move.
Miss Darcy hummed and hawed. She would and
she would n't, but I think she 'd come if she
did n't think her character for strong-mindedness
would be imperilled. I did n't see Darcy. He
was out."

"And the Monsons?"

"Oh, yes, I saw him. He thought there was
no need for his wife to move as they were actually
next door to you."

"H'm! Well, you can go on with this report,
Jelland, and I 'll go and see Colonel Crowther
myself. I want to arrange about that guard.
Just send this down to Elliot, will you. I want
him to pick me out twenty-five of his steadiest
men."

Captain Morton got his guard, but not without a struggle.

Colonel Crowther, backed up by a very angry and towering wife, made it plain that he considered the request insulting, impolitic, unnecessary—an encouragement of the vicious—and several other things.

Richard stood tall and silent in the middle of the room until he had finished.

Then he said:

"Colonel Crowther, do you desire me to report to the Chief Commissioner that you, as officer commanding the troops, decline to comply with my official request for a guard?"

Mrs. Crowther glared.

"Official fiddlesticks!" she said, but her husband caught at her arm, and she felt his hand shake.

"Hush, my dear, I beg you. Really, Captain Morton, I do not know why you should take this intemperate tone. Of course in your official capacity—as Deputy Commissioner—" He paused and put his hand to his head.

"My dear Louisa, I am in very considerable pain. The heated tone of this conversation! I think Captain Morton would do better to retire. Captain Blake can arrange what he wishes. I really do not feel equal——"

And Captain Morton departed with the honours of war, but with no triumph in his heart.

That evening he received the official notification that a mutiny, attended by considerable loss of life, had broken out at Shahjehanpore.

CHAPTER XII

HOW THE STORM BROKE

What is the voice in the wind,
  That calls to me?
Is it a voice of the hills
  Or a voice of the sea?
Is it the breath of a word
  My lips have said?
Or is it the breath of a soul
  That forsakes the dead?

There are four great Winds,
  As all men know.
North, and South, and East, and West,
  The four Winds blow.
The four great Winds,
  We hear their breath,
But no man hears the passing-by
  Of the Wind of Death.

The East Wind, and the West Wind,
  The North Wind, and the South,
They cannot bring the breath again
  Into a dead man's mouth.
The Angels of the four great Winds
  Stand still and hold their breath,
There is a greater Wind abroad,
  The Wind of Death.

BY the morning of June 3d, Captain Morton
had persuaded some at least of the married men to send their families to his house.

Mrs. Elliot was there with the four-months-old
baby, to which she always alluded as "my funny
little monkey," thereby greatly shocking Mrs.
Hill, whose naughty six-year-old boy was always
"an angel," no matter what he did.

Miss Darcy, having been attacked by Mrs.
Crowther, had discovered that true strong-
mindedness lay in defying that autocratic lady.
A row royal had ensued, during which the two
Miss Crowthers sat meekly trembling, and con-
fided to one another in whispers that it would
have been rather fun to join the others at Mrs.
Morton's.

"Mr. Purslake is sure to be there a great
deal," whispered Milly, and Carrie blushed a
very faint pink, and said, "Oh, Milly!" in her
plaintive way.

Adela was by no means pleased with her ill-
assorted company of guests.

"Really, Helen!" she said angrily, "really I
do think Richard is crazy. Fancy asking all
this crowd of people here. Clerks' wives too
—like Mrs. da Souza. Why she is as black as
my ayah. I never did like Mrs. Crowther, as
every one knows, but I declare I think she
shows her sense in staying away. It's a regular
Noah's Ark! I should think all the servants
would give notice."

"We will give them extra wages," said Helen
gaily; "and if they decamp, I will cook, and
all the little Da Souzas shall wash up," and she

ran away to dose one of the said Da Souzas with quinine.

Mrs. da Souza was installed in Helen's own room, which she had already reduced to a condition of incredible disorder. Three of her children were actively engaged in adding to the prevailing confusion, whilst the fourth wailed fretfully upon its mother's huge and spreading lap.

As Helen entered, sounds of strife met her ears, and she heard Mrs. da Souza exclaim in a high-pitched sing-song:

"Oah Johnnee, take thee comb out of thee butter, and do not let thee babee rub it on his face! Oh, verree nahtee babee!" and there was a shrill scream of passion from the youngest Da Souza.

A mingled spasm of mirth and disgust made Helen's voice a little shaky, as she proffered the quinine, and asked how the sick child was.

"He is verree ill," said the mother. Her tears came as readily as her anger. Big drops rolled down her fat dark cheeks and fell upon the little boy's face.

"He is verree ill. Perhaps he will die."

"Suppose you were to lay him on the bed? It would be so much cooler. And perhaps the children could be made to keep quiet. The noise must be bad for him, poor little fellow."

"He shall nott die on thee bed. He shall die in my arms," declared Mrs. da Souza passionately. Then, with no perceptible change in her expression, she screamed at the children on the floor.

"Johnnee, will you fight when your brother is dying? Chup now. Be silent, all of you. Noisee, nahtee children!" The children screamed in reply, and Helen fled. At the door stood Richard Morton, beckoning.

She went to him quickly, and they stood together for a moment in the deep verandah screened off from the garden and the outside heat by a line of hanging bamboo screens.

"Where is Darcy, Helen?" he asked.

"Dr. Darcy? Oh, Lizzie Monson took him over to her house half an hour ago. Her ayah's baby is ill, and she wanted him to see it."

"They must come back. Darcy is in charge here. He had no business——"

Richard had torn a sheet from a note-book as he spoke, and was scribbling half a dozen lines.

"Here, Helen, send this over at once. Add a line to Mrs. Monson. Tell her she must come. Say I said so."

"Yes, Dick, what is it?"

"The 114th lines are on fire. Jelland went, and has sent back for me. I don't know what is wrong. Don't say anything."

"Of course not."

Richard hesitated a moment, shook his head, moved as if to go, and then turned back again.

"Helen, you've a steady head; get all these women together if you can—at the back of the house. Don't frighten them. Darcy will be here at once. If anything goes wrong—with the guard—you are all to get across the nullah, and make for Cawnpore. Do you understand?"

"Yes, is there anything else?"

"No. I must go, Helen."

"Yes, Dick."

She met his eyes and added:

"It's all right."

For a moment his hand fell on her shoulder and rested there. Then without a word he was gone.

Helen watched him out of sight. Then she called a servant, gave him Richard's note, and one from herself to Mrs. Monson, and told him to make haste with them. When the man had gone, she went back to her room and told Mrs. da Souza that the other side of the house was much cooler, and that they had better move at once. She herself headed the procession, carrying the smeary baby, who had evidently been playing with the butter again, in spite of Johnny's efforts.

The whole family deposited in the dining-room, Helen fetched Miss Darcy and Mrs. Elliot to inspect the sick child, and then drafted them into an adjoining room with the suggestion that it would be a charity to assist Mrs. Hill to fan her husband, whose fever was very high.

She was returning to her own room when Adela emerged from her bedroom, very angry.

"Helen, you 've never let that Da Souza crowd into my dining-room? I think it is a most unpardonable liberty! I won't have it!"

"Adie, the child is sick."

"Well, it can be sick in your room. You offered to have them there instead of being firm with Richard, and now, of course, you don't like it, and want to change, and I won't have it! I simply won't!"

"What is that!" said Helen in a curious low voice.

She was listening intently, but not to Adela.

"I don't hear anything except that wretched baby crying."

"Hush! No, Adie, you are to——"

Helen went to the verandah door and opened it. The heat was intense. It came in in a hot gust, and the sleeve of Helen's dark grey muslin dress seemed to scorch her arm as she leaned out and listened, straining every nerve.

A brain-fever bird was calling from the tall peepul tree in the Monsons' garden.

"Brain fever! Brain fever! Brain fever!" he shrieked, and each metallic repetition was higher than the last.

The Da Souza baby fretted on a low whining note, and Mr. Hill muttered from the room behind.

Helen had heard something different from any

of these sounds. She had heard a short, sharp
sound that seemed to rap upon her brain. A
little nerve quivered there still, and repeated the
signal like an echo.

"Helen, do shut that door!"

Helen drew a long breath. It must have been
fancy. She was getting nervous. It would
never do for her to imagine things. She took
half a step backwards, and then sudden and
distinct she heard the sound again—clear beyond any mistaking—a shot—two—three—far
away—but clear—dreadfully clear.

Helen Wilmot stepped out on to the verandah
and closed the door behind her. She went to
the corner which commanded a view of the road
and the Monsons' house.

Imaam Bux rose up, salaaming.

"What is it, Imam Bux?" she said, and she
saw that his hands were trembling.

"God knows, Miss Sahib. Miss Sahib, what
do I know?"

"I heard—shots."

"It is true."

"What does it mean?"

"God knows, Miss Sahib."

Helen caught up a felt hat from one of the
verandah chairs, and walked a few steps clear
of the house.

A sentry was pacing up and down. She could
see the Police picket in the Monsons' garden,
and the guard at their own gate. The men were

muttering—looking up and down the road. There was no sign of Dr. Darcy. Out of the distance came a noise of trampling feet.

" It is the guard. They are coming to change the guard," said Helen to herself, but her heart began to beat, not fast, but very hard, so that she could hear it. It troubled her, because she wanted to listen to that far-off, trampling noise.

Imam Bux went down to the gate, and looked along the road. There was a British officer with the guard, and he spoke to the old servant, and sent him back again.

" The Sahib says it is the new guard. He said, ' Tell the Miss Sahib to go in. The sun is hot.' "

Helen nodded impatiently. She wanted the old man to stop talking. She wanted to listen.

" Helen, you will get a sunstroke," called Adela. Then she shut the door of her room with a bang, and just as she did so Helen heard a new sound, away on the left past the Monsons' house. It was a sound like horses galloping, a great many of them, all together; and she remembered that the Cavalry Barracks lay beyond.

Suddenly Imam Bux spoke in a quavering voice.

" Miss Sahib, ai Miss Sahib! This is no guard that comes. There are some who walk, and some who run. A guard does not come thus."

Helen made a step back, half turning. She

saw the guard at the gate stir, and separate into
two bodies. She saw the officer glance over his
shoulder. There was a revolver in his hand. He
ran a few steps towards her, and shouted:

"Go in! go in!"

The words came faintly, and they were scarcely
spoken when a shot rang out, and he went down.
Helen did not see who fired, but at once there
was a confusion amongst all the men, and a tall
Sikh sprang out of the ranks, shouting and
waving his arms.

Helen's feet clung to the ground. She could
not move. She looked down the road, and saw
a long swirl of dust go up into the air. It hung
in a dark cloud, and through the cloud she could
see fierce faces and waving arms, and a medley
of men in red and men in white who ran and
shouted as they ran. They cried aloud:

"Join us, brothers, join us!" and half the
guard swung forward, and half held back.

Then there was a wild answering cry, "Oh,
yes, we will join you! We will show you how
we will join you!"

It came from the tall Sikh, and at the word
the Sikhs who were with him fired upon the
advancing crowd, and pandemonium was loose.

"Miss Sahib! Miss Sahib!" Imam Bux was
catching at Helen's arm, and at his touch a
panic seized her, and she turned and ran for the
house. She did not see the Police guard charge
the Sikhs from the rear. That happened just as

she reached the verandah, but before she came
to it she heard a great thundering of hoofs, and
she saw Lamington's Cavalry come racing down
the road. Without pause or check they went
crashing past. At the head of the foremost
troop, with lifted head and flying bridle, galloped a riderless horse. With the noise of
thunder they came, and with the noise of thunder
they went. Involuntarily she hung back—her
heart jumped. In that moment Dr. Darcy came
out of the Monsons' house. He had Mrs. Monson by the arm, and was making her run. Helen
saw them running, and her own feet would not
stir. There were more shots. The running
figures fell.

Helen Wilmot drew a quick sobbing breath,
and ran, and as she ran she heard a woman's
scream, and a groaning, and then more shouting, and a noise like hell.

The house seemed very dark to Helen. She
came in out of the strong light, and for a moment she was blind and giddy, and the dusk
seemed full of hands that caught at her dress,
and full of the frightened crying of children.

" What is it? Oh, what is it? "

Every one seemed to be calling out together,
and the noise from the road grew louder. There
were shrieks and oaths, and the clash of arms,
and, high and wild, the battle-cries of the
Sikhs.

" We must run," said Helen. Her moment of

confusion was over. "We must come at once.
To the nullah. Richard said so. Imam Bux,
take that child. Yes, Mrs. da Souza, you must.
That is right. Adela! Where is Adela!"

"My husband—oh, my husband can't! It will
kill him!" wailed Mrs. Hill.

"He must," said Helen. "Miss Darcy will
help you—Adela! Where are you?"

Mrs. Elliot took her baby out of the ayah's
arms, and opened the door to the verandah. The
noise redoubled and she hung back a moment.
Then Imam Bux passed through with Johnny
da Souza, and she followed him. Mr. Hill tot-
tered after them, his eyes hazy with fever, and
his mind confused. He had heard nothing—
understood nothing. His ears buzzed with
quinine, and he thought he could hear a drum
being beaten, but he could not tell the reason
for it, nor why his wife should cling to him,
and weep. "What a lot o' women!" he said
thickly, and stout Miss Darcy caught his arm,
and so they stumbled out into the heat, Mrs.
Hill crying all the time, and Jacky highly pleased
because he was running races with papa, and
mamma, and all the grown-up ladies.

Helen saw them go, and ran to Adela's room,
calling all the time. Something held the door
against her, and then gave way with a shriek.
She pushed her way in, and Adela, wild with
terror, rushed through the room, and crouched
behind the bed.

"Adie! Adie!" cried Helen. "My dear, come. It is Helen—only Helen!"

"Helen, they are killing each other! They are shooting at us. Oh, I saw them. Oh, Helen!"

Helen pulled her to her feet, and once they had begun to run, Adela's panic set her racing, and it was Helen who was put to it to keep up with her.

When they were clear of the house, they had to cross the wide dusty sweep which ran all round it. The dust already raised by all those hastening feet flew up, and hung about them like a mist, only it was dry. It parched their throats, and stung their eyes.

Beyond the sweep a narrow grassy path ran between low rose hedges whose flowers were dead, and whose long thorny trails stretched out across the path, and caught at the women's dresses as they ran. When they had gone twenty yards the path turned off at right angles, and for another twenty yards there was no cover at all, and they were full in view of the black advancing crowd.

For the Sikhs were all down now. Every man of them dead, with the dead he had killed around him. In the gateway the corpses lay so thick that it was easier for the mutineers to climb the outer wall than to pass the gate which was guarded by the dead. They broke over the wall as a wave breaks—Cavalry, Infantry, men in the

English red, with the English rifle in their grip, and hate of the English in their hearts, men in the loose white native dress, high-caste Brahmins, fanatic Mussulmans, bazaar scum, united by a common thirst for blood and loot.

After one glance Helen looked only in front of her. She had to drag Adela along, for panic was passing with exhaustion, and she was thankful that she herself felt neither.

Instead there was an excitement—almost elation—that urged her on, and gave her strength. She found herself noticing everything,—the blazing heat of the sun, the fact that the sky was hazy and showed no blue. She wondered if that were because of the dust of their flight, and a strange and terrible verse came into her mind and stayed there, "And the sun shall be turned into darkness and the moon to blood." Only which of them would live to see the moon?

There seemed no end to the path. There were bright indigo shadows on it, odd crisscross shadows, that changed the colour of the grass, and flickered on the women's gowns. Suddenly the grass at Helen's feet was ripped up. A puff of dust rose from it, and her foot felt a little roughness as she passed. Adela screamed, and hung back, and a loud crackling noise came from the direction of the gate. Helen's mind, working quite clearly and, as it seemed to her, quite slowly, informed her that they were being fired upon, but that they must keep on—because that was what Dick had told them to do.

She dragged Adela forward, and just in front of them she saw some one, Miss Darcy she thought, fall sideways across the path. She made no sound, but she moved a little, and one of the clear indigo shadows became blurred with red. Mrs. da Souza, the fat Eurasian woman, called wildly, and shrilly, upon her Maker, and dropped among the bushes, covering her head, but Helen stepped across the body, and pulled Adela after her by main force.

Helen looked down as they passed and saw the woman's face. It was Miss Darcy, and she was dead. You must be dead if a bullet goes in at your temple, and leaves a strange ragged hole like that. Helen felt no emotion. She was rather glad that Miss Darcy was quite dead, because otherwise she would have been obliged to wait, and try and pick her up, and Miss Darcy was heavy.

It would probably have ended in Adela being shot too, and whatever happened to other people, she must save Adela. Mr. Hill was down now. Not wounded, but too exhausted to go any farther. He lay on his face and sobbed, and his wife sat down beside him, and tried to screen the sun from his head with her small, useless hands. The tears ran down her face all the time, and spoilt little Jacky tugged at her skirts.

Helen caught the child's hand as she went

past, but a yard or two farther on he wrenched
away from her, and stumbled back to his mother.
Adela noticed nothing, and Helen's eyes were
set on the turn of the path only just ahead of
them now.   There was cover there—tall clumps
of oleander and bamboo.   To come into the shade
of them was like coming into safety, but as they
reached it, and pressed on, Helen heard a scream,
and something seemed to cry out in her, with a
loud insistent calling.

She pushed Adela behind the bamboos, and
said in a strained whisper:

" Not a child.   One can't.   It's no good; go
on, Adie—I'll come," and she turned and ran
back.

But when she came to where Mr. Hill had
fallen, he had stopped panting for breath, and
Mrs. Hill lay across him with a bullet in her
breast, and a dead child clutched in her arms.

Helen crouched between the roses, and stared
at them, but none of the three moved, or would
move again.

She felt neither grief nor horror.   They were
dead.   Now she could go on, and that clear insistent calling would trouble her no more.   She
looked towards the house and saw that it was
on fire.   The mutineers were looting it, but it
would not occupy them for long.   A bullet sang
past her cheek, and another ripped the muslin of
her skirt, but she reached the turn of the path
again, and pushed her way into the bamboo

clump to where she could see Adela Morton's white dress.

"Come, Adie."

But Adela was leaning against the bamboo stems half sitting, half kneeling, and her face was white and wet.

"I'm fainting!" she gasped, and Helen's grasp tightened on her arm.

"If you faint, they will kill you!" she said in a low hard voice; and Adela clung to her and trembled, and aided by the slope of the ground, Helen dragged her a few yards, but the weight on her arm grew heavier and heavier, and it was all she could do to keep from falling.

"I can't."

The words were only just audible. They ended in a long shudder and Adela sank helplessly to the ground. Helen let her go and straightened herself. Then she unfastened the large brooch at her neck, and ran the pin very deliberately into Adela's arm.

The blood spurted, and Adela came out of her half-swoon with a scream.

"Get up, Adie," commanded Helen. "They'll hurt you more than that. Being killed will *hurt!*"

Adela stumbled to her feet sobbing, and again they ran. They were quite out of sight of the house by now, and every moment the ground sloped more. It grew very rough too, and seemed damper. Here and there were high tussocks of grass, and there was a quantity of low, dusty scrub, and a few tall trees.

Helen proceeded in a definite direction. She had a clear picture in her mind and kept constantly to the right, calling to Mrs. Elliot to do the same. Grace Elliot's long fair hair had come down, and there was a blood-stain on her shoulder, but she ran steadily, holding her baby, and keeping beside Helen, until the sound of the noise and the shouting died away, and their breath failed them.

At last Helen slackened her pace, and stood for a moment listening.

" No one is coming," she said in a husky voice. " No one is coming," and she let go of Adela, and took a deep breath.

Mrs. Elliot had halted too. She came a few paces nearer, panting.

" Is it safe? Ought we to stop? "

And Helen repeated the same words again.

" No one is coming."

" Are you sure? Is it safe? "

Safe? Nothing was safe any more, but Helen nodded, and Grace Elliot sat down, and rocked her little silent baby.

Helen stood for a moment longer, still listening. Then she too sat down, and laid her head in her hands. So often in the last few days she had wondered what it would be like when it came, what she should feel—and do. She had wondered whether she would be afraid; whether she would run, and scream. The idea had terrified her more than the idea of death. She had had a vision of herself screaming, and running, and a long thin knife coming nearer and nearer, until it touched the flesh—the warm, live flesh. The thought of that knife was dreadful. It would be cold, very cold, and the cold chill of death would slide along the blade, and pierce between the pulsings of her heart. That was the picture—the vision.

The reality was quite different. She did not feel afraid, because all feeling had quite, quite stopped. She did not feel at all. From battle and murder, and from sudden death, good Lord deliver us. She had seen all three, and she felt nothing at all. She had seen women killed, and a little child, and she had felt nothing.

Adela was crying beside her, as if her heart would break, and Helen lifted her head for a moment, and rebuked her coldly and sternly, and then felt vaguely sorry. After all it was proper for Adela to weep, since Adela was a widow now. Widows ought to cry. Dick was dead. Yes, Dick must certainly be dead, or they two would not be sitting there so comfortless in the dust.

Sharp on her wandering thoughts came Mrs. Elliot's voice.

"Helen! Helen Wilmot!"

Helen raised her head.

"What is it?"

" I can't wake my baby."

" Why do you want to wake her? "

It was like a conversation in a dream, all about nothing, and yet instinct with some nightmare quality, which quivered behind the common words.

" I can't wake her," repeated Mrs. Elliot, in a low, hurrying voice.

Helen leaned forward and touched the baby's hand. It was lax and warm. Somehow the warmth of it shocked her. She knew as she touched it that she had expected to find it cold. Dead hands were cold.

" Its hand is quite warm," she said vaguely, and Mrs. Elliot gave a sharp, terrified cry.

" Of course her hand is warm," she said, and then went back to her old complaint; " but I can't wake her! "

Adela Morton looked up with the tears running down her face.

" Is the baby dead? " she whispered to Helen, but the mother heard.

" What? " she said, and gave her a fierce look of hatred. Then she turned away her head, and they could see nothing but the long fair hair that fell all around her, and the smear of blood on her left shoulder.

" Hush, Adela! " said Helen, and Adela began to cry again, whilst Helen sat staring, and Mrs. Elliot rocked and rocked with the baby on her knee.

The heat of the day increased. The sun beat down. The thin shade overhead seemed to be burning away. Helen leaned her head against the tree behind her, and shut her eyes.

CHAPTER XIII

Why do we gather so slowly the strength that must pass
    away,
Wrested in patience from Time and spent in an hour, in
    a day?
Month upon month to the birth, and afterwards year upon
    year,
Fashioned in labour and pain, nurtured in striving and
    fear,
All we have gathered from Time, passes, is gone like a
    breath
Into the vast, unknown, unharvested garner of Death.

IT might have been an hour later, or it might
have been some much shorter time, when
Imam Bux came to them through the bushes,
guided by the sound of Adela's low persistent
sobbing.

For a moment he stood and watched the three
women, with the tears running down his brown
and wrinkled cheeks. Then he called, " Mem
Sahib! Mem Sahib! " and Adela's little scream
woke Helen from the doze into which she had
fallen. At first she saw only a dazzle of glittering light and dusty green. Then her eyes
cleared.

" It is Imam Bux," she said. " Adela, hush!
Do you hear?—hush! Be quiet, don't cry. It is
Imam Bux."

" Huzoor," said the old man, salaaming with
a shaky hand.

Helen got up, pressing her hands upon her
temples. The dreamlike feeling had faded. She
felt clearer, and she was responsible. Dick had
made her responsible. A stab of pain brought
her completely to herself.

" Imam Bux, what must we do? · The Sahib
said ' Go to Cawnpore—' How can we go?
Do you know how we can reach the road? "

" Huzoor, I know."

She drew the old servant aside.

" Where is the Sahib? " she asked. " Is he
dead? Do you think he is dead? " and her voice
was steady because her strong will kept it so.

Imam Bux wrung his hands.

" God knows! " he said. " Many sahibs are
dead. It is a madness. It is the devil's breath.
These sons of Satan have killed many sahibs.
Perhaps my Sahib is dead. They say he must
be dead. God knows."

" Who says? " asked Helen sharply.

" It was Purslake Sahib who said it."

" Where is he? When did you see him? "

" He also is hiding here in the jungle, and
with him is Blake Sahib, very sorely wounded,
and the Colonel's Mem, and one of the Miss
Sahibs."

"Are they far?"

"A half mile, Miss Sahib. Also the child I carried is with them. I returned to look for my Mem Sahib, and my Miss Sahib——"

"We will go to them," said Helen, and she went back to Adela and Mrs. Elliot.

"Imam Bux says that Captain Blake and Mr. Purslake are a little farther on; Mrs. Crowther is with them, and one of the girls."

Adela Morton sprang up with a cry of relief. A man—any man—spelled protection and safety. She had cried until she could cry no more, and was ready now to be saved and comforted. The idea that this was only the beginning of troubles had not presented itself to her mind.

But Mrs. Elliot rose slowly. She was shivering although the heat was so great, and she turned the baby's face into her bosom, so that Helen should not see it.

They came upon the other little band of refugees quite suddenly. Carrie Crowther saw them first, and she came running to meet them, sobbing, and trembling with excitement. Her eyes were bright, and there was a colour in her cheeks. She looked very pretty.

"Oh, Miss Wilmot! Oh, Mrs. Elliot!" she panted. "Oh, isn't it dreadful? Isn't it too dreadful? My poor papa and Milly! Do you know they shot them? They shot poor Milly." She choked and caught at Helen's arm. "Mamma had gone back to fetch the Sergeant's baby, and they shot poor Milly whilst we were running together. We were holding hands, and she fell down, and I could n't lift her up, and then mamma came, and she made me run again. Oh, dear! Oh, dear!"

Adela Morton pushed past her and clutched at Mr. Purslake.

"Oh, I thought every one was dead! Thank God! Thank God!" she cried.

To do her justice it was not the man with whom she had flirted to whom she clung, but to safety, protection, help, all personified in the one able-bodied man of the party.

Mrs. Crowther, on the ground beside Captain Blake's unconscious form, lifted her head heavily, and stared at the new arrivals. She frowned a little at Adela, and then looked vaguely towards Helen and Mrs. Elliot.

Oddly enough Helen's first pang of pity stirred in her at the sight of this woman whom she had so cordially disliked.

Mrs. Crowther's brick-coloured face was now of a uniform streaming crimson. Her brilliant hair hung in wet wisps across her forehead and down upon her shoulders. There were horrible stains, not yet dry, upon the front of the light dress she wore. Her harsh features twitched, and she made two attempts to speak before any words would come.

Then she said in a dull, strained voice:

"It is very hot. It is very, very hot."

She turned her head away, and the effort with which she moved it was pitiable to see. Then she went on fanning George Blake with a wide, dusty leaf.

Helen came up to her, and knelt down.

" Is he dead? " she asked in a whisper, looking at the half-closed eyes and deadly pallor.

" Not yet," said Mrs. Crowther. Then she lifted her own eyes, and Helen saw that they were rimmed with red, and bloodshot—dreadfully bloodshot.

" My poor Colonel is dead, and Milly, and they say Captain Elliot too. No, I don't know who told me."

" And Dick? "

Helen spoke very quickly because she knew that if she waited for a moment, she would not dare to ask.

" Dick—where is Dick? "

Mrs. Crowther shook her head, and went on fanning.

" Mr. Purslake." Helen's eyes compelled him, and it was at her, and not at Adela, that he looked as he replied:

" I don't know. I really don't know. It all happened so quickly."

" Tell me what happened, please."

He passed his hand over his brow.

" My orderly ran in and said that the barracks were on fire, and that Captain Elliot had been shot." He lowered his voice. " Then we heard firing and ran out. Our lines were on fire. There was great confusion. Noise. Blake caught hold of a bugler and told him to sound the assembly, and then some one rushed up and said the Colonel was shot. I don't really know how it all happened. My head—I don't seem able to think. But some one called out Morton's name, and I saw him jump his horse over the ditch and ride towards us with a revolver in his hand. Then Blake was shot, and his orderly was holding him on his horse, so I got up behind him. One of the native officers helped; and I galloped off, and got across the nullah, and found Mrs. and Miss Crowther. That is really all I can tell you, Miss Wilmot."

He passed his hand over his forehead again, and looked vaguely from her to Adela. His hazel eyes had the look of shallow shifting water.

"But Richard. Oh, I don't understand."

This time it was Adela who asked:

"Where is Richard?"

Mr. Purslake looked dreadfully uncomfortable. He was not formed for tragedy. He felt bewildered and confused, like an actor who has learned his trivial part, and finds himself suddenly set to play the hero in some strange unknown drama.

Carrie Crowther broke the silence with a sob, and Adela cried out: "Why did he leave us? It was very wicked of him to leave us. What shall we do now!"

Helen Wilmot took a grip of herself. If this were a dream, an awful, awful dream, she would wake soon, because to every dream there comes the moment of awaking, and if it were not a dream, if it were real, then there was work to do, and a high part to play. By and by this too would end. Life's dream would break, and there would be a new awakening.

Meanwhile she must not let her reason go— must keep at bay the impulse that prompted her to sit down, there in the dust, and let the mists close in upon her brain.

Helen drew a little away from Mrs. Crowther, whose loud, slow breathing was more distressing to listen to than any sound of weeping. She was trying to think. Some one must think, arrange, direct; she was wondering to whom they could look. George Blake—so near that her hand touched his soiled uniform. He would have been their helper, but unconsciousness buried him now, as deeply almost as any grave of earth. She looked around her at the little band of forlorn creatures. Carrie with her high flush, fever-bright eyes, and lips that were never still for one moment. Adela, wearied out, her head against the rough bark of a tree, and a strand of her shining hair all in a tangle across her breast, which heaved with a continual sobbing. Beyond them, just where the shade began, Mrs. Elliot standing quite still, a tense, unmoving figure, with her head bent above the

unmoving child.   Farther off again, under a
clump of bushes, Imam Bux, sitting on his heels,
and swaying distressfully to an accompaniment
of low whimpers from Johnny da Souza who
squatted beside him.

Here was no help, only great helplessness.
Helen's eyes and thoughts travelled back, and
rested upon Charles Purslake.   One shall be
taken and another left.   The words passed
through her mind.   It seemed very strange that
he should be left when so many were taken.   If
only it were he who lay here unconscious, and
George Blake were in his place.   Or Dick.   No,
she must not think of Dick—only of what Dick
had left her to do.

She looked again at Mr. Purslake—at the de-
jected droop of his shoulders, and the nervous
movement of his hands.   One of them hung
down, and the fingers beat upon the ground as
if spelling out a tune.   Continually he cleared
his throat, and every now and then he put his
hand to it, and coughed, and then fell to drum-
ming on the ground again.

Helen got up, and went over to him.   Touching him on the shoulder, she beckoned him a
little away from Adela.

" Mr. Purslake, what are we to do? " she asked
in a low voice.

He threw out his hands.

" We must wait here till nightfall."

" Yes, and then? "

" Heaven knows! "

" I think we must know too. Dick "—her
voice was quite steady, " Dick said to make for
Cawnpore, but it is thirty miles by the road.
We can't walk. That is, you and I might perhaps, but not the others."

Mr. Purslake began to pull himself together.
Helen was looking him very straight in the face.
He did not admire her composure, but it had a
stimulating effect upon him.

" If you could get a cart—one of those big
bullock carts," she was saying, and the consciousness that it was she and not he who was
taking the initiative stung him into making a
suggestion of his own.

" Too slow. Why, a bullock cart only goes
three miles an hour."

" Yes, but it keeps on; and I 've been thinking, it will attract less notice than anything
else. If we start as soon as it is dark, we should
reach Cawnpore in the morning."

Purslake made an impatient movement.

" My dear Miss Wilmot, how are we to get
a bullock cart, or any other cart, for the matter
of that? There is Blake's horse, and that is all
we can count on in the way of transport."

He laughed feebly.

Helen put up her hand.

" Imam Bux must get us a cart."

" And bring those rascals down on us? "

" Nothing is safe, but we can't stay here.

Wait a moment and I 'll speak to him. He will do what he can."

Imam Bux was terribly shaken, and a sickly pallor showed beneath the brown of his skin. He put piteous hands together when Helen made it clear what she required.

He was a poor man. He was an old man. Whence could he obtain a bullock cart? The sons of Satan would kill him. Certainly they would kill him, and then there would be nobody to protect his Mem Sahib and his Miss Sahib.

Helen listened to the wavering excuses, and met each one with comfort, encouragement, and praise. Her heart sank, but she looked kindly at the old man, and by and by when he had talked his fill, he shuffled away through the bushes, and Helen took the little Da Souza boy by the hand, and went back to Mr. Purslake.

"He will do it," she said. "And he will come back here, and let us know. He is very frightened, poor old man, but he will do his best. Now, Johnny, you sit down here by this lady, and no one will hurt you. There 's a good boy."

Adela drew away her soiled white skirts as Johnny squatted down. She gave a little sob, and looked round for sympathy. She thought Mr. Purslake might fan her, instead of talking to Helen. Johnny sobbed too, and Adela pulled at Helen's dress.

"I am so thirsty," she said in a complaining voice. "Helen, I am so dreadfully thirsty."

"Yes, we all are. Perhaps we shall get some water before long. Could you sleep a little?"

"In this heat?"

"Try, Adie. Shut your eyes and try. I must go to Mrs. Elliot now."

"Why can't she sit down?" fretted Adela. "It gets on my nerves to see her standing like that. She has n't moved once."

"Nor has the child," said Mr. Purslake. His eyes went from Mrs. Elliot to Helen, and she saw the shrinking look in them.

"That baby—Miss Wilmot, what is wrong with it? It does n't seem to be asleep."

"It is dead," said Helen, with a catch in her voice.

"How?"

"I don't know. It has n't moved at all. Adie, do you think if you went to her—you lost your baby—do you think——"

"Oh, *no!*" said Adela. "Oh, I could n't—Helen, I could n't; how unkind you are!"

She began to cry again, and Helen without a word left her and went to where Mrs. Elliot stood, like a woman turned to stone.

Helen touched her lightly.

"My poor dear, do sit down. You 'll want all your strength," she said, and then stopped, the other woman's eyes were so terrible.

Yesterday—was it yesterday or all the ages ago?—Mrs. Crowther had said that, for all she pretended to be so girlish, Mrs. Elliot must be

close on thirty. Every feature of the worn
face confessed to more than thirty now, and
the eyes stared out of a strained network of
lines.

"Gilbert?" she said in a whisper.

"They say so," said Helen, crying. The tears
which she could not shed for Dick came hot
and fast for Gilbert Elliot, whom she had
scarcely known. "Oh, my dear, God comfort
you—they say so. Give me the little baby, you
poor, poor dear, and sit down, and cry if you can,
for it helps, it does indeed."

Helen felt a long shudder pass through the
arm which was next her own.

"Gilbert too," said Grace Elliot, in a strained,
choking breath. "Gilbert too"; and with that
she moved forward a halting step or two and
sat down, letting the child fall across her knees,
and clutching with both hands at the rough,
prickly stem of a little tree.

She turned her head aside, and rested it upon
her hands. The long hair covered them, and
covered her face too.

Then like a flood came the tears. Helen Wilmot sat down beside her with her hands folded
in her lap. Her own tears were dry again.
There was a passion of pity and trouble at her
heart, but it was a frozen passion that could
find no outlet.

She sat quite still and waited until a dull
silence followed rending sobs. Then again she

waited for what the endless day might yet bring
forth.

The sun was at its full strength, the heat of
it like a weight suspended overhead. And this
weight seemed to come lower and lower, com-
pressing the air as it came, making it dense and
heavy, so that the lungs laboured and the blood
beat against the temples and the drum of the
ear.

The tree beneath which they were gathered
gave a thin and ineffective shade, shot with
blinding, dusty sunshafts, and beyond it was a
glaring belt of dry, uncovered ground, which
gave back the fierce sunlight with an unendur-
able fidelity. Heat and light struck upwards
from it, and the air above it trembled with a
faint incessant tremor that troubled the senses.

A dreary, pain-haunted sleep came to some of
them. When they roused from it, it was like
waking into some phantasy which the mind could
not accept.

Carrie Crowther lay with her head upon her
mother's stained dress. Her eyes were only half
shut, her hand twitched, and her lips kept moving—moving, even in her sleep.

Adela slept too, and the little boy had crept
up close beside her. Helen watched them, struggling to realise that only yesterday they had
laughed and flirted, chattered and gossiped at
the Club—and now? What new existence did
these awful birthpangs herald? The old life was

gone as entirely as if they too were dead. They
were lost in a new world, a world of flaring light
and pitiless cruelty. What were they to do in
it? and what would be the end?

Helen slipped into a dream of heat and terror,
in which Dick called to her, and she could not
reach him. He kept on calling, and calling, and
she woke gasping, with George Blake's voice in
her ears.

As the day wore on his unconsciousness had
become less complete. Now and then he stirred,
and once flung round upon his side, with so
sharp a cry of pain that a thrill of sheer terror
ran through all the little company. It was this
cry that woke Helen Wilmot. It startled them
all. They had been drifting among shadows,
looking into the past, suffering with a suffering
of the mind, and this sharp cry of bodily pain
was like the voice of reality crying aloud in the
wilderness of the unreal.

Mrs. Crowther stopped her mechanical fanning and a slow shudder ran over her heavy
form. Carrie muttered in her sleep, and little
Johnny whimpered, but there was only that one
cry, and after it the sick man slid into a deeper
unconsciousness than before.

After what seemed like a week of days, Imam
Bux returned. He was shivering with the strain
of the day's work, and a little fever burned in his
blood and made his hand shake as it went up
to make the salaam, but he was full of pride.

He had found a man, and the man would not
fail.   He would bring a cart—a cart with a cover
to it.   In the face of death he had arranged
everything.   As soon as it was too dark to tell
a white thread from a black one, the man would
bring the cart and wait in the shadow beyond
the old bridge.   Blake Sahib they must carry.
He had brought a sheet.   Thus he could be carried without danger.   Also he had brought—
this, and out of the folds of the sheet Imam
Bux proudly produced two bottles of soda-water.

"More I could not hide; I was in fear of my
life," he said, and stood to be applauded, like a
child that knows it has been good and wise.   A
murmur went up from all the parched lips, and
Johnny da Souza put out both hands and wailed:

"Pani!   Pani!"

Helen spoke quickly in the old servant's ear:

"And the Sahib?"

The pleased look disappeared.

"Ai—my Sahib," he said; "God knows.   In
the bazaar they say that all the sahibs are dead."

Two bottles of soda-water do not go very far
amongst eight persons who have had nothing to
drink all day, but each had a couple of mouth-
fuls; and then again they waited, whilst the
shadows lengthened, and the sun-glare waned.

In this time of waiting a strange experience
came to Helen Wilmot.   She was looking out
from the shady patch, where she sat beside Mrs.
Elliot.   She saw the dusty scrub, and the dark

scrawled shadows that lengthened as the sun
went down—and then quite suddenly she heard
a cuckoo call. She heard it quite plainly. It
was very far away, but sweet—so sweet, like a
low laugh heard through a thin clear sheet of
water, falling. Cuckoo—and the notes fell
nearer. And at the third cry the dust was gone,
and the dry jungle scrub, and instead she saw
a pale sweet sunlight falling between fresh
burgeoning trees, upon a sheeted mist of bluebells. A hyacinth splendour, like sea-water in
a bloomy transmigration. A breeze rippled it
into waves, and the waves lapped nearer, nearer,
trembling under the breath of that invisible
sound, nearer and nearer, till with the final
laughing cuckoo note, the flower spray beat
against Helen's outstretched hands. She felt it
cool and exquisite, like a touch of the visible
blue of heaven, and then, with a quick-drawn
breath, she shut her eyes, and broke the vision
midway. When she looked again, the light had
fallen suddenly, and the dusk was about their
feet.

That night as they jolted over the dry road,
packed in the hot covered bullock cart, with the
sick man laid full length and the rest crouched
about him, Helen dwelt on this strange seeing
of hers.

Adela leaned on her shoulder and slept, but
Helen waked. Once only she dropped into a
half sleep, and dreamed that she stood barefoot

in the midst of that hyacinth sea. Her feet
were wet with the rainbow dew of it, and she
plunged bare arms amongst the flowers, and
gathered them to her bosom. Then as she
straightened herself, and breathed divine cool
air, she saw that Richard Morton stood beside
her.

He laid his hand upon her shoulder, and looked
into her eyes. Something broke in her heart for
very gladness, and she awoke into the close heat
of darkness of the covered cart, with a strange
parched laughter in her throat.

Through the opening in the front of the cart,
she could see the driver swaying sleepily, a white
sheet covering him from head to foot. There
was a glare of moonlight that turned each little
shadow to a pool of indigo with an orange-
coloured edge. Helen looked out with dazzled
eyes, and heard the galloping of a horse,
very far away. It came nearer, and as the
rider shouted a masterful "Hut, byle-wallah
—hut!" the drowsy driver started awake, and
pulled the cart with a jerk to the side of the
road.

Adela wakened whimpering. Mrs. Crowther
fell heavily against her daughter, who uttered a
protesting murmur. Captain Blake groaned
once, and drew a long shuddering breath, and
the horseman went by with a clatter, leaving the
moonlight heavy with the dust he stirred.

Helen, her trembling hand upon George

14

Blake's silent pulse, saw his face as he passed, and recognised it.

Fatehshah Khan was out of the burning house. Oude flared in the mutiny behind him, and his face was set towards Cawnpore.

CHAPTER XIV

Would'st thou be Master of Men, then learn to govern thy
  Will,
For if thou rule not thyself, another will master thee still.

ON the morning of the fifth of June, a small
group of men were gathered in one of the
inner rooms of a house opposite the Civil Court
at Cawnpore. The room was high and dark, for
it had no outside door, and was lighted only by
two very small windows, set twenty feet up in
the stained and dirty wall. The untidy matted
floor was only half covered by a priceless Persian
carpet, whose dim, lovely tints could scarcely
be distinguished in the dusk.

In one corner on a native string bed a young
man lay tossing and muttering; his half-closed
eyes were bloodshot, and his face was drawn
and thin. A richly embroidered scarf lay across
his feet, and a brilliant silken cushion supported
his head, which turned continually from side to
side. Other cushions lay upon the floor, their
bright colours emerging from the shadows with
a curious and rather startling effect. Half a
dozen common Mora chairs, made of yellow cane,
and bound with scarlet cotton stuff, were grouped

211

about a table upon which stood a golden ink-
stand studded with jewels, a brandy bottle with
the top knocked off, and a high cut-glass tumbler.

In one of the chairs sat a very stout man,
dressed all in white. His thin muslin shirt was
fastened at the neck by a great red jewel, but it
opened below, exposing two handbreadths of
the fat unwholesome flesh upon his chest. His
small white turban was almost entirely covered
with gold lace, and a thick gold chain hung
down into his lap. Between the gold lace and
the gold chain his face had a yellowish look,
for the skin was fair, and tightly stretched
across the fat cheeks and heavy, sensual chin. He
was clean shaven, and there were lines about
the mouth and eyes which should not have been
on any human face, but in spite of these the
general effect was one of good-natured self-
indulgence. Only the dark glancing eyes were
wild, brilliant, and restless, like the eyes of the
young man upon the bed. Emerald peacocks
perched upon golden pinnacles ornamented the
hookah from which he smoked, and as he smoked,
his eyes went to and fro continually, and showed
a bloodshot rim.

Every now and then he leaned sideways and
spat into a golden bowl which stood on the floor
beside him. Then again he smoked, and again
his eyes looked every way. For this was his
day of fate. This day he must decide whether
he would remain the Nana Sahib of Bithoor, a

mere native gentleman, denied the honour of a
salute, mulcted of the princely rank and pension
of his adopted father, Bajee Rao, last of the
Mahratta line, or whether he would make a bold
bid for power and a kingdom. On the one side
there was sovereignty, the title of Peishwa,
wealth, power; on the other, what was there to
tempt him? An extra slice of land, a little
favour from the lord Sahib, some trifling indulgence in the Courts—the hushing-up, perhaps,
of that business of his adopted sister's death.
Nothing more. Nothing further. Only on the
one side and the other there was danger, there
was ruin, there was death, and who could say
upon which side the menace was strongest?

To be Peishwa—perhaps the most powerful of
all the Peishwas—there was the lure. Up to
now he stood uncommitted. He had proffered
help to the English, whilst sending his emissaries
amongst the native soldiery to fan their growing discontent. He had set a guard upon the
Treasury, and the English Magistrate leaned
upon him. Yet that same night he had listened
for an hour to the counsels and ambitions of
Teeka Singh, the ringleader of the Mutineers.

Now he had come to the dividing of the ways,
for smouldering Cawnpore had sent up its first
tongue of flame in answer to the challenging
beacons of Oude, and the roar and the smell
of burning blew all abroad on the breath of the
rising storm.

Already the sky leaned red and lowering above the city that was to wear for ever such a brand of blood. Already there was a prophetic tinge upon that sacred river, of which the peasant folk were soon to say shuddering, " We cannot look upon it—it is red—all red——"

Dhundoo Punth drew the delicate mouthpiece of his hookah from between his lips, and drank a long draught from the carved glass at his side, whilst about him his followers talked incessantly, and their voices—fierce, arguing voices—echoed high up amongst the dusty rafters overhead.

Tantia Topee, the soldier of fortune; Baba Bhut and Bala, the Nana's brothers; Azimullah, the ex-khitmutghar, the late lion of a London season—they all talked, separately and all together, urging, flattering, cajoling, whilst the Nana swayed, and smoked, drank, and smoked again, with those restless eyes of his glancing from one to another, and seeing now Tantia's fierce eyes, now the heavy stare of Baba Bhut, now the fever-stricken boy on the bed, and now nothing—nothing at all but his own burning, wavering dreams.

Suddenly he spoke, in the slow, mellow voice of a fat man:

" Who broke out first? "

" It was Teeka Singh, Teeka Singh and the 2d Cavalry," said Tantia, leaning on the table between Bala and Baba Bhut. His eyes flashed, his voice was low and harsh.

"They cut down the Subadar Major because he would not give them the colours, and they went away shouting, 'Join us, brothers; join us, heroes!' until the Gillis regiment came out too. To-morrow the rest will come. There is doubt in their hearts to-day, but to-morrow they will come. Then we can kill all these accursed English, and make a kingdom here."

His dark lips lifted a little as he spoke, and showed the white teeth behind them. They were as white and sharp as an animal's.

"There are many of them," said the Nana, "very many. They are a very strong people."

Azimullah, the Mohammedan, leaned his elbow on the table, stroking his handsome chin, with the dark curled beard upon it.

"They were strong, but they have become weak," he said deliberately. "Their war with Russia has used up all their men. With my own eyes I saw their weakness. With my own ears I heard the tales that were told of it, when I was in Roum. They died in that war, as the wasps die when the cold weather comes. They were full of disease and weary to their bones of the fighting. They will not send more men to Hindustan now. They are weary. This is the time to strike. There is no other time. A wise man who finds his enemy weak and wounded, kills him quickly, and goes to his house rejoicing. Our enemy was weak, and we held our hands. Now he is wounded, he is in our hands to kill. If we are wise, we will kill now. Then we shall be in safety, and you will be Peishwa, and we, your servants, will come to honour. That is my counsel. These words are true words. The Rao Sahib also knows if I have spoken the truth."

Azimullah ceased speaking, and looked across at the sick man, who had flung round upon his side, and was listening with a half-dazed expression, his pale face ghastly against the cushion of flaring orange silk.

A strong man's anger finds vent in action, but the resentment of the weak turns inward, stagnating and breeding the creatures of stagnation. Francis Manners, whom they called the Rao Sahib, was full of the fruits of three years' aimless, brooding hatred. When he had fever, and when he was drunk, he dreamed dreams of vengeance. When he was sane and sober his incompetence pressed upon him, and his thoughts were the more bitter.

Sometimes in those dreams of his he saw Adela Lauriston's face. It was mocking, scornful, lovely with the unearthly loveliness of vision, and then it changed. The eyes wept—the bitter tears rolled down—the head bent, and bent to him. Imploring hands rose up from the night of sleep and caught at his. Then his own hands burned, and he awoke to the throbbing pulses of fever.

Out of such a dream as this he awoke now,

and looked at Azimullah with his restless, brilliant eyes. He was full of opium, and his own voice sounded to him as if it came from some great height. He had a vision of the words, falling like knives—like bright flashing knives. They came swiftly, swiftly from very far away, and they fell into the dark room with a ringing sound.

"Curse them! Curse the English! What have I to do with them?" Bala, his fierce uncle, turned an angry look upon him, and he fell again into a muttering silence.

"Yet they are a strong people," said Dhundoo Punth doubtfully. He put his hands together upon his stomach and looked down at the great ruby on the uppermost finger. It caught the light, and sent out gleams like blood.

"They are a very strong people," he repeated, "and if they send many troops, many regiments——"

"Where will they get them from?" said Bala, in his quick, toneless voice.

He drew the fine line of his brows together, and spread out his small, strong hands. He was much darker than his brother, and of a thin, tough make—a small man, very fierce, and pitted with small-pox.

"Where will they get them from? They are gone. They are poured out like ghee, and like ghee the sun has melted them, and the earth has swallowed them up. Be bold, my brother!"

Azimullah had risen. He came near and spoke low, whilst Tantia broke into an argument with Baba Bhut, a fat man with a stupid face.

"The Mussulman folk talk of the Nunna Nawab for their king, if you draw back, Maharaja," he said, his handsome eyes narrowed to a watching look.

The Nana frowned, putting out his hand to the tall tumbler. Suddenly his assumption of calm was broken up by an outburst of uncontrolled anger. With the gesture of a furious child, he flung the glass against the wall, and as Baba Bhut exclaimed, and the splinters flew, he spoke with a kind of enraged vehemence.

"What can I do? How do I know what I should do? Every one says something different! You say that they are not strong, but I know that they are strong, and if we go against them, and they prevail, they will blow us from guns, and what will it then avail us that I have been called the Peishwa for a month,—two months —who knows? "

Bala had risen too. He came softly behind his brother, and plucked Azimullah by the sleeve.

"What is this talk of the Nunna Nawab? " he said, and his eyes were small and intent.

Azimullah moved a little to meet him, and spread out his hands.

"The talk is as I have said. There are many of the Mussulmans who desire a Mussulman to

be their ruler. They talk of the Nunna Nawab.
If the Nana Sahib does not speak quickly, they
will talk more. In the end they will act also."

The Nana went on speaking:

"Who is the Nunna Nawab that I should fear
him? If I fight for the English, I will tell
them that he is disloyal. I will tell them that
he sought to lead away the Mussulman folk, that
he sought to make himself a king! They will
listen to me, and he will be blown from a gun
—I will swear it on the burning oil, and they
will listen."

"Why should we fight for them?" muttered
Francis Manners from the bed.

A sweat came out on his face, and he flung
out his hand, and cursed his father's people in
a wild, shaking voice. He was the Rao Sahib
now, and not Colonel Manners's son.

Bala drew Azimullah a little farther off.

"Presently, when he has talked, he will say,
'Do as you please, then'; is not that his custom? And afterwards he will be angry, but his
anger will pass. He has taken brandy and
opium. In the night did he sleep? Now he
will desire to sleep, to be in peace, to go to
Oula and let her fan him "; and Bala's face
contracted scornfully.

"That is true talk," nodded Azimullah.

"But what of the Nunna Nawab?" asked Bala
quickly. "What is best? There must be a proclamation. Send and fetch Moulvie Salamutul-

lah—he shall raise the Jhunda, and proclaim
Jehad. That will bring the Mussulmans to us.
They will come to the holy flag, and they will
fight in a holy war."

Azimullah looked doubtful.

" I have seen him already. We spoke for an
hour in the dusk last night, after I came from
Teeka Singh. He will not proclaim Jehad."

A fierce exclamation broke from Bala.

" Will not! "

The Mohammedan shrugged his shoulders.

" He is a priest. This is a priest's matter.
He says there is no Jehad. Also what he says is
true. There can be no Jehad, no holy war against
people of the Book—the Christians and the
Jews. The Jehad is against the infidel. The
Moulvie speaks the truth." There was a pause.
Then he added with his eyes on Bala's face:
" The Moulvie is instructed, but the people
are ignorant. They know nothing. And the
Kazi——"

Bala looked up eagerly, and the Mussulman
went on:

" If the Kazi were to raise the green flag, and
the Moulvie stood below it and prayed? Prayer
is always good. If he stood with his rosary in
his hands, and prayed—doubtless all who be-
held would cry ' Jehad! Jehad!' Also they
would feel their hatred towards the English
much strengthened. Yet the Moulvie need say
nothing."

Azimullah smiled a little as he finished speaking. He drew his hand down over his beard, as was his custom. Then he said, " I will send Fatehshah Khan to the Kazi. He is a useful man. Also he is related to Moulvie Salamutullah."

" Fatehshah Khan? "

" He came in from Urzeepore yesterday. I sent him a message to come away. The regiments there have killed their officers. They will come here and help us, if the Nana Sahib declares against the English."

Francis Manners started up upon his elbow; his voice shook. " Urzeepore? " he said. " What do you say of Urzeepore? Who was killed? "

" Many, they say," said Azimullah carelessly. " But some of the women escaped. They came into the entrenchment yesterday. Fatehshah Khan passed them upon the road. He should have made an end of them then, and saved us a little trouble "; and Azimullah smiled again.

Francis Manners put his hand to his throat—not like this—oh, no, it could not end like this. In his dream—in the dream of this very night—she had wept, but she was alive.

" Who escaped? " he stammered.

And Azimullah shrugged his shoulders, and said:

" How do I know? The Deputy Commissioner's wife for one—Fatehshah Khan said it—perhaps he knew."

Bala played impatiently with the dagger in his

belt. He turned from Azimullah and looked at
where the Nana Sahib sat swaying his great
bulk, and talking all the time, though only Baba
Bhut took any heed of what he said.

Baba Bhut, stout as his brother, swayed a
little too, as if in sympathy. Sometimes he said,
"True words, brother." Sometimes he merely
nodded his heavy head. Bala watched them
both with a hard look of contempt.

Suddenly there were sounds from the outside
world. There was a distant shouting, the clatter
of horses' feet, and a hum of voices. The smell
of stirred-up dust came into the room, and the
smell of burning with it.

The air was full of it, and full of a clamour
of confused noises, out of which came a cry
of "Maharaja! Maharaja! Maharaja!" that
mounted and mounted still.

With feet that slipped on the rough matting,
a barefoot servant ran in, too frightened to
salaam, and close on his heels there pressed two
men with reddened hands, stained clothes, and
fierce, excited faces. Without ceremony they
pushed the servant aside, and Teeka Singh, the
foremost, raised his cavalry sabre in the salute.
It was his moment of triumph. Behind him in
the verandah clustered his comrades of yesterday, his followers of to-day. He spoke loudly,
insolently, without deference:

"Here I am, Maharaja, and the Army waits for
my word. When I give it, they will kill the

English, and all who hold by the English. Say now, Maharaja, will you join us and take a kingdom, or will you join our enemies and take death?"

Dhundoo Punth ceased his swaying; here was decision clamouring at the doors red-handed. The sabre with which Teeka Singh had saluted was red too. Half-way up the blade the dull stain showed, and Dhundoo Punth, beholding it, let this insistent menace outweigh all fear of the white man's possible vengeance. Fate and his own ambition beckoned, fear pricked him, and he took Fate's way. Who was he to fight against Fate, that real, unchanging deity of the East?

As the man finished, he spoke, straightening himself, seeking a more kingly pose.

"What have I to do with the English? I am altogether yours!" Tantia and Bala came forward. They stood one on either side of the Nana.

Teeka Singh spoke again.

"Will you swear it, Maharaja?" he said.

"By the holy Godavery, I will swear it."

"Swear it on our heads," said Teeka Singh.

Dhundoo Punth hesitated no more. The two men bent before him, and he put his right hand on the head of Teeka Singh, and his left hand on the head of Gopal Singh, Brahmins both, and took the oath which a Brahmin cannot break.

"I swear that I am yours. On your heads

I swear it," he said, and a murmur of approval broke from his followers.

Teeka Singh rose, and fell back a step. His manner became more respectful.

"We go to Delhi," he said briefly; and, saluting, he passed out on to the verandah, and called aloud to his men. A burst of cheering and shouting came in through the doors which he had left standing wide.

Azimullah bent quickly to the Nana's ear.

"What are you in Delhi?" he whispered. "Here you would be Peishwa—at Delhi nothing. This is your kingdom. What have we to do with Delhi?"

The vehemence of the low words disturbed the new look of satisfaction upon the Nana's heavy face.

"What can I say?" he demanded. "If I say I will not go, they will be angry. They will go all the same. And what am I without them?"

"Bid them sack the Treasury here," said Tantia Topee. He was the soldier of fortune—alert, resourceful. "I will see that we get our share"; and he smiled, remembering the elephants brought from Bithoor, the carts and the waggons stored near at hand. He and Azimullah had made their plans well.

Bala touched his brother's arm.

"When their hands are full of rupees, they will think less of Delhi," he said. "There are English to be killed here too. You shall tell them that their faces will be blackened before all Hindustan, if they leave these accursed people in their entrenchments. Let them slay these first, and then we will think of Delhi."

The others nodded, breaking into voluble assent.

The Nana rose from his seat.

"I will go with them. We will go to the Treasury," he said. "We will go on elephants. I and my brothers will go. We will open the Treasury and take what is in it. I will fill their laps with rupees. We will make a proclamation also. Bid Jowala Pershad see to it. Bid him draw out a proclamation in the name of the Emperor of Delhi, and in my name; Azimullah, see to it."

A thunderous shouting broke upon his speech. For a moment he turned pale, then as he caught the sound of words amongst the tumult, he passed with his brother Bala at his side into the outer room, where a long open door showed the empty verandah, and beyond a wild, disordered crowd, all leaping, waving their arms, and shouting vigorously. Some one had fired the Court-house, and a dense cloud of smoke hung over it, shadowing the strip of road and the fierce, angry crowd which filled the compound of the Nana's temporary abode. The sun slanted beneath the smoke with a lurid effect. It glittered on the gold in the Nana's turban as he came out on to the raised verandah, and looked down on his

new followers.   When they saw him they shouted
louder still.

"Victory to the Maharaja!   Victory to the
Nana Sahib!   Victory to the Maharaja!"

CHAPTER XV

THE FANNING OF THE FLAME

O Love, if you were dead, would you not come to me
In breath, and change, and sleep, in dream and mystery,
Close as the blood of the heart, and dear as the heart's
    desire,
Vision, and Essence, and Flame, till we met and mingled
    in fire?
Yet if I find you at all it is only in memory,—
If you were dead, O Love, would you not come to me?

THE mid-June sun beat down on the light haze of heat and dust which hung above Sir Hugh Wheeler's entrenchment. The Christian population of Cawnpore—to the number of about one thousand—was collected within an irregular space some two hundred and fifty yards square. A four-foot mud wall enclosed the entrenchment, and within its bounds were two barracks, built of bricks, the one thatched, and the other roofed with masonry. To the left, at rather more than a mile's distance, lay the city of Cawnpore. To the right, eight partly finished barracks of hot red brick ran in a slanting line down towards the road that led from the city to the Grand Trunk road. All round the entrenchment lay the enemy. Their guns commanded every point of the low-lying camp.

Their pickets were drawn about it in so close a ring that it was fast becoming impossible for even a native spy to pass between the besieged and the outer world.

With the blindness of the fated, General Wheeler had made his stand in a place where defence meant exposure, where no supplies from friendly natives could reach him, whence no retreat was possible. It is said that he staked all on his expectation that the Mutineers would immediately proceed to Delhi.

Doubtless his spies had informed him of their intention of so doing; but he reckoned without the factor of the Nana Sahib's ambition, and his desire to found a kingdom of his own, rather than to swell the train of a Mohammedan Emperor.

The mutinous troops, their pockets full of rupees from the looted Treasury, were easily worked upon to remain at a spot which had already rewarded them so richly. They had pleasing visions of looting the city and of squeezing the bankers. Delhi was far. They would first sweep their own house clean, purge it with blood and fire from the foreign taint, and then with something to show for their time, they could move Delhiwards. and continue their conquering career.

So the Nana held his state in Cawnpore, his batteries rained a dreadful hail upon the doomed entrenchment, and his chief ally, the terrible

June sun, poured down his maddening floods of
light and heat, killing the weakly, and weakening
the strong.

On the afternoon of June 14th, Helen Wilmot
came out of the thatched barrack, which served
as a hospital, and ran quickly across the angle
between it and the second building. She drew
a breath of relief as she slipped in at the open
space from which the door had been shot away,
and stood for a moment accustoming her eyes
to the dim light.

The long barrack room, which she reached by
a second open door, presented a very curious
appearance. It resembled the deck of an emi-
grant ship, for the whole of the available floor
space was taken up by groups of women ·and
children, sitting, lying, or standing. One or two
had fastened a sheet, or a shawl, across some
corner, in order to obtain a little privacy, but
for the most part they remained in full view, the
women reading, writing, or attending to their
children. Smaller rooms opened from the main
room, at intervals; the roof of these only rose
to half the height of the main building, and
above its level were the windows that had lighted
the long room. They were wide, gaping holes
now, with the framework almost entirely shot
away. Sometimes a brick fell down amongst
the little groups below. Sometimes a glancing
bullet followed it. Sometimes a round shot
crashed its way through the masonry, and

brought a quick, terrible death to man, or woman, or child.

There was a continual crackle of musketry, a continual sharp rattle of bullets against the heated brick of the walls. Some of the women still winced at each fresh impact, but the children took no notice at all. After the first day no one cried out or made a noise.

Even when the torn air whistled overhead, and shell or round shot went screaming past, there were perhaps clasped hands, pale lips, and beating hearts, but no spoken tribute to terror. So soon do terrible things become a custom.

The children took no notice. The boys played marbles with the spent bullets, and the little girls arranged a mimic hospital, and nursed poor wounded soldiers made out of scraps of rag or splinters of bamboo.

Helen heard two of them talking as she picked her way across the crowded floor.

"Your man's dead, Nellie"; and Nellie whimpered:

"He isn't, then; I say he isn't."

"'Course he is. He's got a bullet right frough and frough of his head. Just like my daddy had; he had a bullet right frough and frough of his head, and he died, so 'course your man is dead."

"He's got a new head. A new mended head," said Nellie with the immovable obstinacy of the weak, and Helen patted the child on the shoulder as she passed on.

She found Adela Morton sitting in a corner, fanning herself. Helen sat down, too, and leaned against the wall. A level beam of dusty light traversed the darkening room, very high overhead. A cloud of flies hung floating in it. They made a slow continual buzzing sound. Helen watched them for a moment with uplifted face. She looked very tired.

"Helen, you will kill yourself," said Adela fretfully. "Every time you go over to that hospital, I think you are going to be shot. You don't know what I go through. And even if you don't get killed that way, you will wear yourself out with this dreadful nursing."

"Some one has to do it," said Helen with a gleam of humour.

"I should let it be some one else."

Helen sighed.

"Oh, it is easier to be doing something," she said. "Adie, I came to ask if you would come over for five minutes when the sun is down. Mr. Purslake was hit last night. He is very bad, and he keeps on asking for you."

"Oh, I could n't." Adela stopped fanning, and turned terrified eyes upon her cousin. "I could n't really, Helen."

"Adie, I think he is dying."

"People would think it so curious," faltered

Adela, and humour and anger together flashed
from Helen's eyes.

"I don't think it will compromise you irre-
trievably," she observed.

Adela hung her head a little.

"Helen, don't. Some one might hear you. I
don't think you ought to say things like that.
One has to be so careful. People do talk so,
and you know it is different now—now I am a
widow. Richard might——"

Helen lifted a perfectly colourless face, and
looked at Adela with an anger which she herself
did not understand.

"Hush!" she said imperiously, and Adela fell
on a plaintive note.

"How unkind you are! I am sure, Helen,
you might think how dreadful it all is for me.
To be a widow at three-and-twenty, and not even
proper mourning to put on, and no one to look
after me or do anything. You are most unfeel-
ing, I do think"; and she began to weep a little,
silently.

"Richard wouldn't ask me to go out to that
horrible hospital and see a lot of dreadful
wounded people and be shot dead," she sobbed;
"and you know he never liked poor Mr. Purslake—you know that quite well."

That new anger shook Helen again. She
pressed her lips together, forcing them to be
silent. But she could not silence her thoughts.
Dick? What right had Adela to speak of him at

all—Adela who had never loved him, who had
troubled him so—had hurt him so. Now he
could not be hurt any more, or comforted any
more, and Helen's heart was like a thing in torment because there was nothing that she could
do for him now, and she began to know how
much she could have done. A fortnight ago—
that fortnight that was like an age—it would
have shocked her to look into her heart and find
it full of the image of another woman's husband. Now she had come past that. Dick was
in her heart, but if there was passion there, it
was like the passion of thwarted motherhood.
It ached only to be spent, to give, and to console—and Dick was dead. With each ebb and
flow of her breath the thought ebbed and flowed.
With each beat of her pulses, it beat upon her
brain and upon her heart.

Adela had said that she was killing herself
with work, but it was not the work which
weighed so heavily upon her strength. Work
was salvation, but whenever she tended any
wounded man, her old enemy, the imagination,
showed her Dick so torn, so hurt, and alone, with
no one to ease the pain and bring him water, or
take the hand that had once grasped life so
strongly, and now relaxing—letting it go for
ever—yet groped for one human touch before
the utter darkness closed.

Adela dried her eyes and looked curiously at
Helen.

" You *do* look tired," she repeated. " Oh, dear, won't it be nice to sleep in a proper bed again, and have a bath. How long do you think we shall be in this dreadful place, Nellie? "

" I hope not very long."

" Yes, you hope, but why does n't some one do something to get us out of it? That is what I want to know. I am sure I should do something if I were a man. I suppose anyhow we should have to wait till September before sailing for home, though I am sure I don't know what I shall do when I get there, now that I have n't got poor mamma to go to. Of course I shall have to keep very quiet for a year, and I don't know what money there is. I suppose poor Richard's life was insured. Mamma is sure to have insisted on that."

" Adela, I can't bear it," said Helen suddenly.

" Really, Helen, what did I say? And as to bearing it, I don't know what you mean. You have n't lost your husband, and I shall have to wear black, which never suits me, and a frightful widow's bonnet, and those bonnets make every one look forty; I 've often noticed it. And I shall be burnt to a cinder in this dreadful heat. I try to be cheerful for the sake of other people; but I am sure it is enough to depress any one."

" Of course it is," said Helen in a curious voice. " Poor Adie, a lost complexion would be the last straw, would n't it? "

It was almost dark in the long room now, and almost silent too. Helen got up, wearily.

" The firing has stopped. I must go back," she said. " Will you come? "

" Helen, I told you I could n't, and oh, I wish you would stay here. It is so lonely, and I know you will be killed, and I shall have no one left."

" Poor Adie," said Helen again.

Her voice was quite gentle now.

" I will try not to get killed, my dear. It would be rather like deserting, would n't it? "

She moved away, retracing her steps amongst the fanning women and the pale, fretful children.

The shaft of sunshine was gone, for the sun had dropped, and the thick, hot darkness was coming down upon the room like a suffocating blanket. Beneath it some of the children were already beginning to fall into a restless sleep.

The firing had ceased at sundown, and the room was full of small fretful noises. Here and there a baby wailed, here and there a mother crooned some little cradle-song.

Helen stopped just by the door, and spoke to a small cross child of four, who was being undressed by a tired little lady in a soiled green gown.

" Good-night, Jenny," she said.

" Not good-night, welly bad night," said Miss Jenny with conviction. The mother gave a sad half-laugh.

"She does so hate not having her bath," she
explained. "But I've got a lovely plan. I am
going to undress her, and take everything off,
and we will pretend a beautiful bath, and rub,
and scrub, and go to bed ever so clean and
comfy."

"Jenny wants real bath—Jenny hates pertence
bath!" wailed Jenny.

Helen stooped again.

"This is a very special sort of pretence bath,"
she whispered. "Just for Jenny. When Jenny
has had it, she will go ever so fast asleep, and
dream she is swimming in a lovely silvery sea,
with pink fishes, and blue fishes, and sparkly
goldy fishes, and to-morrow Helen will tell her
a story all about real mermaids."

"Now! Tell Jenny now."

"To-morrow," said Helen, nodding wisely.
"First Jenny will have the pretence bath, and
then she will have the lovely swimming dream,
and to-morrow Helen will tell her the mermaid
story; and she must have a kiss or else the dream
will stay away."

The child put up her face. Only the eyes were
visible in the half-light, and they were full of
pleased anticipation. Helen kissed the little
damp chin, and passed on.

A very young girl with her fair hair in a
loose plait was waiting by the door. She caught
timidly at Helen's dress, and then drew back
colouring.

"Oh, Miss Wilmot," she breathed; and Helen smiled and said:

"What is it, Lizzie?"

"Oh, Miss Wilmot, don't you think I might come and help in the hospital? Do ask them to let me."

"My dear, you are too young."

Lizzie Carthew made a hesitating and yet impulsive movement.

"I am *nearly* eighteen," she said. Her voice was the voice of a child who has always had all that it wanted.

"I shall be eighteen in September, and I am engaged to be married, you know, and mamma always said I was a good nurse."

Helen laughed.

"Wait till you are married," she said teasingly.

Lizzie pouted.

"Papa said I must wait till I was eighteen to be married. Mamma was married when she was seventeen. Oh, Miss Wilmot dear, do you think they are being very unhappy about me? I do wish I could write and say I was safe. Perhaps they have heard that poor Aunt Martin was killed, and don't know that I am safe. And John, perhaps he thinks I am dead. Oh, Miss Wilmot dear!"

"Poor little Lizzie," said Helen.

"Dear Miss Wilmot, if you could get them to let me go to the hospital and help; if I might

be doing something, I should n't fret so. You
don't know how terrible it is to sit here all day
long and think about poor Aunt Martin. I had
only been staying with her for a week when it
happened, and we were going to the hills a week
later. I do want something to do so badly."

"Why don't you help with the children?"
said Helen. "They are such dears, and some
of the mothers have more than they can manage."

Lizzie pouted again.

"Oh—children," she said. "No, I want to be
like you. I do think you are so splendid. I
want to nurse the wounded, and be useful, and
for John and mamma to know I was quite
grown-up and sensible. They do treat me like
a child, really they do, and if I were like you,
they could n't."

Helen laughed, and kissed her.

"I sha'n't be splendid if I am late," she said.
"Don't be in too great a hurry to be grown
up, Lizzie," and she passed out through the
shattered doorway.

It was a relief to come out of the close, unwholesome room, even though it was almost
hotter outside. The trampled mud underfoot,
the piles of rubble, the brick walls of the barracks, radiated the day's heat to an almost
unbearable degree.

Helen had left the hospital thermometer standing at 126 degrees, and the air had not yet grown
perceptibly cooler, though the absence of the

sun's glaring light was a relief to eye and brain.
She stood for a moment in the angle between
the two buildings, and looked at the sunset. A
belt of dull, yet glowing orange lay along the
horizon. The black mass of one of the unfinished
barracks rose against it and the trees on the
road beyond. Above, the dusty air was all full
of a crimson glow which deepened into great
streaks and blotches, like smears of new-spilled
blood. One narrow purple cloud lay like a
menacing bolt between west and south, but all
the rest of the sky was cloudless, hazy, and
penetrated with soft dying shades of blue and
green, that failed as the eye rested upon them,
and darkened into shadowy grey.

Helen stood and looked. She remembered the
crimson light behind the tamarisk trees at Urzeepore, and how she had watched it with Dick.
It was the same sun—the same light—the same
glow, but everything else was changed. Of the
little party of eight who had escaped the massacre at Urzeepore, three were gone already:
George Blake, who had died in the cart, with
her hand in his; Mrs. Crowther, dead of heat
apoplexy; and Grace Elliot, struck by a flying
bullet. Carrie Crowther's reason was gone, and
Charles Purslake was dying.

Helen felt a weary reluctance to return to the
crowded hospital, where the tainted air was full
of groans and the breath of dying men. To
suffer oneself was not much—at least, it occu-

pied the mind—but to see children suffer, and brave men who had been strong once—from these things her flesh shrank.

Some one came to the hospital door and opened it. A confused murmur of sound came out, a sound of muttering, a sound of groaning —a man's voice singing.

Helen caught the words as she lifted her stained skirt out of the dust, and moved across the open space.

It was Charles Purslake, who sang in a voice high with delirium:

> "Dey try for to sleep, but it ain't no use;
> Sing song Kitty, can't you ki me oh,
> Dere legs hang out for de chickens to roost,
> Keemo, kimo, dar oh whar,
> Wid my hi, my ho——."

The voice strangled on a groan, and as Helen came to the doorway she heard the man in the next bed to Mr. Purslake praying aloud in a harsh and melancholy voice. He was the runaway son of a Methodist minister, and the unheeded prayers of his wild boyhood thronged his clouded mind. He, too, was dying.

Helen turned for a last breath of air before she went in. As she did so, one of the lights that marked the enemy's lines seemed to rise swiftly into the air. It travelled towards her with an inconceivable rapidity that paralysed her reasoning faculties. As it came she heard a loud whistling, hissing noise. Then it passed overhead, so close that she thought she could feel the heat of it. A man came behind Helen and pulled her through the door.

"You shouldn't stand there with the lights behind you," he said.

"What was it?" asked Helen.

"That? They are trying to set us on fire. That's all. I should like to wring the neck of the man who roofed this old death-trap with thatch! It will burn down as sure as fate some day."

It was burned down that night, and with the burning of the hospital, horror rose to its height.

Helen never forgot the roar of the flames, as they lifted in a pillar of fire and smoke to the arch of the midnight sky. It was like the roar of all the waters of the world falling over some high and dizzy precipice. They fell thundering, and sent up a continual blinding spray, that shone, and showered, and burned the living flesh of any creature upon whom it came down. And it came down on many.

Heroism had become part of the daily round. The men who all day long endured the sun, that they might defend the low mud wall, and braved a drift of bullets to draw water for the women, were trained to a courage beyond the common. They met the furious heat of the fire, as they met the tropic heat of the day, and all the time, as they went to and fro, dragging out the wounded, and struggling with the flames, the

16

enemy's fire poured in on them, and man after man went down, with a shattered limb or some wound more mercifully mortal.

Some of the wounded perished in the fire, and all the medical stores, all the surgical instruments were destroyed. To be wounded meant an almost certain death henceforward, since it was impossible to extract a bullet, perform an operation, or dress wounds.

At the very height of the fire, the enemy attacked in force; the crackle of musketry and the roar of the guns were added to the tumult, and children woke screaming to see their mothers upon their knees. The slate-roofed barrack stood, but it was soon overcrowded, and many women and children and wounded men were driven into the open, where they cowered down in any angle of the wall which could afford a temporary protection from the stinging drift of bullets, and the gusts of scorching air which blew from the blazing hospital.

Helen found herself on the south side of the barrack, with two wounded privates, one of them in agony from a broken thigh, and the other the man whose bed had been next to Charles Purslake's; Charles Purslake himself was dead. It seemed to Helen that he had been dead a long time, but this man was not dead yet, and whilst he lived he raved wildly about the burning lake of torment, and the worm that dieth not, the fire that is not quenched.

Jenny and her mother crouched beside Helen, and Lizzie Carthew was with them. They had moved from their place near the door, and had been unable to get back to it. There were also two other women whom Helen did not know, one of whom had a baby in her arms, and two trembling children at her skirts. The baby fretted, and Jenny cried all the time, but the other children did not cry. Only they shook all over, and in the lurid light that failed and flared, and flared and failed again, Helen saw their eyes wide with a dreadful unchildlike terror, and their faces fixed in a dreadful unchildlike self-control.

"Hell—burning, burning hell," whispered the delirious man, and the intense horror in his voice made the words audible through all the din. "Burning, burning hell; and the smoke of their torment going up for ever and ever and ever. Amen, so be it."

Jenny gave a loud, terrified scream.

"I dare n't move," said the mother. "But this is so dreadful. Will he die soon, Miss Wilmot?"

Then she broke off with a quick "God have mercy!" as a cluster of drifting sparks showered down not a couple of yards away, and with a loud and terrifying concussion which shook the ground upon which they sat, the guns of Ash's battery broke upon the assault.

At once there was a loud, wild outcry and a

shrill, screaming sound that sank away again into the common clamour of battle, as the men in the trenches poured out successive volleys of musketry. Helen was past being afraid, but her heart ached for the children. She crawled a little nearer to the two who sat and trembled, and slipped an arm about each.

"I am going to tell Jenny a story," she said, "such a nice story. Come and listen."

The children shook a little more when she touched them, and the mother said under her breath:

"Don't take them away. Don't take them away."

"Oh, no. I will sit just here. Jenny, don't you want to listen? It's a story about a palace made of fire, a beautiful golden palace."

There was less noise now, and here in the angle of the building they could hear themselves speak.

"Don't like fire," fretted Jenny, who had almost cried herself to a standstill.

"Oh, but it is ever so beautiful," said Helen cheerfully. She pulled the strange little boy and girl close down on either side of her, and this time they yielded, and pressed against her like silent, frightened animals.

"It is ever so beautiful, you know. Let us count the colours in the sky. I have counted eight already. That is one more than the rainbow has, and the eighth colour is the fire colour

—the beautiful rosy pink colour—there, see, Jenny, up there. And just look at the golden, golden birds flying up there in the sky. Look, quick. I saw a whole cloud of them go by, and there comes a swarm of shining bees. I wonder what hive they belong to; I expect they will fly right on, and on, and on, till they come to the golden sun, and then they will hang down all in a cluster on the sun tree's topmost branch, till the Angel of the Sun throws them one by one out into the dark sky, to shine in the night, and be beautiful golden stars."

Helen had a very full, soft voice. It filled the children's ears, and their terror of the flying sparks was changed into interest.

"They are sparks, not bees," said the little boy doubtfully. "And they hurt. One hurt my hand. It fell on it, and hurt it."

"He does n't ever cry, because he is a boy, and boys don't cry, but it did hurt. It hurted dreadful," said the little girl.

"Bees sting," said Helen wisely. "All bees sting if they are touched; but we forgive them, because of the honey they make, and these bees made star honey for the baby angels."

"Is there baby angels?" demanded Jenny.

"Oh, yes! Little darling baby ones, with baby wings, and baby hymns to sing."

"And do they eat the star honey?"

"They do. And then they grow up big and strong, and able to take care of the little earth babies, and sing them to sleep at night if they are frightened."

"Sing a baby angel's song," said Jenny imperiously. "Jenny's sleepy, sing to Jenny."

The sick man in his delirium threw out his hands and groaned lamentably.

"Water!" he cried. "Across the great gulf —one drop to cool my tongue, one single drop— Lazarus, Lazarus——"

Helen crawled to him on her hands and knees, and when she came near he snatched at her dress, and she felt the burning fever in him strike through its tattered folds. She put her hand on his forehead, and he gave a sort of gasp, and said in an altered voice:

"Mary—is it Mary? I have had such a dream. But it is all—right—now."

The words came slowly and sleepily. With the last he turned his head. There was only a strip of sacking between it and the trodden ground, but he lay still and slept Death's sleep. The man beside him was drawing the long breaths of endurance. He never spoke nor moaned, only lay staring at the sky, and drawing those deep breaths.

Helen stayed for a moment longer, bending her head, and praying. Then she came back to the children and sat down.

"Has the noisy man gone to sleep again?" said Jenny. "Jenny wants to go to sleep. Sing to Jenny."

Helen's own throat was burning, but the sleepy little voice was insistent. She put an arm about each of the stranger children, and sang:

> "I dreamed a dream the other night,
>   And long before the dream was done
> I had seen the Angel of the Moon
>   And the Angel of the Sun.
>
> "The Angel of the Moon was white,
>   He had the strangest, kindest eyes;
> I looked at him, and all at once
>   I too was very wise.
>
> "There came a golden, singing wind,
>   It blew so long, it blew so loud,
> It hid the Angel of the Sun,
>   All in a golden cloud.
>
> "I could not hear the Angel's voice,
>   It blew so loud, it blew so long,
> And yet I know that Angel sings
>   A holy, burning song.
>
> "Because the Angel of the Moon,
>   He looked so deep into my eyes
> That I could hear the echoes fall
>   Far off in Paradise."

Jenny's mother put her hand softly on Helen's arm as she finished. The children were asleep, Jenny with her head upon her mother's lap, and the other two children cuddled up against Helen. Lizzie Carthew was crying to herself.

Helen leaned against the hot brick wall at her back, and the noise and the clamour of the

attack died away.   The glare of the burning
barrack fell lower and lower.   The thick smoke
drifted away northwards on a light breeze, and
the stars looked down again out of the hush of
illimitable space.

CHAPTER XVI

THE WAITING

It's look your last on the Sun, my Heart,
   And look your last on the Moon,
And look your last on the Stars of Heaven,
   For the dark will be coming soon.

The Sun, and the Moon, and the Stars are far,
   And only the dark is near,
And the dark may be full of the dream we crave
   Or full of the dream we fear.

WHEN Richard Morton had fired the last
shot in his revolver, he backed his horse
against a high mud wall, and got out his sword.
He saw Colonel Crowther fall, and he saw a
Naik cut down Major Marsh, and go on cutting
and cutting at him as he lay on the ground.
Then a shot struck his horse, and it reared
up, and fell over with him, and he became
unconscious.

When he opened his eyes he was in a small
room with mud walls and a mud floor. He lay
on a string bed, and one of the native officers
was bending over and looking at him.

Richard Morton sat up and recognised the
man. There were two other men in the little
room, and he recognised them both. One was

his old orderly, Issuree Singh, and the other two were Durga Ram, subadar, and Jowahir Lal, two of the four native officers who had come to see him upon his arrival at Urzeepore.

The man by the bed saluted and stepped back. Richard Morton looked at him in silence, and he put up a protesting hand.

"It is a madness, Sahib," he said.

"And are you mad too?" asked Richard Morton.

"God forbid," said the man. "We are your servants. Am I a dog that I should forget? When the river carried away my son, did you not save him?"

"And your son?" asked Richard Morton.

The man hung his head and fell back.

"He is young," he muttered.

In that hut Richard Morton remained three days and nights. Neither threats, persuasions, nor promises would induce the men to let him go. They had saved him at their own risk, and were determined to keep him from destroying himself and them. When he heard that some of the ladies had escaped, and were believed to have reached Cawnpore, he gave up attempting to persuade them, and waited quietly for the next move. After three days they sent him by night to Aunut Singh, the grateful zemindar, and the whole body of Mutineers flocked into Cawnpore to join the Nana's standard.

At Cawnpore things went badly enough.

After the burning of the hospital, there was no longer sufficient shelter for all the women and children. The one barrack which still remained standing was riddled with shot, but at least its battered walls gave some slight protection from the flying bullets and the blaze of the midday sun. But only a limited number could be accommodated under its roof, and if the wounded had not died almost as quickly as they were brought in, still more of the women and children would have had to seek the shelter of the trenches. Shelter is the word one uses, but the facts make a mockery of it. What shelter does a four-foot wall afford? At first the men put up frail canvas structures, so that the women might have a little decent privacy, a little shade from the sun; but as fast as they were reared up, the enemy marked them, and shot them down again with deadly fire, that tore the ruined canvas into shreds, and brought it fluttering down upon the crouching forms beneath. Only too often a glancing bullet would tear its way through more than the canvas, and the tattered cloth would be stained red as it lay.

When the firing slackened at nightfall, some of the men dug holes and trenches, and here the women spent the hot, dreadful days. Some died of apoplexy, and some of their wounds. One, at least, found that death came too slowly, and ran with her children into the open, waiting there for a quick end.

A day or two after the fire Helen Wilmot was sitting in the trench beneath the eastern wall. For about five yards the earth had been dug away to a depth of three feet, and in the hollow thus formed, she and others were crouching. The sun was directly overhead, so that the wall no longer afforded any shade. A narrow strip of canvas stretched between two low sticks was their only protection, and as it barely cleared their heads, the heat of the sun struck through it with torturing intensity.

The two grave-faced children whose acquaintance Helen had first made upon the night of the fire sat beside her. Their mother and her infant were dead, and they had attached themselves to Helen in a matter-of-course way, which at once amused and touched her. Little Jenny was dead too—of dysentery. Her mother sat by Helen. She had not shed a tear—no, not one, and every now and then she smiled.

Helen pressed her hand, and looked at her with brimming eyes, and the mother said in a low voice:

" I am so thankful—so thankful."

After a moment she spoke again:

" They can't hurt her now. No one can. My little lamb. She's with her father. Oh, Helen, I have been so terribly afraid of dying and leaving her all alone to be hurt and frightened. She is so little to be frightened—my Jenny. Now I am only thankful."

Helen could only turn away her head.

Lizzie Carthew, crouching behind the other woman, met her eyes with a tired little smile. She looked very white and thin, and her fair hair was rough and dusty.

" I 've been counting up," she whispered, " and I do believe my wedding dress will be coming out next week. All my other things were being made out here, but mamma would send home for that. My godmother was giving me a Brussels flounce to put on it, and mamma had saved her own wedding veil for me to wear. Papa said I was to wait till September, when I shall be eighteen, but mamma sent for the dress a long while ago, and if John could have got his leave the wedding would have been early in August. Mamma does n't ever argue, but things are generally done her way. She just lets papa talk, you know, and when he has finished talking, he gets tired of the whole thing, and says, ' Oh, do as you like, Bessie.' Mamma's name is Bessie. I am Elizabeth after her. So, you see, I think it *would* have been August, but now "—her lips quivered childishly—" now I think it won't be ever at all."

She stopped suddenly, pressing her hands tightly together and struggling for self-control.

The woman beyond her made a weary movement.

" It 's terrible hot," she said, " terrible hot it

is. I heard a man swear at the heat a while
ago."

She spoke in a hoarse, gentle voice with a
strong West Country accent.

Mrs. McNeil, a Scotch sergeant's widow,
looked up with reproof in her wild eyes.

"Is this a time for swearin', an' for takin' the
Lord's name in vain?" she said. "The heat is
the Lord's judgment, an' we should a' be thinkin'
o' our sins."

The other woman sighed in a depressed
manner.

"I don't hold with swearing," she said.
"And I don't swear myself, though I 've known
pious folk that did."

"This is no' the time for swearin'," repeated
Mrs. McNeil. Her face was deeply flushed, and
she stammered a little in her speech. "Seek ye
the Lord, whiles He may be found. Call ye
upon Him whiles He is near. Let the wicked
forsake his ways, an' the unrighteous man his
thoughts, for the hour is at hand, an' the great
an' terrible day of the Lord is at hand."

Helen leaned across Lizzie Carthew, and laid
her hand on the woman's arm.

"Please," she said. "Oh, please. You are
frightening the little girl."

Mrs. McNeil turned her eyes upon Helen.
They were so wide open that the iris could be
seen as an unbroken circle, with a rim of white
around it. And the white was all bloodshot.

She shook her head, and went on in a rapid, yet halting fashion. " I had a dream last night —an' I saw a great wall, a great high wall, an' there came out as it were three fingers o' a man's hand, an' wrote upon the wall. An' the writin' was red, an' the hand—was a' bluidy."

She fell back against the side of the trench muttering to herself, and the West Country woman shivered and drew away.

" She 's a terrible frightening woman," she whispered to Helen. " There was one like her in our village, and my mother never would let us go by her cottage. There was a young man, she said, would live to be hanged, and hanged he was, in Exeter gaol, on the day that I was born. Edward Carey his name was, and that gave my mother a fear of her, though there were some that thought she was a wise woman, and maybe if she had told me what was to come, I 'd have stayed to home with mother."

She paused, sighing deeply.

" It 's terrible hot," she said. " My father he was a miller, and there was a stream ran by our house. I never thought anything of water then, but oh, my dear soul, if I had a drink of it now! Many 's the time I 've drunk out of my hand, and splashed the water about, and been punished for it. It was very cold water, and there was rats in it. We had a cat used to catch them. There 's not many cats can. But the rats they used to come up by the mill, after

the grain, and the cat she used to sit and watch,
and there was a little hole so big as a tea-cup,
and when the rats came out through it, she'd
catch 'em. Oh, my dear soul!"

The woman's face worked pitifully.

"Don't," said Lizzie Carthew. "Oh, don't,
don't!" and she put her head down on her knees.
The children stared at her, round-eyed and
interested. They saw her thin shoulders heave.

"Oh, I shall never see John and mamma again,
I know I sha'n't," she said in a thin little voice.

Helen whispered in her ear, but the poor child
pushed her away.

"I sha'n't, I sha'n't," she gasped.

"Oh, John! Oh, mamma!" and the exceed-
ing bitterness of the last word brought the tears
to the Devon woman's tired eyes. She began to
pat the girl's shoulder timidly, and after a while
Lizzie's sobs grew fainter, and Helen became
aware of a low-voiced conversation at her elbow.

"She could," the boy was saying. "She
could, Lucy."

And the little girl said gravely:

"You ask her, then."

They both fixed solemn eyes on Helen's face,
and she smiled at them.

"What is it, Ernest?" she demanded.

"Lucy says you can't, but you can, can't
you?" responded Ernest in the voice which so
exactly suited his name.

"What can't I do?"

The little boy threw a reproachful glance at his sister.

" I say you can," he exclaimed.

" Well, what can I do? "

The children looked at each other, and then again at Helen.

" It is so hot," said Lucy piteously, " and we are so very dreadfully thirsty, and he says "— with an accusing glance, " he says you could magic it away, like you magicked away the being frightened when the fire roared so loud, and we thought we should be all burnt up. But I said if you could magic it away, then why did n't you? "

Helen felt the most absurd inclination to burst into tears. If she could, why did n't she? She felt as if she had been weighed and found wanting.

" It has to be a very strong magic," she began, and Ernest's face fell.

" Can't you make the strong sort? " he asked, and Helen knitted her brows and said:

" Yes, if I try very hard."

Lucy edged nearer.

" Oh, please try," she whispered. Her lips trembled. " I don't want to cry, because it makes you so much more thirsty, but if there is n't a magic soon, I 'm afraid I shall cry, I 'm really 'fraid I shall."

" There 's going to be magic," said Helen quickly.

17

She scrambled on to her knees, and got up very cautiously, stooping so as to avoid exposing herself. Then with a quick swing of her body, she stepped on to a big stone, and looked out over the wall. The sun's heat struck her like a blow, as her eyes went out to the flat, dusty plain that reflected so much light and heat. To the left lay an arid space, bare and blinding in the sunlight, but away on the right there brooded the strange mirage which she looked for. Almost daily now it mocked these weary prisoners with its visions of green trees which they might not reach, and soft dim shade which would never fall on them again.

Helen lifted her head recklessly, and a bullet went past her cheek. The air which it stirred beat like a wave of fire against the parched skin.

"Get down, what are you doing!" called a man's voice angrily, and Helen dropped again to her old place.

"It is there," she said, nodding.

"Oh, what?"

"I'll tell you. I thought it would be there."

"Oh, what, what?"

"The enchanted forest," said Helen in a thrilling voice.

"Really—truly?"

"Yes, ever so really truly."

"Where?"

"Right over there." She waved her hand. "I saw it quite plain. It looked lovely—all

green, with high, high trees and a little blue
sparkling lake, and singing birds in the bushes,
and wet blue violets to walk upon. Oh, they
smell so good, and the white May hangs down
till it touches them, the branches are so heavy
with flowers."

" I have seen May, but Lucy has n't," said
Ernest in a superior tone, and the little girl
fretted:

" Does it smell good? I 've forgotten what
nice things smell like."

" Oh, no—just think." Helen breathed the
heavy, tainted air, but her voice carried conviction with it.

" Just think. All the sweet-smelling things in
the whole world live in the enchanted forest.
Lilac, and lilies, and sweetbriar, and myrtle
trees, and down amongst the violets there are
balm, and thyme, and very sweet lavender
bushes. And there 's a dew on them like the
baby beginnings of a rainbow. I do think we
might take off our shoes and stockings, so as
to feel it all cool and lovely on our feet."

" Mine 's off," said Lucy.

" And so are mine."

The tattered edge of Helen's dark grey skirt
disclosed a bare brown ankle.

" I made a present of my stockings to Mr.
Ash yesterday, and what do you think he wanted
them for? To fill up with bullets and fire at
the enemy. I am sure my stockings never did

think they would live to be fired out of a gun. I hope it won't make them proud."

" You can't be proud if you are in bits," said Ernest, with the dogmatism of early youth.

But Helen replied that it all depended upon how you were made.

" Now, my left stocking was quite horribly proud—that was its disposition—and jealous too. It wanted to be a right-foot stocking."

" How did you know it wasn't one? " asked Lucy.

" I didn't. They got mixed when they were babies, and no one ever, ever knew the truth, and now they are in bits, and no one ever will know, but I don't believe even being in bits will keep the left-hand stocking from being proud."

" Oh! " said both the children, and Ernest made a gentle correction:

" Left foot—not left hand."

" Of course," said Helen very gravely, " I meant left foot "; and she continued to talk nonsense whilst the children listened and were magicked out of three parts of their suffering.

The interminable day passed through an hour of strange sunset splendour into night, and then the little company crawled out of their trench, and lay down in the open, where the air stirred a little and sleep might visit them.

The day's allowance of food was about half a pint of split peas and flour, which was served to all alike, and could be made into a sort of gruel. The day's allowance of water cost more than one man's life in every day. Even the wounded and the children had to endure the extremest pangs of thirst for hours at a stretch, for the well was the enemy's most constant mark, and even at night they fired upon it continually.

Helen never drank her scanty portion without remembering King David and the water from the well of Bethlehem which is beside the gate, poured out before the Lord, because, he said, "Is not this the blood of men that went in jeopardy of their lives?"

One day Helen woke in the hour before the dawn. Every limb ached from the day's cramped confinement and the contact with the hard, sunbaked ground at night. She rose, stretching herself, and began to walk up and down.

Overhead the stars were still bright against the blue-black arch of the sky, but gradually they grew dim, and the blue turned slowly to a faint misty grey.

Helen walked to and fro, moving softly, so as to disturb no one who could sleep. She felt a new restlessness which she could not explain.

Fifteen days of siege were past, and how many more were to come? She wondered how long their scanty food would last. Yesterday a rumour had gone round that a relieving force was close at hand. Helen tried to realise what it would mean if this were true. Perhaps it was true. Perhaps to-morrow relief would come.

She stared at the eastern sky, and saw how the darkness thinned and a faint flesh-coloured tinge spread upwards, whilst all along the horizon, the grey sky turned to a pale, clear, lily green.

Perhaps relief would come to-day. Perhaps it would come before the hidden sun had reached its terrible noon. Helen turned away. The fierce continued courage of the last fortnight, would it outlive relief and a return to the ordinary conditions of life? She felt as if the natural terror of death had changed into a sharper terror of living.

Life was a hard matter. She saw hers stretch before her unendurably grey and desolate, and she had a moment's passionate envy of the dead who lay in the well beyond the unfinished barracks. Only yesterday she had heard an Irishwoman pray in an anguish against the pains of death, but they ceased and had an end. How long—how long were the pains of life?

A dizziness came upon her as she looked ahead along the unmeasured years.

Far away a jackal called, and farther still another answered him. Then they fell silent, and through the silence came a faint sound. Helen stopped in her walk and listened. She saw a little stir run along the wall, and the man nearest her reached for his loaded musket. Through the listening hush came the clatter of hoofs, very sharp and clear, on the hard,

parched ground. The noise of them jarred
the stillness of that hour of truce. They came
with a headlong rush, and a smell of stirred-up
dust rose in the heavy air. The dim light
yielded the flying vision of a horse, spurred to
his utmost speed by some half-seen rider.

An outcry ran along the wall. The man near
Helen fired. Two other shots rang out.

Then out of the morning dusk came a changing shape that seemed to scatter the dust and
the darkness as it came. An English voice
shouted, and the horse rose at the wall, and
came crashing down with a bullet in its shoulder,
whilst the rider flung himself clear, with a laugh
and a cry of:

"Don't shoot! Don't shoot!"

There was a clamour then, and a crowding.
Helen was pressed up against the wall.   She
leaned there, both hands on her heart, shaking
from head to foot.

That shout had first stopped her pulses, and
then set them racing—racing.   A spasm of incredulous joy held her.   It was a moment before
she could push her way through the questioning men.   The dawn was coming fast.   The sunrise flowered in palest rose and amber.   All the
grey was gone.

Helen looked and saw Richard Morton's face
cut clear against the sky.   It was very hard and
thin and brown, but she could see the blue of
his eyes.   His black hair was covered by a native

turban, and his black brows made a thin straight
line.

"I 'm Morton, Deputy Commissioner of Urzeepore," he was saying, and a man took hold of
his hand and wrung it.

"You, Dampier? Do you know if my wife—
if Miss Wilmot—" said Richard's voice, a hard
steady voice.

Something in Helen Wilmot answered to the
steadiness in that voice. She took a grip of herself and moved a pace forward. The men who
were between her and Richard Morton fell away,
and she came through them, and rested her hand
on Dick's arm. "Adela is quite safe," she said,
and so they stood for a moment and each looked
the other in the face.

CHAPTER XVII

HOW THE NANA SAHIB SWORE BY THE GANGES

The Rajput's word is a rock, but the false Mahratta's
  faith
Is the sand that shifts, and the dust that drifts, as the
  maker of Proverbs saith.

ON the twenty-fifth of June, at sunset, the
Nana Sahib held council.   He had pitched
a kingly camp under the trees of the Savada
house, and the soft wavering shadows of their
leafage lay slantwise across the white outer cov-
erings of the many tents.   Inside the Nana's
tent, there was a riot of luxury.   There were
Persian carpets and wonderful embroidered silks.
There was goldwork from Delhi, and carving
from Kashmir.   A low wide native bed with
silver legs was heaped with cushions of orange
and vermilion.   Amongst the cushions sat the
Nana, cross-legged, with a string of pearls like
hazel-nuts about his thick neck.   They circled it
three times, with the skin showing yellow between them, and then fell into his lap, and were
lost amongst the folds of the white muslin which
he wore.

The long tube of his hookah lay unheeded beside him, the ivory mouthpiece resting on a cracked china plate.

Every now and then he reached out his hand to a small silver tray at his elbow, and took up one of the little packets of leaf-enfolded betel-nut which were piled upon it. His jaws worked with a slow, continuous motion, and the bright red juice stained his lips. Every now and then a drop ran out at the corner of his mouth, and dripped upon his fine white shirt, for in the past weeks he had taken much opium, and there was a haze about him.

He stared half sullenly through it. The west was reddening to the sun's descent. The air was hot and heavy. The Nana looked towards the sunset and frowned. There—yes, there had stood the hundred and seventeen Englishmen from Furruckabad. There they had stood. There they had died. He had had high words with Bala, his brother, about those Englishmen, but Bala had had his way. They had all died—some with a groan and some with a curse, some with a prayer and some quite silently. The dust covered their blood, and their wives and their little ones sat in slavery in the Savada house close by. Once in a while the Nana would send for one of them that she might sit for an hour or so and grind the corn for his horses' food. Such was the usage of conquerors; and was he not a conqueror and a king?

He fell to twisting the ring with the great

ruby in it, which he always wore. The sunlight slanted across the mouth of the tent, and a faint breeze just stirred the looped-up curtains that hung there. They had the colour of spilled wine, and they were covered all over with an embroidery of silver stars and little golden fish.

Bala, the Nana's brother, sat by the right-hand curtain, with Tantia Topee beside him. Bala leaned on a crimson cushion. He had a long dagger across his knees, and his small, delicate fingers played with it all the time, following the fine gold tracery that was bitten into the steel. The sunlight followed it too, and shone on the ruby velvet scabbard, which lay on the carpet's edge.

Bala's look was alert. He sat well in view, and a man who was passing the tent salaamed to him, bending his whole body in abasement. And the Nana Sahib's heavy, sullen face grew heavier and more sullen still. The look of easy good-nature was gone from it, never to return.

Already the terror which haunts the Oriental despot had touched him with its finger. It was the sharpest terror of all, the terror of his own kin, and it watched beside him in the noon and in the midnight, and walked in all his ways from dawn to sunset. He looked at his brother Bala, and remembered that once already he had been forced to yield to him.

The Englishmen had been butchered, and the army—the army had applauded. Since then they had grown restive. Only two days ago they had been beaten back from the entrenchment with great loss. Now they murmured openly. They said they would attack no more. There was talk of going to Delhi. There were rumours of a mutiny within a mutiny. And Bala smiled, and sat with his dagger on his knees, whilst all men bowed themselves to the earth before him.

Dhundoo Punth made an abrupt movement with the hand that wore the ruby, and spoke in a thick voice:

" They are devils, these English. They will never surrender. Why do we sit here and wait? "

Azimullah stroked his beard. His keen glances had been going from one brother to the other. He noted now that Tantia Topee scarcely turned his head to listen to the Nana's words. Bala had some plan, he knew that, and he had begun to wonder whether the time had come to change masters. He was not sure, and until he was sure he would do nothing.

" Why do we sit and wait? " repeated Dhundoo Punth heavily.

" The army asks that," said Tantia, and Jowala Pershad, the new commander of the forces, nodded, and echoed the words. He sat opposite to Tantia, and they looked at one another. The Nana seemed to rouse himself. He met Azimullah's eyes for a moment, and began to say his lesson as he had learned it.

"Why should we kill our men? Why should we sit here and wait any longer? Let us offer them terms. Let us say that we will give them boats, that they may go down to Allahabad. They will accept gladly, since there is no longer food enough for the half of them."

"He whom we caught yesterday, Shepherd, the half-caste, he said there was food enough, and to spare," said Bala.

"Yes, and he looked like a starved jackal," returned Azimullah.

"That is true," said Jowala Pershad. "Also, the women servants who were taken three days before, they said that there was no food and no water, and that the women and the children died like the flies die when the cold comes. It was on that account that they tried to escape. Their words were true. If they had not been very much afraid, they would not have dared to come out of the entrenchment. Only a very great fear will cause a woman to forget a lesser fear."

"And, therefore," said the Nana, "therefore I say they will all come out gladly if we say that we will send them to Allahabad."

Baba Bhut looked up in his heavy way. He had grown stouter, and his hands, which were folded before him, rested on roll upon roll of flesh.

"Ai, brother," he said, "will you then let them go? What profit is there in letting them go?"

Bala flashed him a glance of contempt, but Azimullah said politely:

"I do not think that the lord's meaning is such."

Tantia Topee moved impatiently.

"We will let them go," he broke in. "Oh, yes, we will let them go to hell."

A laugh went round. Baba Bhut looked stupidly from one to the other. Then he took up the mouthpiece of his hookah, and began to smoke, swaying a little as he did so, with half-closed eyes. Bala shifted his position, turning towards his brother. The movement brought his head and shoulders into strong relief against the glare of the sunset.

"They will not come out," he said.

"And why do you say that, lord?" asked Azimullah.

Dhundoo Punth leaned forward, spat a mouthful of the red betel juice into a golden spittoon, and said loudly:

"Why should they not come out? Do they wish to die? Do they wish to stay until they can count all their ribs, until even the vultures and the jackals will refuse them? I say they starve, and if they were not devils, they would have surrendered long ago. Did we not say to the army that the entrenchment should be theirs in three days? Have not twenty days gone by? Will the men go to the assault again?"

He looked at Jowala Pershad, who cast down his eyes.

"If the army will not go in and take them, then I say, I will bring them out, and deliver them to the army. We will order boats. And we will promise them food and a safe-conduct to Allahabad. They will come out gladly. Then, when they are come to the boats, we will kill the men and save the women and children alive. These are good words."

Bala smiled sneeringly.

"What is this that you say? If any are killed, then all should be killed; where there is a woman, there are sharp eyes and a long tongue. Let them all be killed. Then we shall have peace."

"That is true," observed Tantia, and Azimullah nodded, and quoted the poet Sa'adi:

"'It is not wise to put out the fire and keep alive one spark, or to crush the serpent and to feed the serpent's young.'"

The Nana's eyes flashed.

"Who is the master?" he exclaimed angrily. "If I say I will save the women, then I will save them. If I give the men into your hands, have I not done more than the whole army could accomplish?"

"They will not come out. They will not believe," said Bala, playing with his unsheathed dagger.

Dhundoo Punth spat again, and waved his

hands. Bala had killed a hundred, he would kill a thousand men. Then the army would see who was their lord. Then he would go to Bithoor in triumph, and take his seat upon the throne of the Peishwas. Then the Brahmins would affix the sacred tilka to his forehead, and the army, drunk with slaughter, enriched with silver coins and golden armlets, would acclaim him as their king.

"They will believe," he said. " I will swear to them upon the Ganges. Upon the burning oil I will swear that they shall go down to Allahabad in safety."

Baba Bhut withdrew the mouthpiece of his hookah and stared into his brother's face.

Jowala Pershad stood up, salaaming.

"Maharaja, would you break the oath upon the Ganges? " he said, and Azimullah covered his mouth with his hand, as he too looked at the Nana and waited for his reply.

The Nana threw out his hands as if pushing something tangible away.

" What is an oath to an enemy! " he exclaimed.

Jowala Pershad salaamed again.

" Maharaja, if the troopers hear that you have sworn by the Ganges and afterwards that oath is broken, their minds will be troubled. They will expect some great misfortune—and when an army expects misfortune, misfortune will surely come."

The Nana's manner became suave.

The smile that had caused generals and commissioners to trust him parted his stained lips.

"You will tell those whom it may concern that this is a sacred cause," he said softly. "To annihilate an enemy, any means are lawful. That is the creed. At such a time as this, a hundred artifices may be employed and any oath may be taken. Is it not to save the lives of Brahmins? This is a lawful expedient. These are true words. Also, when it is finished, and these insolent English are blotted out, I will give presents. To every man a rupee and a golden bangle. Tell them that this is my order. Ask them also what kind of face they will show to God, if they are guilty of any neglect in this matter. Do they wish to wait idly until the English send more regiments from England? Do they desire to be made Christians of? Tell them all these words."

He gave a sweep of his hand, and said:

"You have my leave to depart."

Then as Jowala Pershad and Tantia Topee went out, he took another of the little green folded packets of betel-nut and crushed it between his strong and even teeth. The red juice ran out and dripped upon his hand.

In the dim and failing light which came all red from the crimson west, the stains upon hand and dress showed prophetic, like the stains of half-dried blood.

18

CHAPTER XVIII

THE END OF THE PATH

This is the end of the path.
Since hope is gone,
We, with unfaltering feet,
Must travel on.
On, and over the brink
Of the gulf we know,
And down in the rush of death
To the dark below.

ON the twenty-first day of the siege the Nana's envoy came into the entrenchment with the Nana's terms—a strange and most miserable envoy, with terms that were to be broken after a strange and most miserable fashion.

Sir Hugh Wheeler sat amongst the men he trusted, with a letter in his hand—a letter in Azimullah's handwriting.

It was very short, but he read it again and again.

" All those who are in no way connected with the acts of Lord Dalhousie, and are willing to lay down their arms, shall receive a safe passage to Allahabad."

Sir Hugh let the hand which held the letter,

fall upon his knee and fixed his tired eyes upon
the half-caste woman who had brought it. She
had been fainting, and she was ghastly under
the brown of her skin. There was a little sickly
baby at her breast, and she hugged it and
trembled. A strand of black hair fell across her
shoulder, and over the bosom of the torn and
ragged gown which was her only garment.
Tottering, and in terror of her life, she had
come across the sun-scorched plain, only to fall
in a swoon at the first barricade, where she had
narrowly escaped being shot. Now she met the
General's eyes, and tears gushed from her own.

"Mrs. Greenway, who gave you this letter?"
said Sir Hugh.

She caught her breath, her voice came unsteadily. After the manner of her kind, she had
many words. Also it eased her to complain.

"Azimullah gave it to me," she said. "Oh,
he is a great budmash, that Azimullah. All the
world knew that we were rich, and he has taken
our money, and he has promised to let us go,
and always he is verree, verree sorree, but we
must give more money. Already he has had one
lakh of rupees, and my children have not enough
to eat, oh, he is a verree great budmash."

Captain Moore, the big fair Irishman, held up
his hand.

"You saw Azimullah? He gave you the letter? Did you see the Nana Sahib?"

"Oh, no—no, I did not see him. Oh, he is

a monster, that one. God will punish him. Oh,
yes, some day God will punish him. He is verree
wicked. They are all verree wicked, wicked
men. See, even my ear-rings they have pulled
out. They have torn the flesh of my ears and
pulled them out. Oh, my God! I screamed,
but they tore them out. And they took my
clothes and the clothes of my children. Oh,
yes, certainly God will punish them."

The men moved farther away, and spoke in
low voices.

"Why did they send this woman?" said Sir
Hugh.

Captain Moore gave a half shrug of the
shoulders.

"Heaven knows. Poor creature, she was
nearly shot by Mowbray Thompson's picket. He
only just knocked one man's musket up in time.
Perhaps the Nana was thrifty and did n't want
to risk a man."

Sir Hugh Wheeler made a restless movement.
He was an old man and irritable. Only a few
weeks ago Henry Lawrence had spoken of him as
a tower of strength. But he had served in India
for more than fifty years, and under the strain
of the siege he had grown conscious of his age.
His small, spare figure was no longer erect, and
his brown skin showed line upon deep-carved
line of weariness, illness, and suffering. Private grief had laid a crushing weight upon his
over-burdened shoulders. It was only ten days

since he and his wife had seen their son torn to pieces by a round shot before their very eyes. His hair had turned quite white since then. Fate had struck him too hard, and though his spirit was still brave, it was with the courage that faces death because it dare not look life in the face any more.

His hand shook now as he moved it, and his eyes were very heavy.

"What are we to say, Moore?" he said. "What are we to do?"

"Have we any choice, sir?" said Captain Moore.

"You would surrender?"

"Sir, we have only food for three days now."

"Relief." The word was almost a groan.

"I am afraid not."

"Moore, it must come. Our last letters were urgent. They must be pushing on."

"We don't know what is happening down country, sir. Even if we had the food, there are the rains to be thought of. They may break any day now—any day—and the moment they break, we shall be flooded out. But we haven't got the food. Relief, to be of any use, must come within three days' time. Can we for a moment deceive ourselves into supposing that it will do so?"

Captain Moore's merry blue eyes were very grave as he spoke. All through the siege, his voice, his smile, had heartened the fearful, the despondent. He had been leader of forlorn hopes, deviser of cunning stratagems, comforter of the sorrowful, friend to the bereaved, and through it all, hopeful, buoyant, and confident. Now that his face was grave, the lines upon it showed; now that he smiled no more, an instant conviction that the situation was indeed desperate, came upon all who watched.

There was a pause. The other officers spoke among themselves, but in low voices. Then Sir Hugh Wheeler brought his shaking hand down with a crash upon the table, beside which he stood.

"No, by Heaven, no!" he exclaimed. "I don't trust them. I can't trust them. Does any one trust a Mahratta? Better blow up the magazines."

The younger men looked at one another. A murmur of protest broke from them. Some of them had wives and children in the entrenchment. Hope dies very hard, and when hope for oneself is dead, there is still a little left for those we love. If it is more prayer than hope, it is none the worse for that, and it lingers until the last spark of life has gone.

Captain Moore had a wife—and children. He spoke quickly.

"Sir, only the very last extremity would justify— There are the women."

And Sir Hugh flared up.

"Do I forget them? My God, if I could.

Is n't my wife here, and—and my daughters?
But you are all against me. Have it your own
way, gentlemen, but at least let us take what
precautions we may."

He made an effort and controlled himself. If
the indecision of age was upon him, its caution
was also his. The flare of anger died down,
and he began to speak quietly, soberly, discuss-
ing details, going over the old arguments once
again, and coming in the end to the old
conclusions.

"This letter is not signed," said Sir Hugh
at last. "We must have the Nana's signature
—and all reasonable safeguards. Some one
should inspect the boats, and we must have
hostages. Send this woman back to her children, and say that they must send some responsible
person, if they wish us to treat with them."

When all was arranged the council broke up.
One by one the ragged, haggard men went away
to busy themselves over this forlornest of forlorn
hopes. Sir Hugh watched them go.

Captain Moore and a civilian were the last.
Just as they reached the shattered doorway, the
old General stretched out his right hand and
spoke in a weary and yet passionate voice:

"Gentlemen, this is against my judgment," he
said. Then he sat down by the rickety table and
put his head in his hands.

Silence and heat brooded over the entrenchment. ɔ There was no firing all through that long

day, and the jackals and the vultures came up
close under the walls to feed upon the dead, who
had lain unburied since the great attack on the
night of June 22. There was little left now but
gleaming bone and tattered cloth, but the jackals
slunk and yapped over the fragments of their
horrible feast, and the great white vultures
brooded obscenely over the dead.

Backwards and forwards across the scorched
plain went the messengers of the Nana.

Now it was a mounted trooper, who galloped
across with a written message demanding the
immediate evacuation of the entrenchment and
threatening a renewed bombardment. Now
again it was Azimullah and Jowala Pershad,
who assured the Englishmen of the excellence
of their master's intentions, and agreed with
polite compliments to the safeguards demanded
by Sir Hugh.

Finally the messenger was an Englishman,
who carried the treaty of capitulation into the
Nana's very presence, and saw him sign it, after
many courteous compliments and expressions of
his admiration for such a brave defence.

An intense excitement pervaded the entrenchment towards sundown. The unwonted silence
pressed strangely upon nerves which for so long
had been strung to endure the ceaseless sound of
firing. The women whispered among themselves,
and every now and then, a man would pass
through the long barrack-room and be asked a

hundred questions, which neither he nor any one
else could answer. For once no one was thirsty,
for the well was no longer a point of danger.
Double rations were served out, and Ernest and
Lucy played at feasts and made merry.

Richard Morton had fetched them out of their
trench when the firing stopped, and they sat in
the shade of the barrack all through that day.
It was not so hot as the trench, for there was
more air and they were out of the sun and had
room to move and play, but they kept as far as
they possibly could from the ruined steps which
led to the barrack-room. A girl with wide,
vacant eyes and long floating hair sat there,
twisting her fingers in and out, in and out, in
some pattern which no one but herself could
follow. At regular intervals she laughed, on
one high tone that never varied. Then when
she had laughed, she threw back her hair, stared
for a moment at the sky, and fell to twisting
her fingers again. It was Carrie Crowther, and
she knew no one, and never spoke at all. Lucy
and Ernest were very much afraid of her, though
Helen told them that they need not be.

Helen had been busy. She had saved a spoonful of water at the bottom of her cup, and dip-
ping a rag into it she washed the children's faces
and her own. For three weeks no one had been
able to wash at all. Even this spoonful was
luxury and added to the holiday feeling. When
Helen had used every drop of the water, she set

down the cup and began to comb out Lucy's hair with a pocket comb, borrowed from Lizzie Carthew. She had just finished when Captain Morton came by again.

He paused beside them, and Helen forced a smile.

" Do we really go out to-morrow? " she asked. " We are making ourselves as tidy as we can, you see. When we get to Allahabad we shall have clean clothes, shan't we, Lucy? Then we shall be so beautiful that you won't know us."

No one was beautiful now. Dirt, hunger, and terror had done their work too well. Lizzie Carthew squeezed Helen's arm.

" I shall put on all my trousseau things when I get to them," she declared. " No, Captain Morton, *not* all at once, of course not, but one at a time, one after the other. I shall change my dress five times a day. Mamma often scolded me for being lazy about putting on an afternoon dress; she 'll never have to scold me again."

No, Lizzie, never again—never again any more.

Helen saw something in Richard Morton's face that made her drop the comb into Lucy's lap and get up. She walked a few paces beside him in silence. Then she asked:

" Is it settled, Dick? "

" Yes."

Neither spoke for a moment. Carrie Crowther's wild, high laugh rang out.

" We 've surrendered," said Richard Morton.

"Todd has just come back with the Nana's signature. We march out at dawn. They are giving us boats, and Delafosse, Turner, and Goad have gone down to the ghaut now to see that they are all right."

Helen hesitated for a moment, and then said in a low voice:

"Will it be all right, Dick?"

He had begun some cheerful speech when he met her eyes. Something in them—an intelligence, a courage that equalled his own—spoke and was answered, in silence.

They stood for a moment, and then he turned away, and she went back to the children.

The poor mad girl upon the steps laughed on her high, wild note.

That night the shattered guns of Eckford's, Ash's, and Dempster's batteries were still, and the guard that was set, was a guard of the Nana's men. They stared about them in surprise, wondering how this handful of starving, dying men had fought these ruined guns.

"Devils—yes, they are certainly devils," was the word that went from one to another as the garrison of Cawnpore lay wrapped in the sleep of their last night on earth.

CHAPTER XIX

THE SUTTEE CHOWRA GHAUT

Are you afraid, my heart?
See, this is Death.
He will come very near,
And take your breath.
He will come very near,
And close your eyes,
Lest they should look on him,
And become wise.
He will come very near,
And touch your hand,
Then you will fall asleep,
And understand.

THE twenty-sixth of June dawned greyly, and
the hour before the dawn was full of mist.
Away to the south the clouds were gathering, and
the smell of rain came drifting on a chill small
breeze. The rains were coming, but as yet no
drop had fallen in Cawnpore, and the road to
the river was ankle deep in a white stinging dust,
which rose in clouds about the feet that stirred
it. Many feet were stirring it in the hour before dawn. Great softly-treading feet of elephants whose loaded howdahs swayed to their
rhythmic tread. Slow feet of patient bullocks,
straining forward drawing rough country carts,

each with its load of wounded men, who groaned and cursed as the wheels jarred and the dust flew up.

Bare feet of dhoolee bearers and blistered feet of men who had stood at their posts through twenty-one days of sleepless horror and privation.

The blistered feet stumbled along—some bare, some wrapped in rags, a few with boots that gaped and showed the skin beneath. One helped another forward upon that halting march to death. They were a feeble company, but when the gathering crowd of Sepoys pressed nearer, the weakest straightened his bent back, and the most suffering kept in the half-uttered groan.

Hardly a man was unwounded; all were weak with hunger and lack of sleep, and many were haggard with private grief.

The children and the women went—some in carts, some in palanquins, and some on foot—in the midst of that sad procession. There were mothers who sobbed bitterly as they left that Fort of Despair, because their children lay buried there. And there were mothers who smiled to their children as they went, and spoke of meeting daddy, and being at home again. There were women who chattered restlessly, keeping thought at bay, and there were women who watched as silently as if this were a dream and the haze around them the haze of sleep.

So they went down to the river, their river of Death.

Adela Morton had a place in one of the carts. She had altered less than most of the other women, and excitement had brought a little of the old colour to her white cheeks. Helen's hat covered the limp chestnut curls, and in the crowded cart one could not see how ragged and filthy her fine white muslin dress had become.

Helen Wilmot walked by the cart, holding Lucy by the hand. Richard Morton had brought some money with him into the entrenchment, and Helen had given a native five rupees for his coarse white cotton sheet. It was fairly clean, and she was glad to cover her head and her rent gown with it, since the Sepoys pressed so close and stared so hard.

"You look like an ayah," said little Lucy very seriously; and Helen laughed and said:

"Very well then, I'm your ayah, yours and Ernest's. You must be very good children, or I shall take off my slipper and beat you."

Whereupon Ernest peered down into the dust and said:

"They're not slippers, they're shoes, and there's a new hole since yesterday, Miss Wilmot."

Lizzie Carthew was walking too.

"Oh, Miss Wilmot," she exclaimed, "how long do you suppose it will take us to get to Allahabad? Three days? Four? How long do you think it will take?"

"Nearer five than four," said Captain Morton.

Adela turned her head in his direction.

"Richard, is that you?" she said complainingly. "This cart does jolt so dreadfully. I believe I'll walk after all."

"Very well."

"Or at least I would walk if my shoe had n't a hole in it. Is it very dusty?"

"Is it, Lucy?" said Helen. She looked straight at Adela for a moment, with a kind of bitter humour.

"It is very dusty," observed Lucy in her deliberate fashion. "Very dusty, indeed, Mrs. Morton."

Richard came up close to the cart and spoke in a low voice:

"Change with that child for a bit, Adela," he suggested. "She looks ready to drop, poor mite."

"But my shoe has a hole in it," was Adela's reply, and her husband fell back again.

"Like a ride, Lucy?" he asked, and without waiting for an answer, he swung the child up on to his shoulder, whence she looked with a patronising glance at Ernest, walking in the dust.

"I can see the river," she cried; "I can see it quite plain."

They had turned off the high-road into the

deep sandy lane that led to the Suttee Chowra Ghaut, where the boats awaited them.

"I can see boats too," said Lucy, jigging up and down. "Oh, Captain Morton, I can see the boats! Miss Wilmot, I can see the boats."

"I should think Richard would be tired, carrying that great child," said Adela. "You and he are so strong, Helen. I only wish I were. No one knows what I have gone through. The shock of Richard's return alone. Now, Helen, what *is* the good of pretending it was n't a shock. Why, even you felt it, and imagine what it was to me. My heart is n't at all strong. It might have been really *dangerous.*"

Adela had made this remark a great many times since her husband's return. Once Helen flashed into speech and asked if she thought true consideration for her feelings should have led Richard to remain dead, in order to spare her a shock. Adela had sobbed and replied that Richard never did have any consideration for her feelings. Now Helen said nothing at all, but plodded on in the dust.

A ravine ran down to the river and the landing-stage. The landing-stage was thronged with a dense crowd of spectators. Upon its right-hand side at the top of the steep bank stood a small Hindu temple, scarcely larger than an English summer-house. It overhung the water and a flight of steps led down from it to the river. On a masonry platform outside the temple a group of men were waiting.

At the eastern end one of these men had spread a small carpet. He looked towards the dawn, and as the first pale ray of sunlight gilded the dusk, he fell upon his knees with his face towards Mecca, and bowed himself with his forehead to the ground. It was Azimullah, very gorgeous in a green and gold brocaded coat, and his morning prayer would not be omitted because there was murder to follow.

At the other end of the platform there burned a small charcoal brazier, and the Nana's brothers squatted beside it, with embroidered shawls drawn close, for the mist from the river was damp and chill in this hour of dawn.

As the light strengthened, Bala rose and joined Tantia Topee who stood upon the edge of the platform, looking fixedly inland. Bala's eyes took the same direction, and both together heard the sound of trampling feet coming nearer in the silence. Tantia swung round, his white teeth showing.

" They come," he said.

And Bala answered him.

" Yes, they come."

Upon Tantia's other side stood a young man muffled in a thick white shawl with a gold embroidered edge. Every now and then, in spite of his shawl, a slight shudder passed over him. The morning chill had crept into his bones and

19

was heralding an attack of fever. He too leaned forward as Tantia spoke, and looked eagerly towards the cloud of dust which could be seen at the head of the ravine.

"Why is my uncle not here?" he asked; but the two men made no reply, and he did not repeat the question.

The sun lifted clear of the horizon. The boatmen waiting below stood up, breaking the silence with their chatter and busying themselves about the boats. The first of the little band of English came down through the crowd to the waterside, and Azimullah having finished his devotions, arose from his knees and came to the edge of the platform to look at them.

There was a crowding and a confusion. The mass of spectators were driven back by Sepoys. Carts blocked the way. The Sepoys themselves gathered and pressed nearer. Just below the temple two of them were talking.

"Yes, they come out grandly. See how they come, with elephants and with palanquins and all. Let them now ask God to pardon them."

"They are devils," said the other with conviction.

Bala smiled as he caught the words. He moved his head a little, and the sunlight danced upon the pearl and diamond aigrette showing white against the white turban. Under it his small, dark, pitted face seemed almost black.

Francis Manners, beyond him, drew a little

away. A long shiver shook him, and he clutched his shawl close, drawing. it forward so as to cover his head.

The boats, to the number of forty, lay all along by the landing-place. They were heavy boats, lying deep in the water, wide and roomy, with thatched roofs as a protection from sun and rain. Most of them were grounded, for the river was at its lowest and the bed of it was full of ridges and banks of sand which showed in the muddy stream like the bones of derelict monsters.

Richard Morton lifted his wife out of the cart in which she had ridden, and hurried his whole party through the crowd and down to the water's edge, with what Adela thought most unnecessary haste. In a business-like way he picked out a boat which lay in deeper water than the rest, and issued his orders.

"That boat," he said. "Yes, Adela, I'm afraid you must wade. I must carry the child. Take my arm. It is not really deep. Helen, are you all right? Can you manage, and you, Miss Carthew?"

Helen nodded and caught Ernest by the hand.

The boat which Richard Morton had indicated lay in about three feet of water. It was of rather lighter draught than most of the others. About half a dozen yards separated it from the bank. The shallow waters were full of people by now, and the cool current seemed to give new strength and vigour to the scorched and weary limbs it washed.

"I want to paddle too. Oh, let me paddle," cried Lucy, and turned away from Helen, who had scrambled first into the boat, and was holding out dripping hands to take her.

"The boatmen—why are they all going ashore?" called Lizzie Carthew.

She stood up in the boat and uttered a piercing scream.

"Oh! there is a boat on fire—the other boats —they are burning—the thatch is burning. Oh, Captain Morton!"

As she spoke, Bala, the Nana's brother, leaned from the temple platform and fired the pistol which he had kept hidden under his shawl. The sharp report hung for a moment upon the air, and the shawl itself, a brilliant scarlet square, patterned in a dozen exquisite shades, fell from Bala's shoulders, and fluttered down upon the yellow waters below.

Then with a crash that seemed as if it must dissolve the very heavens in wreck and wrath, the hidden guns broke out, and from behind each patch of grass, each dark tamarisk clump, the liers-in-wait poured upon the helpless English a paralysing hail of lead.

The wood of the boats was splintered, and the thatch of their roofs broke out in flame. The thick grass along the river's edge caught alight and the noise of the fire went up to heaven with

the crash of the guns, the shattering rattle of
musketry, and the wild, agonising screams of
those who died in the water and those who died
in the fire.

It was not like the surprise of an ordinary
ambush. It did not come with the common
shock of war. They had endured all things already—these men, their women and their little
children. They had become used to suffering.
Nerves, strained to the utmost tension through
weeks of fear, had grown numb and unrespon-
sive to any common dread. But this thing came
as the lightning might come upon the eyeballs
of one half blind. It tore the dimness with a
rending flare of horror. It woke the dulled
nerves to feel, to suffer, and to agonise afresh.
Suddenly, and very terribly, they felt—they saw.

They saw the house of life shattered, and the
streams of life mingled with this yellow river of
death. They saw flames that crept and leaped
and hissed in the blood of the dying. They saw
those red, hissing flames reflected from water
that ran horribly, vividly crimson, until between
the fire above and the blood below, there came
a drifting smother of thick black smoke that
was like a horror of darkness made manifest,
because the deeds that were done in it were the
deeds of that outermost darkness, where there
are weeping and gnashing of teeth, the worm that
does not die, and the fire that none can quench.

Helen Wilmot had expected, she knew not

what—but when it came her heart seemed to stop beating altogether. Richard thrust the child into her arms, and she crouched there in the forepart of the boat, holding a limp little body that never moved again. She did not know that the child was dead. She did not know where Ernest was. He had been with her in the boat, and then suddenly he was not there any more. She knew nothing, except that this was the end, the very end of all, and that it was dreadful, unexpectedly dreadful, because she must look with her eyes, and see Dick die before she died herself. They had been saved for this, that she might see him die.

These thoughts passed in her mind instantaneously. They were there as Richard straightened himself after leaning towards her with little dead Lucy in his arms. She saw him turn to Adela, who had fallen on her knees in the stream, and at the same moment he uttered a cry, which she rather felt than heard, and fell across the side of the boat, with the blood streaming from his head. In an instant Helen's heart began to beat again and she came back to life. She thrust the child aside, and caught him by the arm, but strain as she might, she could not drag him in. He had fallen face downwards and lay across the side of the boat, half out of it and half in, with the lower part of his body in the water. Helen tore the sheet from her shoulders and passed it twice about him, under the arm-

pits. Then she held it tight with both her hands
and knelt there waiting for the end. That hour
was like one of the hours of Eternity. One hour
was all the hours, and all the hours were one.

There was no time any more. Helen looked
through the smoky air and her brain played her
a strange trick. She lost all sense of perspec-
tive, all sense of distance. Near and far were
confounded, and she perceived all these fated
and fatal things, all these faces of wrath and
fear and vengeance, all these forms distorted by
passion and suffering, as if they were ranged in
one long, straight line that had no end. For
ever afterwards she thought that that was how
the nations of men and the untold souls of the
dead would appear upon the great Day of
Judgment. None before or after another, none
greater or less than another, but all equal, all
terribly equal, as men are only equal in death
or in the eyes of God, who kills and makes alive.

Helen saw everything after this strange fashion. Bala, dark and fierce, upon the temple platform, seemed as near as poor young Lizzie
Carthew, with her dead face only a yard away
—as near, and as infinitely far.

Something which was neither mist nor smoke
was between Helen and all that she looked upon.
It was like a sheet of impalpable glass. It was
like the veil which hangs between the living and
the dead. Through its intangible film she heard
the screams that were like one long, unending

scream. Through it she looked upon terrible
and tragic things.

She saw Mr. Moncrieff, the chaplain, standing with two or three others. He stood deep in
the stream, and it eddied about his waist, and
he rocked a little as it swayed him. He had a
book in his hand. It was a prayer-book, and
he turned the pages as if he were in church.
When he had found the place that he wanted,
he bent his head, and began to read. Helen
saw his lips move, and then a mounted sowar
came driving through the stream with the water
splashing up before him and behind. It made a
cloud of spray and foam, and the lifted sabre
caught the sunlight very brightly once, and then
went down through the cloud into the water,
and was dimmed.

There was a woman clinging to the chaplain's
arm. Helen heard her scream, and then they
were all down, and the water was rolling over
them and covering them from sight. The trooper's wild shout rose high above the din as he
rode on, and as he rode, he laughed and waved
his bare arm, which dripped with blood and
water.

There was less shouting now. The nine-
pounders were silent, and the musket men had
ceased to fire; but the sandy lane and the landing-place seethed with a wild confusion of murderers and the murdered, and the turbid waters
were beaten into red waves as the wild troopers

rode their horses into the shallows, slashing and
shouting and calling to one another.

It must have been at this time that desperate
hands succeeded in pushing Major Vibart's boat
off the sand-bank into deeper water. With a
great jerk it swung round, and that jerk sent
Richard Morton slipping back and over the side.

Helen had braced her muscles for the jolt.
She held the sheet desperately, but her hands
slipped inch by inch as his weight came heavily
and yet more heavily upon them. They were
strong hands and there was a frantic courage
behind them, but they were only a woman's
hands, and Richard Morton was a heavy man
for all his leanness.

As she knelt there, straining and panting, the
boat swung round more and more, and suddenly,
as it moved, she caught sight of Adela.

Adela Morton had remained upon her knees,
close under the side of the boat. She seemed to
have no power to rise or move, and her eyes
stared over the water, and saw it beat against
her breast and sometimes rise almost to her chin,
yet she never raised herself nor stirred. Now
as the boat swung away from her and slid out
into the channel, she looked around her like a
terrified animal.

It was at this moment that Helen saw her
and called to her loudly:

"Adie, Adie, come this way!"

But Adela stumbled to her feet, blind and deaf

with fear. In the wild panic that knows nothing of direction she struggled forward, her wet clothes dragging at her limbs. She felt the ground rise under her feet and gained the shore. Then she screamed and began to run, and as she ran she heard a man shout and laugh, and saw above her head a red sword raised to strike. Helen saw it too. She had called and called with all her strength. She was powerless; she looked and could not turn her eyes away. She saw the sword rise and begin to fall, and then with her own instinctive shudder, the weight upon her hands slipped lower, and in an instant she forgot Adela and looked to see the water come up against Dick's shoulders, against his chin, against his mouth. His head had fallen back, and the stream seemed to be drawing and pulling it under.

Then Helen cried aloud. They had drifted out into the open channel, a little away from the confusion, and there was something in that cry of hers that rose above the other sounds of misery. She cried again and again, and two men crawled out from under the thatch and stared at her in amazement.

"What are you doing?" said one.

"Help me! Help me to pull him in!" gasped Helen.

The second man drew Lizzie Carthew's body out of the way and looked over the side.

"He's dead!" he exclaimed.

" No, no. Pull him in—for God's sake—for
God's sake."

" We 've no room for dead men," said the first
man, not brutally, but as one who states a fact.

Helen turned her white face, with its terrible
blazing eyes, upon him. They were like. darkness with a flame in it.

" Help me," she said, and as she spoke she felt
the sheet slip a little more. Then she looked
back to the river, and saw the awful tinged
water flowing like death itself between her and
Dick. His face looked through it—his dead
face. It sank lower and it was as if the whole
world slipped away from her with it, leaving
her unimaginably alone in a space where neither
God nor man would ever come. Her anguish
broke from her in another cry, not loud, but so
bitter, so full of misery, that the second man
stretched down and caught at the sheet.

" But he 's dead," he said, yet he pulled
strongly.

As he pulled Helen saw the veil of the water
grow thin and part, giving Dick back to her
again, and her soul came back with a rush from
that strange lonely place.

The two men pulled Richard Morton in and
lifted him on board. He lay there with his head
on Helen's lap, and Helen bent above him and
tore a strip from the sheet to bind the wound
on his head. It was a long, ragged tear, and
it crossed the line of an old, deep scar.

"What's the good o' that to a dead man?" grumbled the man who had lifted him over the side; but Helen made no answer. She had felt the little pulse that beats in the temple; she had felt it throb as she touched him on the brow, and every pulse in her own body answered it.

CHAPTER XX

THE STAYING OF THE SWORD

If thou take oath in a matter, and thou presently break
    thine oath,
Thou shalt pay thy dues to the Brahmin and he shall
    pronounce thee clean.
But if thou have sworn by the Ganges, then the most high
    Gods are wroth,
And all the waters of Ganges, they shall not purge thy sin.

SEREEK DHUNDOO PUNTH was alone in
his tent. The door hangings were drawn
aside and the early morning light stole past
them. It took a reddish tinge from their rich
colour, and struck upwards faintly, losing itself
by degrees in the orange-coloured dusk that
filled the upper part of the tent.

There was no one before the doorway, which
framed a rectangular patch of dusty ground. A
man walking to and fro inside the tent would
have nothing else before his eyes. Dhundoo
Punth had sent his servants away. He wished
to be alone and he walked to and fro continually.

When he looked towards the tent door he saw
that empty, dusty space with the pale, hot sunshine on it, and when he looked down at his

feet he saw the same sunshine lying in a square upon the carpet and striking all the colours of the seven great jewels from its dyes—sapphire, emerald, turquoise, topaz, amethyst, pearl, and ruby.

The colours flashed as he paced to and fro, but the red of the ruby prevailed. It spread and spread until it swallowed all the rest, and the ground tone of the silken carpet swam before his staring eyes, until it seemed as if he walked in a bloody mist that rose about his feet.

Up and down walked Dhundoo Punth, and the muslin of his thin garments was damp with sweat.

He was listening, listening intently, and the strained nerve throbbed to sounds that were only counterfeit and not real at all—the roar of guns, the clamour of many voices and a noise of groaning that burdened the heavy air.

Suddenly the sound of a horse galloping came to him sharp and distinct. This was a real sound, and it relieved the tension. It came on, faster and faster, then stopped, and on the instant a man covered with dust broke in upon the Nana's solitude, a man whose face was so pale that it seemed as if the dark pigment had been driven from it by sheer horror.

It was Francis Manners, called the Rao Sahib. He came in panting, crying out, "My uncle— my uncle!" and the Nana stood aghast with the sweat on his face. What had chanced?

What had befallen? Were broken oaths so quickly heard, so quickly punished by the high gods?

" What is it? Speak! " he stammered, and the young man moistened his pale lips and threw out his hands.

" They kill every one. Is this your oath? All the women—all the children—and she is there —Adela. They said she lived. Is this your order? It is not to be borne. Is it your order? Is it your order, my uncle? "

Dhundoo Punth looked at him with his wild, brilliant eyes. They had the same eyes, these two, and in each there was a spark that might blaze some day in madness. The Nana frowned, drawing his brows close.

" It is Bala. It is Tantia," he exclaimed. " Ai, Bala, my brother, you are not master yet! "

He broke into a fury and cursed, striding up and down, a terrible, unwieldy figure that seemed to fill the tent. His face was convulsed. Fear and rage looked out of his restless eyes. Suddenly he stood still.

" Go back, and take them an order," he said. " Take them an order from me, from their lord. To-morrow I shall be Peishwa. It is not Bala who shall sit upon the throne. It is not Bala who is lord. The women are to be saved, and the children. They are to be saved and brought to me here—to the Savada house. As for the woman you desire, take her. What is that to me? The men I have given to the army. In a month they could not take them. Then I spoke. Then I made my plan. I gave them these men who are as brave as devils, whom they could not subdue, no, not with all their force. I gave them into their hands. Let them be content. Take my order to them. Show them my ring. Tell them it is their master who speaks. Tell them to obey. If any one will not obey, he shall be blown from a gun. Yes, if it were Tantia himself, or Bala, my brother. These are my words."

He pulled at his finger and dragged off the ring in which the great ruby shone so red, and the Rao Sahib took it and went out quickly, like a man pursued, and again the sound of galloping hoofs came back to the Nana as he paced back and forth across the sunlit patch upon the ground.

Down at the ghaut the bodies lay piled, one on the other, the dying with the dead. Far down, far down the stream the shuddering villagers turned from the sacred water and said tremblingly:

" We cannot drink of it; we cannot look upon it."

Here by the landing-stage, the burning thatch smouldered away and the firing and the shouting died.

As the Rao Sahib came down the ravine, riding furiously, the lightest of the boats swung

out into the deeper channel.   One of those who
pushed her off was Captain Moore, and as he
pushed he fell, shot through the heart and the
waters of the Ganges closed over him.   At the
same moment the Rao Sahib saw a woman who
had been crouching in the water spring up and
falter blindly towards the shore.   She had a grey
felt hat upon her head, but as she ran it fell off
and he saw her hair—her floating chestnut hair.
The sun shone on it and on her face distorted
with terror.   She came stumbling to the shore
with the water splashing about her, dragging
her back, and as she gained the sand a sowar
rode pelting up behind with his sword raised and
a shout of " Maro—maro—kill—kill—kill."

The Rao Sahib spurred forward.   He too
shouted, and as he reached the water's edge and
reined in his horse the woman flung herself
against the animal's shoulder and gripped the
saddle-cloth, pressing blindly against the warm
heaving life, as if it could screen her from the
sword which she had seen raised up and ready
to strike.

In every quivering limb she felt the thrust of
it already, along each shrinking nerve there ran
the anticipated anguish.   But the trooper rode
past with a shout.

"Victory to the Maharaja!" he cried and
galloped on, raising his dripping sword in a
salute as he passed his master's nephew.   The
Rao Sahib looked down and the woman looked

20

up. On the hot air between them memory flung its strange mirage. Both saw the green of springing plants and the cool gleam of a sleeping pool. A woman stood by the pool and smiled. There were crimson flowers at her white bosom and in her white dress. There was a man who caught her dress and groaned.

The air trembled and gave up its vision. The past was gone and the dead years were dead.

Here was a woman with lips that had forgotten how to smile. Her dress was white no more, and the red that stained it was not the red of flowers.

Her hands caught at the man's garments. Her eyes held the extremity of terror as she raised them.

Francis Manners and Adela Morton recognised each other.

CHAPTER XXI

THROUGH THE WIND

Death has brought me alone, to a dim and terrible place.
I have forgotten Sun and Star.
I cannot see.
The darkness is all around me, the darkness covers my
    face.
This is no land where the living are.
Let me go free.

A DAY, and a night, and the hours of another
    day——.

Major Vibart's boat still floated. She had
always drawn less water than the other boats,
and now she was lighter than she had been, for
many who had set out in her were dead, and
the dead had been thrown overboard. The
thatched roof was gone. During the night,
arrows, weighted with blazing charcoal, had been
showered upon it until it caught fire and had
to be thrown over into the river.

Those who remained alive were now quite
without shelter from the sun or the enemy's fire.
They were oarless and rudderless; they had no
food to eat, and their drink was the water of
the river into which they threw the dead.

The winding channel had brought them to

Nuzzufghar, twelve miles from Cawnpore. Of the times they had struck the shelving shore, of the times they had swung in the slow current and borne down upon some hidden sand-bank, of the hail of bullets by day and the blazing arrows that fell at night, there is no space to tell.

They drifted inshore near Nuzzufghar under a deadly fire, and then the rain came down upon them so heavily that it made a truce.

At sunset there came a boat from Cawnpore, full of armed men, but they too ran upon a sand-bank, and the little desperate band of Englishmen fell upon them and destroyed them. Then the sun went down, the rain ceased, and it was night. No efforts would stir the grounded boat, she lay heavily in the shallows, and her occupants lay down to sleep wearily and without a hope in the world.

Helen Wilmot was still in the stern of the boat. The bullets had passed her by, and she was unwounded. By her side was a man who never lifted his eyes, but sat staring and muttering. Sometimes she gave him water, and he drank it without looking at her. Sometimes she broke a piece of native bread and put it to his lips. She had saved it in the entrenchment that the children might have food after their walk to the boats, and she kept it hidden, taking a mouthful now and then, and feeding the man beside her who ate and fell again into his ram-

bling talk, of which she could not understand
a single word.

The man was Richard Morton.

After lying unconscious for hours, he had
awakened into this half-delirious state. He had
no fever, but his mind wandered, and Helen
watched him continuously with a heart-break in
her eyes. The rain had ceased, the sunset had
gone out like a quenched torch, and the darkness
of a heavily-clouded night came down. The men
and women in the boat slept. There was no
hope to trouble them now. They were too
weary to care whether they lived or died, and
too faint to keep wake any longer. Crouching or
lying one against the other, they slept, huddled
up in one common misery, beneath the blanket
of the dark.

Helen Wilmot woke suddenly.

Her sleep had been dreamless, or rather her
dream had been of the vague empty places beyond the reach of thought. White formless mist
pressed in upon her brain. Closer and closer,
nearer and nearer it came, bringing nothingness,
annihilation—the end. Then, to the sound of a
sharp cry of agony it was gone. Her eyes
opened and saw the dead blackness of night
stretched like an impenetrable curtain between
the invisible heaven and the dark invisible earth.
Some one had called her she thought. Some one
had called her name—not Helen, but her own
name—the essential name which she had had

from the very beginning. Dick—was it Dick who had called? She sat up. Her shoulder was very stiff and her arm was numb.

The side of the boat was so hard. But her shoulder had been against Dick's shoulder when she dropped asleep, her arm had touched his and her hand had clasped his hand.

She slipped her hand along the edge of the boat and touched nothing but the splintered wood. Richard Morton's place was empty. Helen rose upon her knees and began to grope in the darkness. She touched a woman's dress and a child's hair. She touched a face which was cold and did not shrink, though her fingers brushed across the open eyes.

Helen's own hand was as cold. A numbness ran up from that cold face and dulled the pulsing of her heart as she forced her stiff fingers to feel for the bandage and the scar which must be there if this were Dick—if it were Dick who had died whilst she was sleeping. There was no scar, no bandage. All at once she conceived a stark horror of the dead man whose face was so near to hers as she leaned above him in the gloom. She drew away with a shudder, and the blood ran tingling back into her finger-tips. It was at this moment that she heard something moving in the water with a slow, careful movement. She strained her eyes, but she could see nothing, the darkness was so sheer. Only through it came that lapping, whispering sound, growing fainter and fainter as she listened for it. A man wading very carefully and cautiously would make just such a sound.

"Dick," said Helen in the quick whisper that will carry farther than a louder tone.

There was no answer. A quick gusty breath came ruffling up the stream. As it did so Helen heard a little gurgling splash farther, much farther, away, and on the impulse she took the sheet from about her shoulders, swathed it tightly round her body, fastening it with the strong brooch from her throat. Then she slipped over the edge of the boat where the wood had splintered away, leaving a gap, and felt the water rise cold in the darkness until it lay about her waist, chill and close. She moved forward half a dozen paces, with a slow wading motion. The cold edge of the water ran up a little higher and fell back again as she moved. It felt like a sharp edge of steel pressing upon the heart. Again she heard a faint splash, and again moved on, and the current of the deepening stream beat hard against her breast till her heart answered it.

She had lost her sense of direction then in the black gloom, and could not tell which way the boat lay or where was the shore. Out here in the deep channel the river seemed full of strange sounds. Ripple answered ripple and the wind stirred the night into broken speech.

The wind rose momentarily and brought with

it the smell of wet earth and the noise of the whispering of trees. To Helen, these land scents and land noises brought a sudden overwhelming horror of the river and the brooding dark. The chill about her struck inwards, and with an increasing tremor she remembered the guardians of the stream, the alligators who haunt the fords and the shallows of the Ganges. She had seen one only a few hours before, and as it moved in the water, the long ripple that followed it had made just such a sound as the one which had brought her here.

She stood quite still and did not dare to stir, and then again something moved in the water and she pressed forward without knowing whether she was going towards the sound or away. Almost immediately the shelving sand-drift rose beneath her feet. Trembling and shivering, she came up the bank and stood there wringing out her drenched skirt and wondering where she was and what she was to do. As she wondered, the wind took her loosened hair and drove it across her eyes. It was like a bandage over them, and she pushed it back, looking and listening, straining eyes and ears, straining and straining still. Through the deep continuous murmur of the wind, she heard the sound that a dog makes when he shakes himself free of the wet in his coat. It was quite close, and she ran forward and struck against something that moved, but which she could not see. There was a moment of sheer dread. Then her hand touched another hand, and it was one she would have known for Richard Morton's, even upon the edge of death.

"Dick, come back. What are you doing here?" she said, in a low insistent voice, but he shook himself again, roughly, and moved away from her.

"Dick," said Helen. "Oh, Dick!"

She caught his arm and moved with him, and then quite suddenly, the murmur of the wind rose into a loud whirling roar and the air was beaten down to the earth by the torrents of the rain.

Helen's voice was gone in the noise and the pelting rush of wind and water. Her lungs laboured for breath, bare breath, but she kept her desperate hold of Richard Morton's arm, and her feet stumbled after him along some path that she could not see at all.

But Richard Morton walked as if he saw. He went steadily forward, and seemed neither to know fatigue nor to be aware of Helen's presence. Once she lost her grip of him, and a terror of the night came over her so that she cried aloud. The wind carried away her cry, swelling it, but the next gust drove her against him in the darkness, and she clung very close to his arm and did not lose her hold again. He noticed neither her coming nor her going, but held on his way without a pause.

The tempest filled all the black vault of heaven with its clamorous outcry. It beat about their heads with its strong, invisible wings, and the great gusts of it caught them and drove them forward, so that sometimes they ran and scarcely felt the ground, whilst before them stretched a darkness that wavered in the wind.

Once when the breath of the storm failed between two shattering buffets, Helen heard Dick's voice. There were no words, only a wild, strange utterance that seemed to answer the wind. Once when a long pale tongue of lightning leaped from cloud to surging cloud, she caught a glimpse of his face. It was burning white, and his eyes burned too. They looked at the lightning and never shrank or closed.

A strange exhilaration came upon Helen. It seemed to pass into her from Dick, like a current flowing between them. This rain was the water of their cleansing. It fell from heaven and washed them free from memory. The stains of horror and the taint of blood, the touch of pain and the brand of agony, all vanished, all dissolved, and went down in dew to the earth which is man's grave, and the wind blew upon them and made them strong. It came leaping from the uttermost part of heaven, and the breath of it beat on their souls like the breath of life.

That which was washed was also strengthened, and in that strength they ran and were not weary, they walked and were not faint. Of

the path they followed and the way they took,
Helen knew nothing at all.

Consciousness was extraordinarily heightened,
sensation extraordinarily vivid. Sometimes the
clashing trees beat out the music of a march
for them. Sometimes the wind blew a trumpet-
call in their ears. Sometimes their feet were
among stones and rough places, and once they
went down, down in the darkness into some
ravine where water dashed from rock to rock,
and then again they climbed and Helen caught
her dress and tore it from hem to waist
upon some thorny bush. The flesh of her bare
ankle was torn too, and a sharp pain shot
through her as the hot blood ran down and was
chilled by the rain. But they went on and on,
and farther on, and never slackened nor stayed
at all.

It was stranger than any dream. The black
midnight watched them, and time and again the
lightning came out of its secret place and flared
across their way, but they saw no human soul
and were seen by none. It was a night for closed
doors and fastened latch. Men did not come
abroad, and even the beasts crouched low. And
whenever the hurricane paused between two of
its mighty breaths, the darkness was filled and
whitened by a rain that stretched unbroken between flooded earth and streaming sky. Then
the liquid mud rose about their ankles and
clogged their path, and again the wind would

break upon the water and cast it in broken
gouts far out above the straining trees.

In the hour before the dawn a grey pallor
changed the face of the sky. The wind swept
the clouds into a heap and left them, like a
pyre that waits the torch. Suddenly the storm
dropped. The wind's breath failed like the
breath of a dying man. The rain ceased.

Richard Morton slackened his pace and stood
still. Dim stretches of sodden ground lay before
them. Farther on, dark trees. Farther still,
darkness itself.

It was Helen who moved.

She drew Richard with her and he yielded to
her touch, and came haltingly. Slower and
slower they moved. The light that filtered
through the clouds showed feet that stumbled,
scarcely serving to tread another pace.

Grey changed to silver in the east and silver
kindled into gold. The sun's flame struck upon
the piled-up clouds and they sent up a flare of
orange, shot with tongues of scarlet fire. Helen
and Richard stood amongst the trees and saw
facing them a small brick temple, with three
doors to it.

They came to it swaying upon their feet. In
the middle of the brick floor there was a tiny
well, for this was a temple to Kuanwala, the
spirit of wells, he who frightens the children,
and brings misfortune, unless he is propitiated
with an offering of food. Such an offering lay

upon the rim of the well now. Flat cakes of wheat flour and a heap of soft-boiled rice.

Helen rallied the last of her consciousness and filled Dick's hands with the food. Half swooning they ate, and when they had eaten they crouched down, and the deep, deep sleep of exhaustion came heavily upon mind and body.

CHAPTER XXII

THE TWO SCARS

Let be the past of Shadow, let be the past of Pain,
  Are we to squander the gold of our Youth for what is
    not?
Now we are come from the darkness into the light again,
  Is death to be remembered and Life to be forgot?

HELEN WILMOT slept for nearly twelve
hours. When she awoke the shadows of
the trees were lengthening towards the east. It
was already dusk in the little temple. Outside,
birds were chattering as they do at sunset all
the world over. Helen sat up, and found that
her clothes had dried upon her whilst she slept.
She had a vague recollection of heat—of the sun
upon her stiff limbs. They were very stiff. She
was unutterably weary, and her joints ached.

Richard Morton was lying on his back about
a yard away. Helen crawled to his side. The
light came through the middle door of the
temple and fell upon his face, and she was frightened at the look of exhaustion which it showed.
The sunburn was like a brown film over its
pallor, there were deep hollows beneath the
closed eyes, and his hand when she touched it

318

was chill and clammy. His breath came very
slowly and his lips were dry. Water—there
should be plenty of water after last night's rain.
Helen limped to the temple door, and looked
about her. To the right, the stony ground fell
away into a hollow, shaded by a tree that had
big, twisted roots. There was a little pool there,
and another beyond, larger and deeper.

Helen crumpled up a corner of the linen sheet
which was wrapped about her, soaked it in the
nearer pool, and then ran back and squeezed
the moisture on to Dick's parched lips. Her
own were almost as dry, but she did not know
it until she saw him suck at the wet cloth and
felt the water upon her hand. Then her tongue
seemed like a cinder in her mouth, but she went
on squeezing steadily until all the water was
gone, and Richard Morton muttered, opened
blank eyes for a moment, and then fell again
into an exhausted sleep.

Helen went again to the pool. This time she
drank herself, and bathed her temples. Then
she came back and looked at Dick, touching
him to make sure that his clothing was dry, and
that this was only sleep which held him. It was
food he needed. She knew that very well. She
looked at the dry chupatti on the well's edge, at
the few grains of rice which they had left beside it. She tried to get some of the rice between
Dick's lips, but he only muttered and turned his
head, and she abandoned the attempt. A terror

of the coming night seized her. All those hours
and hours of darkness, and Dick must have
nourishment, or this sleep of his would pass into
the final sleep of all. She watched his grey face
in the grey twilight until she dared not watch
any more. Then she went back to the temple
door and crouched there, looking about her in
a dazed fashion for some help, some hope.

The birds were making so much noise that
she found it hard to think, or to collect her
thoughts. The thoughts fluttered in her brain
as the birds fluttered in the branches. They
seemed to have a life of their own, and not to
be under her own control any more.

Sometimes they rose about her with a whirring
noise; then she found it hard to decide which
were her thoughts, and which were the fluttering birds. At last she discovered that her
thoughts were grey and dull, but the birds were
vivid and gay. They were parrots. There were
a whole troop of them, small and brilliant and
loud of voice. Once, half a dozen flashed from
one tree to another, and a slanting beam of sunlight set their wings ablaze with emerald and
sapphire, until the thread of light seemed strung
with jewels. Then the shadows swallowed them
up, and only their loud, harsh talk came down
to Helen, and beat against the confusion of her
brain. She listened to it, and through it she
listened for Dick's breathing, and thought that
it grew fainter.

Helen sat very still, and the shadows of the
temple covered her from head to foot, but a
yard or two away the sunset light touched the
damp earth, and showed a white speck or two
of rice which had fallen from her dress as she
came to the doorway. Suddenly there was a
stir of beating wings. Two of the little green
parrots came down with a whirr, quarrelling,
striking at one another, greedy, curious, angry.

Helen drew in her breath. She became conscious that her right hand was resting on a piece
of broken brick. She had been leaning hard
upon it, letting the sharp edge cut her palm,
because the pain eased her heart a little.

Now she withdrew her weight, and with a
swift instinctive movement with which her consciousness had no concern, she flung out her hand
with the brick in it, and let go. There was a
quick outcry and an uprushing of bright wings,
but only one of the birds had flown away. The
other lay half-stunned, with a broken wing, and
in an instant she had it fluttering in her hands.
Helen had never killed anything in all her life
before, but her hands were quick and strong
enough to kill now. She felt the short struggle
of the terrified creature, she felt its heart fail
under her hand. Half a dozen sharp little
hammer strokes, that tingled all through her,
and then it was dead, a limp warm handful of
emerald feathers.

Helen looked at it stupidly, and then remem-

21

bered that Dick had a knife. It was hung about
his neck on a strong cord. She remembered
how he had cut a soldier for Lucy out of a
splinter of wood. It seemed a very long time
ago.

She turned with the bird in her hand and
went into the temple. Half an hour later she
came out into the dusk again, and went down
to the pool. She was trembling all over, but
Dick was fed, and sleeping as people sleep when
they are going to wake again. Helen's hands
were red, because she had to grind the bird's raw
flesh between two stones. Then she had moistened it to a pulp with water, and forced it between Dick's lips. It had been rather horrible,
but after the first he had taken all that she gave
him. Now she rubbed her hands in the mud,
and then washed them clean. She was glad that
it was getting dark, so that she could not see.
She had a dreadful feeling that her hands were
still red, still stained with blood. O God, there
had been so much blood—so much agony.
Strange, that after all the horrors of Cawnpore,
she should feel like a murderess because she
had killed a bird. And she was so weary, so
unutterably weary. She drank deep of the
first pool, then forced herself to eat some of
the stale chupatti, and again sleep came upon
her.

Fourteen hours later Richard Morton opened
his eyes. He saw a reddish shadow over his

head. He lay quite still, and kept on looking into the shadow. Presently he saw that it had concealed an arch of brick, and he began to count the bricks. Some of them were in a disgracefully broken state. When he had counted up to fifteen, it occurred to him that he was very stiff, and he began to stretch out his limbs. He was lying upon something uncommonly hard too. Ah—more bricks, but there was something soft under his head, and, O Lord, yes—his head must have had a pretty hard crack on it to feel like this. He put up a hand and discovered the presence of a bandage. Then a voice said, " Oh, Dick!" and he sat up, leaning on one hand, and holding the other to his head.

The daylight was coming in through three low doors, and just inside the middle one was a woman.

Richard Morton passed his hand across his eyes and stared at her. The woman had a very pale, thin face of an oval shape. Her lips were pale too, but they were firmly cut, and she had eyes that looked black. There were dark lashes over them and dark circles beneath. She wore a native sheet wrapped closely about her body, but the remains of a tattered grey muslin dress showed at breast and ankle. Her arms were bare to the elbow, and she seemed to have been washing her hair, for it hung in damp black curls all about her shoulders. As he stared at her, her face changed. She looked at him as no woman had ever looked at him since his mother died.

" Oh, Dick! " she said again.

Her eyes were full of a mist, and he saw that they were very beautiful eyes, and that they were not black at all, but grey. Richard Morton kept on staring for a moment. Then he sat bolt upright, dug the nails of one hand into the palm of the other, shut his eyes tightly, opened them again, and finding that the woman was still there, he said:

" Where on earth am I? "

The sound of his own voice reassured him a little, but it seemed to alarm the woman.

She came nearer, knelt down upon the brick floor, took hold of his wrist, and began to feel for the pulse.

Richard felt uncommonly like a fool.

" Do tell me where I am," he urged.

" But I don't know," said the woman; " I really wish I did. We ought to know."

Apparently his pulse pleased her, for she smiled as she let go his hand. When she smiled, Richard saw that she was very much younger than he had thought at first. He liked her face very much.

" Yes, we ought to know," he said. " But why don't we? " And the lady shook her hair back and said:

" Because we came here in the night. Don't you remember at all, Dick? Oh, you had better not try," she added, as he wrinkled up his forehead, and was reminded of the fact that there was a bandage across it.

"But I do remember," he began. "Of course I remember everything. Blake and I were together, and his horse went down. I grabbed at him and a great ugly brute hit me over the head."

Helen began to unfasten the bandage. She kept her hands steady, but her voice shook a little as she asked:

"Where did this happen?"

"Don't you know?" He looked at her curiously. "Why at Multan, of course."

Helen cried out. She could not help it. The two scars, the old and the new, swam together before her eyes.

"What is it?" said Richard Morton quickly.

Helen pulled herself together.

"Nothing—oh, nothing—your wound has healed. Fancy already——"

She hardly knew what she was saying, but the "already" brought a gasp of hysterical laughter to her lips—already—and Multan was how many years ago? Seven?

"That was not why you cried out like that," said Captain Morton. He looked her straight in the face, turning his head to do so, and drawing back against the wall. "It was not anything to do with my wound. You cried out when I said Multan. What has happened? Of

course I can see that something has happened.
Why are we here? Tell me at once, please."

Helen put out her hand, and drew it back
again. She felt quite dizzy. Then she said in
a low voice:

"Multan was seven years ago, Dick."

There was a long silence.

After a minute or two she replaced the bandage. He could feel how unsteady her fingers
were. Yet they moved gently, and never hurt
him. When she had finished, he caught her
wrists and pulled her round to face him. She
met his eyes with a sweet, anxious look. The
sweetness and the anxiety were both for him.

"No, you don't look mad," he said in a voice
he could hardly have known for his own.

Helen began to laugh.

"I should think I must," she said, catching
her breath. "I saw myself in the pool, and I
thought that I looked quite mad—you can't get
very tidy without a comb or hairpins. I'm clean
though, quite, quite clean, for I've washed all
my things. There is quite a deep pool in a
ravine close by, and there is a sort of cave there
too. It might be safer than this."

Helen was talking to gain time, but Richard
did not seem to be listening.

"Am I mad then?" he asked, and though he
smiled as he said it, there was trouble in his
eyes.

"Oh, *no*, Dick, how foolish—your head was

hurt, and you have forgotten. Grandmamma knew a man that it happened to. He forgot everything—even his name—you have n't done that."

"Richard—Vernon—Morton—no, I have n't done that."

"You did hurt your head at Multan, you see," said Helen. "And it happened just in the way you said. Captain Blake told me—not you—you saved his life. That was at Multan, so you see, now that you are wounded in the same place again, it is quite natural that you should get confused."

"But I am not at all confused. It 's not that. I could understand that. My head is perfectly clear. I could tell you what Blake and I had for dinner last night—only, I suppose it was n't last night."

He broke off, and asked abruptly:

"What is the date? "

"The 30th—yes, it must be the 30th of June, 1857."

"Seven years." He put his hand up to his head. "It is inconceivable."

Then his hand came down and felt his chin— "Lord—what a beard! I was smooth enough yesterday. This is a fortnight's growth—since yesterday."

He went off into rather shaky laughter, and Helen looked at him with troubled eyes.

"Don't think about it. Please don't," she

said. "It will all come back in time, I am sure it will all come back." But even as she spoke, it came over her with a rush that she would be glad if it did not come back, if it never came back at all.

"Seven years," said Richard Morton again, in a dazed sort of way. Then he put his head in his hands, and Helen began to be afraid of her own thoughts.

After a while he looked up.

"How long have you—have I—have we known each other?" he said, and she saw a little glow of colour rise in his cheeks.

"Three years," said Helen, and she looked at him because she would not let him see her look away.

"Three—then four years are gone altogether; but you can tell me about the last three, at any rate. What have I been doing?"

He watched her face, and saw it change.

"You were in England in '54," she said.

No, that brought back nothing, but he could see that she expected it to stir some memory. She kept her eyes upon him, and every moment she thought that memory would wake, and show him Adela, his marriage—all the unhappiness.

"In England? You are sure?"

"Why, yes. Quite sure. We met there, you see."

Was that what he was expected to remember? His meeting with her?

Richard Morton experienced a strange sensation.

"And then?" he said.

"You returned to India, and went into Civil employ. You were at Peshawur under Colonel Edwardes."

Richard gave a short laugh.

"Good Lord, how queer that sounds. D' you know I could go into court and swear that Edwardes and I talked for an hour in his tent last night, with the lights of Multan in front of us —big, yellow, winking lights—camp-fires, you know—and Peshawur, you say I was at Peshawur? This is n't Peshawur?"

"No, we are somewhere near Cawnpore?"

"And why are we here?"

Helen faltered.

"Don't you remember anything at all, Dick?" she said almost imploringly.

If he had really lost seven years out of his life, then the years of his marriage were gone too. What would that mean? How should she tell him? What should she tell him? He saw her eyes dilate, and the colour just touch her cheek and fade again. Once more that strange sensation awoke in him. This time it brought a hot embarrassment in its train. Who was she, this girl who called him Dick, who looked at him as no one else had ever done? The mist was in her eyes again now. He spoke quickly.

"Who are you?"

"I am Helen."

It was a relief to have something so easy to answer, but a restless look came into his face.

"You say you have known me for three years. You call me Dick? Then you know me very well. I ought to know you."

"Yes, you ought to know me," said Helen, and in spite of herself her eyes fell and her lips trembled a little.

At her words he broke out:

"My dear girl, for Heaven's sake tell me who you are? Can't you see what I am wondering?"

Helen saw. A burning blush ran up to the roots of her hair. In a strange confusion of mind she remembered how Adela had told her to learn to blush. Well, she had learned now. That blush seemed to scorch her.

"I am Helen Wilmot," she said. "And we are friends, Dick." She kept her head high, but her voice shook.

It was so curious to hear her say his name. He could not remember that any woman had ever called him Dick. It had been Dickie with his mother. Men called him Dick, but never a woman before. He looked at her and could not help seeing her colour, her agitation. She said they were friends, and she called him by an intimate name, and looked at him as if—he caught himself up.

"And do I call you Helen?"

"Of course you do. I suppose it seems strange."

His eyes twinkled.

"I can bear it, thank you—Helen. Now won't you tell me what has happened, and how we came here?"

Helen put her hands to her face for a long minute and thought. He had really forgotten.

Those years were gone and all the horrors. How good it was to see any one look cheerful again—really cheerful, not pretending, with a smile that covered a despairing courage. How good it was to see the laughter and the life in his eyes, to see him look like the old Dick. What was she to tell him?

Adela? Her heart seemed to stop. The tears came hot against her fingers. Adela was dead. Poor, poor Adela. She was dead with the others in Cawnpore. Words shaped themselves in the pain and confusion of Helen's mind: Let the dead bury their dead. They seemed to bring a clearness and a vision.

He had been so ill—and still was weak. If she were to tell him, who knew what might happen. He had been near death—so near that seven years of his life were dead. Why not listen to the floating words? Why not let the dead years bury their dead sorrows, and turn to the living?

If God Himself had blotted memory from Richard's brain, who was she to bring it back?

The tide of temptation took her off her feet. This was her hour, had it come to her only to be renounced?

With a sudden movement she dropped her hands in her lap and spoke.

And in all she said there was no word of Adela at all.

CHAPTER XXIII

THE DREAM

Over the edge of the world, away from its fear and fret,
  We eat the enchanted fruits, we drink the enchanted
    stream.
We look in each other's eyes, and what we will, we forget,
  And what we will, we remember, till the breaking of the
    dream.

THEY moved from the temple that same day,
and took up their abode in the cave that
Helen had discovered. It was only just large
enough to shelter them, but by scraping away
the earth at the back, they made it a little larger,
and at least it kept the rain out. For now it
rained every day and all day, only clearing for
an hour or two, usually at sunset. The country
paths and tracks rapidly became quite impass-
able, and stood a foot deep in liquid mud. It
was doubtless owing to this fact that no more
offerings were brought to Kuanwala's little temple, though there were, as Richard soon discovered, a couple of villages within three or four
miles of it.

The cave was high up in the side of a deep,
rocky ravine, down which there poured a torrent
of muddy water, drained from the surrounding

country. With the moisture, green life sprang everywhere—in the ravine, on the trunks of the trees, about the mouth of the cave.

After three days' rain, the open plain looked as if some one had drawn a gigantic brushful of green paint across it, leaving here a smudge and there a thin clear wash.

" It looks like a heat haze or thunder clouds turned green," said Helen. " I don't believe it's grass. It's just part of the dream we are in "; and she laughed.

After a week Helen ceased to be astonished at this transformation of the dry and barren earth, but she had begun to be astonished at the change in herself. Cawnpore seemed to be a hundred years away. She looked back on it through a mist that blurred the details.

Long afterwards the woman who became Helen's most intimate friend said to her:

" I suppose you can't speak of it. It was too dreadful."

And Helen's answer was a strange one.

" Mary," she said, " it's not because it was too dreadful that I can't speak about it, but because it came not to be dreadful at all—you can't understand that? Thank God, you can't. That is what terrifies me when I look back. One got callous, got used to it all. The people who did n't get used to it lost their reason. I saw things that ought to have killed me, and I did n't die, and I did n't go mad. Once Dick was safe,

I did n't even care. That is why I never let
myself look back." Once Dick was safe! There
is no one on this earth quite so callous as a
woman in love. Half humanity may be blotted
from the face of the globe, and she will not care
so long as the man she loves is amongst those
who are saved.

Richard Morton was very weak for a time,
but he was a very hard and healthy man, and
he got strong quickly. Helen watched him as
a mother watches a child who has been ill. It
was just that with her—the protective mother
instinct which is behind all a woman's best love,
whether for her child or for her child's father.
To know that he was safe, to see him getting
stronger, to be with him, these things filled her
consciousness and left no room for any other
thought. She would wake half a dozen times
in the night and listen to his breathing, until
her heart throbbed so loud that she was afraid
it would wake him too, and every breath she
drew was a breath of thankfulness and praise.
The shadow of death lay only a handbreadth
from them, but Helen was in the sunshine, and
she forgot everything in the joy of its light and
warmth.

It was a most precarious sunshine, but they
lived in the present. In that present, their most
pressing anxiety was for food. At first they ate
roots and frogs, which was rather dreadful, but
you got used to it.

Richard had a precious box of lucifer matches. It was a metal box, so the matches had kept dry, and they used them in a miserly fashion, and tried to keep a small fire smouldering in a second cave, where they cooked their frogs, and so found it possible to eat them.

"I don't really think I *could* eat raw frog," said Helen, to which Richard responded that you could do most things if you were starving.

He practised diligently with a sling, assuring Helen that he had been a first-class shot with one as a boy. After a couple of days he succeeded in bringing down a good many birds, whereupon they renounced frogs and began to put on flesh. Both pigeons and parrots are excellent eating and very wholesome.

"Helen, you are getting quite fat," said Richard Morton one day.

There was a definite break in the rains, and they had wandered half a mile up the ravine. Helen sat on a rock at the edge of a deep pool. She leaned over the water, and looked at her reflection.

"I can't quite count all my bones now," she said lazily. "I was getting quite good at anatomy, only I did n't know the names of the things. Now they are all returning decently into private life, and I shall forget them again. One does n't want to *be* the family skeleton, does one? If ever I get too fat, I can always go back to frogs.

I shall write and tell Aunt Harriet about them when we return to civilisation. I shall say, 'Dear Aunt Harriet, lost waists may be restored in a week, by a diligent diet of batrachians.' Then she will go and look up batrachians in the dictionary; Aunt Harriet is the sort of person who always keeps one on her writing-table, and refers to it when she writes letters—a dictionary, I mean, not a frog—and then she will never speak to me any more for ever. Then we shall all be quite happy."

"Shall we? You see I don't know your Aunt Harriet," said Richard, laughing.

"Yes, you do. I mean you did."

Helen's face clouded, and Richard watched her curiously.

"Did I like her?"

"No, not at all. She isn't the sort of person one *likes*. She is a Disagreeable Relation. Worthy, you know, dreadfully worthy, all the unpleasant virtues. Of course, I ought n't to say so, but one gets so detached from one's relations in a jungle."

"It is a good thing that one does n't acquire new relations at my age, or I should have got detached from mine, with a vengeance," said Richard.

He threw a little stone into the pool, and watched the ripples spread like rings of crystal on its smooth brown surface.

Helen watched them too. They opened, wid-

22

ened, touched the edges of the pool, and came back in tiny waves.

She had not meant to speak, but she did speak.

" Men of your age do form new relationships sometimes," she said.

As soon as the words had passed her lips, her whole body tingled. She knew that he had turned and was looking at her, but she could not meet his look.

" You mean they marry? Or get engaged? "

He spoke very slowly and thoughtfully.

" Yes," said Helen, her conscience urging her.

" One would hardly forget a thing like that," said Richard. He stared at her left hand, as he had stared at it once or twice before.

" No," he said again, " one would hardly forget that."

Suddenly his glance leapt to her face.

" Helen, was I engaged to be married? "

Helen felt the blood leave her heart. It beat noisily against her temples and against the drums of her ears. Through the noise she heard Dick's voice repeating his question, and she heard her own voice answer: " No; oh, no! "

And then there was silence and a mist all about her. Presently it cleared, and she saw the green shadows and brown depths of the pool below her. There was a quick play of light and shade upon its surface, a mingling of many reflections which yielded to one another by beautiful gradations of colour. A brilliant butterfly danced by, beating the hot, moist air with exquisite iridescent flutterings.

Below, in the water, its faint, lovely shadow danced too. It flickered from sun to shade and from shade to sun again. Then it was gone.

Richard Morton's chin was in his hand and his lips smiled. He still wore the native dress with which he had come into the entrenchment, and Helen had torn her sheet in two to provide him with a turban for his head. He had grown a short, black beard that was curly, though his hair was not, and his face was burned so brown that he might very well have passed for a native, until he looked up, and you saw how blue his eyes were.

He had been doing some hard thinking in the past days. He still remembered nothing, but the situation had begun to have a charm for him. Behind the dark curtain which had dropped across his life, he suspected—Helen.

She watched him, but had not guessed that he was watching her. He had not forgotten the look on her face when she found him waking in the temple. That look and his name upon her lips. A girl like Helen Wilmot did not call a man by the name which his intimate friends used, unless he were more to her than a friend. From the first he had suspected, but now he began to feel sure, quite sure. It was not for nothing that their natures fitted at every point. Richard was at that stage in which a man feels that he has always known, and always loved, the one woman in the world. From the first she had been friend and comrade. Closer friend, dearer comrade than any that he could recall. After three days he found it impossible to believe that he had known her for three years, and had not loved her. He could not guess that the Helen she showed him here in this solitude was not the Helen whom he and the world had known. No, he could not believe that this love was a new thing. Her presence was too dearly familiar. They had been lovers in the years he had forgotten, and death had spared them that they might be lovers again through all the years which he and she would remember together. He grudged those past, forgotten years, and yet as he peered back into them, he thought he could recall the love that had filled them. As every lover believes that there was no time before his love began, so his love reached backwards now and filled the empty past.

Past, present, and future caught and held the glow. Life was very pleasant to Richard Morton as he lay by the sun-flecked pool and looked at Helen Wilmot.

The coarse native sheet wrapped her closely. Even the half of it was sufficiently wide to reach from breast to knee, confining the torn, limp folds of her grey dress. Her arms were bare, and her hair fell in a thick plait to her waist. Over the brow it lay in deep waves. Mrs. Middleton

would have called it very untidy. Richard
thought it made her look very young. Then she
moved a little, and he saw the colour stir under
that white skin of hers which never burned at
all.

" Helen," he said, in a new voice, and she
turned startled tragic eyes on him. Their looks
met, his ardent, hers imploring. She got up with
a quick nervous movement.

" Oh, it is going to rain again ! " she exclaimed.
" Dick, we must go back. We really can't afford
to get wet, with no clothes to change, and it
would mean fever, to a certainty."

Richard got up too. He laughed a little, and
did not speak. His look of tender amusement
followed her as she ran before him to the cave.
That night Helen could not sleep. Her conscience was awake, and it stabbed deep. When
she was sure that Richard slept she got up and
knelt at the narrow mouth of the cave.

A jutting boulder sheltered the opening from
above. The rain came down in a steady sheet,
and there was not a breath of wind. Helen
tried to pray, but her prayers seemed shut into
the low cave. The rain hung like a curtain at
its door, and her prayers were shut in with her
—with her and Dick.

She stopped praying.

It was very dark—very, very dark. Somewhere behind all that blackness there was the
soul that had been Adela. Helen's eyes strained

against the gloom. Her spirit strained too.
Her lips moved.

"Adie," she said, on a low gasping breath.
"Oh, Adie, are you there? Can you hear?
Can you understand? You did n't love him.
You did n't make him happy. I love him so
much. Oh, Adie, poor Adie, do you know?"

The tears sprang hot from her eyes and ran
down to her moving lips. The rain never ceased
and they kept on falling, those salt, hot tears.
Suddenly they came with a rush:

"I ought to have told him—I ought to tell
him now. Oh, I ought—I ought—I ought——"

She said the words over and over until they
lost all meaning, and all the time she knew that
she dared not tell him now. The courage was
all gone out of her.

CHAPTER XXIV

THE AWAKING

Over the edge of the World, away from the noise of its
    strife,
  We walk the enchanted Woods, we wander with things
    that seem,
Till we come to the Garden of Eden, till we handle the
    Tree of Life,
  And the knowledge of Good and Evil comes with the
    breaking of the dream.

DURING the days that followed, Helen was
in torment. She could not look at Richard Morton without seeing that he loved her.
And Adela was not dead a month. If he knew
—when he knew—— She kept her eyes from his,
and walked in a mist of pain. To him this new
timidity, this withdrawal gave her the last touch
of virginal charm. She had been friend and
comrade, but now she was the heart of his dream
as well.

He thought he read her mind.

He was to remember, to catch up the lost
thread before he could come to the centre of the
maze and find her waiting. How could she, or
any other woman, say to a man:

"You loved me, and I loved you. We were

to have been married, but you have forgotten."

How she must have suffered—his proud, fine Helen. And now as he read her, it was the old lover, the old familiar love that she wanted, not this new love which was all that he had to give until he could remember. Well, he would give her her way, he would wait, and be patient for a while. These days were happy ones, and it would not be very long.

Already the darkness that had settled over his memory was beginning to be shot with light. Flashes came and went. Sometimes he was on the point of remembering. The black curtain stirred, as if about to rise. Then just as anticipation rose to its height the moment passed, and all was a blank again.

One day as they sat in the cave, and the rain poured down outside, he asked Helen:

" Where did I meet you first? "

And she answered him, without turning her head:

" At 'Aunt Lucy's house "; and she gave the street and the number.

" And who is Aunt Lucy? " His voice held a teasing note. " Another Disagreeable Relation? "

This was the turn of the screw, but Helen steadied herself to say the name that had been Adela's.

" Mrs. Lauriston."

" Oh ! "

He was silent for a moment, and she felt giddy with fear. Not here. Not now. Not whilst they were shut up in this narrow space, so close that they touched one another if either moved. Oh, she prayed that he might not remember now.

"That is curious," he said at last. "That name—and I suppose I could n't have known it very well; but when you said it—I had a sudden feeling—I thought everything was coming back to me. I do have that feeling sometimes now—but just then it was strong. It has never been quite so strong. Lauriston—Lauriston—no, it has gone again. Well, we met at Mrs. Lauriston's house? Did you live with her?"

"No, I was only staying there, after my grandmother died. I told you about my grandmother, you never saw her. Then I came out to India to my father, in the autumn."

"Did you like the voyage?" inquired Richard conversationally.

"Very much. I love the sea."

"Oh!"

Then he leaned over her shoulder as they sat and asked with one of his quick thrusts:

"Was I on board?"

Helen was startled into turning her head. His eyes laughed into hers, but behind the laughter they were keen.

"How did you know?" she stammered.

"I did n't," said Richard, quite pleased with

himself, " I guessed.   I expect I enjoyed the
voyage too, did n't I—Helen? "

Helen felt as if her heart would break.

" Dick, please, please don't," she said, and then
she wondered what he must think of her.   Her
mood changed.   If he would only guess, would
only find out.   It had come to that with her now.
Tell him she could not.   But this daily torment.
It was her punishment, but it was more than
she could bear.

Richard meanwhile had drawn back, and was
fitting another fragment into his mental puzzle.
They must have become engaged upon the voyage.   That was it.   But why had they not been
married?

He pursued his inquisition.

" So you came out to your father?   Where was
he? "

" At Mian Mir."

" That was when I was in Peshawur.   And
then what happened? "

" Papa died—last autumn.   I came to Urzeepore, to stay with cousins.   Please, Dick, I don't
want to talk about it.   You 'll know why some
day."

Richard Morton thought he knew now.   He
had got what he wanted.   The father's illness
must have delayed their marriage.   An only
daughter of Helen's type would scarcely leave
her father if he were ill.   And then she had come
to Urzeepore to be near him.   They must have

been on the eve of their marriage when the
mutiny broke out. They would have had to
wait a few months after Colonel Wilmot's death
—but not more than six, he decided.

He remembered Colonel Wilmot.

How strange that was. To remember Colonel
Wilmot—the man whom nobody particularly
liked, or respected—and to forget Helen, who
had been almost his wife. Why, no wonder it
hurt her to talk of it. One day he would make
it all up to her. One day she should forget it
all—in his arms. He felt tempted to put them
about her now, but, instead, he folded them
across his breast and stared out into the rain.
His thoughts of her were very tender.

In the middle of July there was a substantial
break in the rains. Richard Morton began to
go off upon long expeditions. He was often
away for hours at a stretch. He told Helen
that he was foraging, and sometimes he brought
back a couple of doves or a little wild honey.

One day he came back with news.

Helen had come some way down the ravine
to meet him, and was sitting under a dhak
tree, whose large dark leaves gave a pleasant
shade. The shadow lay on her black hair, and
made her eyes look black too. Richard came
up the bank, and threw himself down beside
her.

"I did n't say anything before, because I
thought you would worry," he explained. "But

I have been trying to pick up news, near the villages. There are those two, five miles apart, and I found a place where I could watch the road. I wanted to hear what was said by the passers-by. Of course as long as the paths were all slush, very few people came along, but the last two days the ground has dried up a lot, and there have been quite a number of people coming and going. Most of them talked about the weather and the crops, but to-day I saw two men meet. If one of them was n't an old Sepoy, I 'll eat what 's left of my boots. Well, they sat down in the shade, quite close to where I was, and they gossiped."

Richard paused, and laid his hand on Helen's arm. They were out in the open, with the trees about them.

" The relief had reached Cawnpore," he said.

" Dick ! "

" Too late to save any one," said Richard.

" I did n't think—oh, Dick—was there any one left to save, after that awful day? "

" Yes, apparently there was. There were women and—and children—and they killed them all before the relief got in. My man said there was a great vengeance taken. It seemed to have put the fear of death into him anyhow, for if ever I saw a man badly scared! "

There was a pause.

Then Richard said:

" If I knew where we were! "

"I don't see how we are to find out. Don't run risks, Dick."

"He pointed over there when he was talking about Cawnpore," said Richard. "And then he said, 'What is twenty kos to such shaitans? If they eat their food in Cawnpore, they will wash their hands in Lucknow. I go to my village.' So I think I know more or less, and I think that we must be moving on one of these fine days, Helen."

"It's a great risk," said Helen, leaning her chin on her clasped hands. Her hair fell over her left shoulder, and she shook it back again.

"My dear girl, we can't stay here for the rest of our natural lives!"

"I suppose not."

"I believe you would like to." His eyes rested on her, with a sudden mischief in them, and to her horror Helen felt the burning colour rise and sting her cheeks. She put up her hands and covered them.

"Why do you tease me, Dick?" she said, with a quick, desperate courage.

He laughed outright.

"And why do you tease me, Helen?" he demanded.

"I don't."

"Yes, you do. You know it too. How long are we to play this game of make-believe?"

"I—don't—understand."

"Don't you, Helen? I think you do. I think you understand very well, dear."

"Dick—please—please——"

She could not control the trembling words, and now she knew that she could not control Dick either. Her command of herself was gone and her command of him with it. It was coming. She could not help it—could not keep it back.

"No, I don't please," said Richard Morton. He had risen and stood over her, very tall, blotting out the sun.

"I don't please at all. I want to have it out. You can't say I have n't been patient. Now it 's done with. We have played long enough. I knew that when I heard what I heard to-day. Anything might happen. I have waited long enough. When are you going to give me back those lost years, Helen?"

She got up, and stood before him, shaking.

"What do you mean, Dick?"

He put his hands on her shoulders.

"I mean that I can't—I dare n't wait any more for what may never come back to me. If I can't remember that I loved you before, at least I love you now. Why, I guessed at once. The minute I saw you, the minute you spoke. The love was in your eyes. And you know—you know I love you."

She could only repeat the same low question:

"What do you mean?"

"That I love you. That we have always loved each other—my heart."

"Oh, Dick, wait."

"No, I won't. I'm going to kiss you, this very moment. Heaven knows I've waited long enough. When did I kiss you last? Oh, my dear—my dear." His voice fell low and changed.

Helen forgot everything but the love in it. It seemed to lap her round with healing and with peace. The pain was gone, the world was gone. In a dream she lifted her eyes to his and saw them nearer, dearer than ever before.

His arms held her close. They kissed.

And as the lightning flashes from the east to the west, tearing and searing the midnight, so recollection flashed upon the darkness of Richard Morton's brain. With his lips still on Helen's in that first kiss, the flash came. It lit the lifting tides of memory, and as he raised his head she saw remembrance flood his eyes and drown the love in them. The arms that held her grew rigid, but they did not loose her. Embraced and embracing they stood, so close that she felt his heart beat hard against her breast, stroke upon stroke, slowly, like a passing bell. And each stroke set its own deep bruise upon the spirit that shrank within.

Helen could not move or look away. No

merciful faintness swept between them.   The
light was full.

For a time that seemed endless, Dick's eyes
looked through and through her, to her very
soul, whilst love changed in them to judgment
and judgment into condemnation.

" Why did you do it? " he said at last, in a
voice that was not like his own.

She looked at him. He judged, and he
condemned. Let it be. There was nothing
for her to say. She did not know what a
heart-break of love and pride was in that look
of hers, but Richard Morton could never
forget it.

" Helen, why? " he said with a groan, and
when she had still no answer, except that dear,
unbearable look, he let his arms fall, and stepped
back a pace.

Then Helen moved a little and leaned against
a tree.   Now that he had let her go, she felt as
if she were going to faint, and she would rather
have died than faint, or make any appeal to his
pity.   She was humiliated enough.   She was in
the very dust of death.   She waited, and he sat
down on a great stone and buried his face in
his hands.   After a very long time he lifted his
head and saw her standing there.

" I must—ask you—" he began, and then broke
off.

Helen tried to speak, but her lips were too
stiff.   After three efforts she wrenched them

apart, but no words came. When she found that she could not speak, she bowed her head.

Richard gave a sort of groan, and looked away from her.

"It is all clear—down to a certain point," he said, breathing hard—"down to—to the river —I must ask you—what happened to her? "

Helen made another effort, and this time a dry hoarse sound came from her lips. She shuddered, and tried again.

"Dead," she said at last.

He could not spare her.

" How? "

" She was—under the boat, you were turning to lift her in—when you—were hit. Then—a long time afterwards—I can't remember—I saw her again. I called. I did call. She ran— towards the shore. There was a man—a sowar. I saw his sword go up."

" You saw——"

" I was—holding you—you were half in the water—slipping. Just then you went down. The boat swung round—I thought you were drowning. You went down—under the water —I—told you."

" Yes. You told me that."

He looked at her again. " Helen, why did n't you tell me everything? O God, why did n't you? Do you know what I thought? What I have been thinking? That we were engaged— lovers—married almost. I thought that——"

Again Helen was silent.

It was the end. There was nothing more to say. She would have been very glad to die, but Death does not come when we would be glad of his coming.

CHAPTER XXV

HOW HELEN CAME TO CAWNPORE

> Love is a dream that's over,
>   We must part,
> Not as lover from lover,
>   Heart to heart.
> We have no troth nor token,
>   You and I,
> Love is a dream that's broken,
>   So Good-bye.

AFTER what seemed to her a long, long time, Helen took a deep breath, and said very faintly:

"That is all, Dick. *Please*, let me go."

The words were like a child's words, and the voice was the voice of a child that has been ill —weak and simple.

A curious rush of emotion came over Richard Morton. He would have given the world to have taken her in his arms, not with the passion of a while ago, but as he would have taken a child —to comfort and console. Between them there were Adela, his self-respect and hers. If he were to go to her now, neither of them would ever forget it.

He got up, looked hard at Helen's white face,

then turned and walked quickly away, until he was out of sight and hearing. Helen did not move at once, but after a little while she went slowly to the cave, and sat down there with her head in her hands. A man in trouble seeks the open, but a woman has the animal's instinct to creep away into some closed-in place. She desires the dark and solitude, four walls about her, and a locked door. Helen had no door to lock, and her enclosing walls were walls of earth and stone, but she had no other place to go to, so she crouched in the cave, and let the thoughts that were in her have their way.

At first she was too numb and bruised to heed them much, but presently there came to her an instinctive knowledge, a realisation. And what she began to know, and realise, was the strength of the marriage tie. There was a power in marriage, something apart from the law, or from religion, something apart from passion, love, or romance. Romance died, passion faded, love passed, yes, even love, but there remained the intimate memories, the unforgetable impress of one life upon the other, and that strange compelling power which she felt but could not define. In some deep eternal sense, that which had once been joined could never be set asunder any more for ever.

And Helen's instinct told her that she had sinned against this union and this power. Adela was dead, but she had been Richard Morton's wife. Not all Helen's love could bring her as near to him. The thought burned, and she held it close as if to burn away the shrinking of her heart. Helen looked back, and saw Adela as a bride, with the white veil over her curls, with the smiling lips that never faltered as they took the vows. And she heard Dick promising to have and to hold from this day forth, for better and for worse. He had loved Adela then, even if he loved Helen now. And Adela was his wife. Adela had borne his child.

Helen forced the flame nearer.

The baby, the little forgotten baby which she had never seen. She had no part there. She was neither wife nor mother. She had only her love, and her love had hurt Dick more than Adela's indifference.

She pressed her hands upon her eyes, but the inner vision remained, the vision of Adela, whom she had loved, whom Dick had loved. Dick had forgotten, and she had tried to forget. Now the vision showed her only Adela—Adela with a smile, leaning against Helen, trusting her, kissing her—Adela with a frown—Adela in tears. Last of all, it was Adela with that frenzied terror on her face and the river swirling about her. Helen sat shuddering, and her cup of punishment filled drop by drop as the slow hours went by.

It was getting dark when Richard's step made her start. He came slowly up to the cave, and she had a feeling that he was waiting for the dusk, so that neither he nor she need see the other's face. When he was beside her he paused for a moment, and then spoke in his usual quiet voice:

" I have been thinking things out."

She trembled a little, but he went on:

" I believe I know more or less where we are. We cannot stay here. Now that we know that there is a British force at Cawnpore we must move in that direction. As there is nothing to be gained by delay, I propose that we start in the morning, three hours before it gets light. There are risks, of course, but we incur greater risks by staying here. Once the rains slacken there will be more people about. I did n't tell you, but as a matter of fact I was seen to-day. The surprising thing is that it has n't happened before. Of course the man may have taken me for a native—or he may not. He took to his heels at once, which is a bad sign. It 's another argument for moving. Will you be ready? "

He paused for a moment, and as Helen bent her head without speaking, he added:

" Will you eat something, and then try to sleep? I will wake you when it is time to start. If the sky keeps clear, I think that we should take advantage of the starlight."

Helen got up then, and brought a cold pigeon out of the hole in the rock which served them for a larder. They ate a strange silent meal together, and the light failed more and more, until it was quite gone.

Afterwards Helen lay down in her accustomed place, and to her surprise she fell asleep almost at once, and slept deeply until Richard Morton touched her, and she woke in the darkness, and remembered all that had passed.

They came out of the cave into a still air, and a night full of the diffused radiance of stars. There was no moon, but the sky was a clear, dark sapphire colour, and it blazed with constellations, and was powdered with the fine dust of infinitely distant suns.

Richard Morton and Helen Wilmot left the ravine without looking back, and walked fifteen miles before the dawn halted them at the edge of a wide desolate tract, that sparkled with alkaline crystals under the rising sun.

Neither upon that day nor upon the next, did they meet with any one. Folk kept close to their villages in those days. When armies were in the field, it was best and safest to stay at home. Also there was ploughing to be done, and the poor man's crop of pulse to be sown.

On the second morning Richard Morton drew a breath of relief, for he had recognised his surroundings. He altered his course a little, and pressed on, making a longer march than they had done yet, and halting in a mango grove until the third morning dawned. As soon as it was light he walked into the village upon whose outskirts the grove lay, and demanded the headman, who came salaaming, recognised Morton Sahib with joyful tears, and announced that he was the slave of the Huzoor.

"Evil times, very evil times, Sahib," he moaned. "Here in my village we are poor men. To the Sirkar we are loyal. The Sahib knows it. The Sahib will speak for us, and say that we are loyal, and that we have had no dealings with the Nana budmash. The Sahib is my father and my mother."

Captain Morton nodded, and was graciously pleased to accept a draught of milk. He learned that there was a British force under General Havelock at Mungulwar, some seven miles distant, which accounted for his host's access of loyal zeal. Captain Morton signified that his zeal would be best proved by the provision of transport for himself and his companion.

Helen, awaiting him in the mango grove, saw him return, accompanied by four men, bearing the most ancient and ramshackle of palanquins. She then for the first time realised that her feet were almost raw, and that she could not have walked another mile. They went forward in the dusk, Richard riding, and the palkee bearers grunting as they shuffled along. Helen had rested and been fed. Just before starting she had drunk a deep, delicious draught of milk, and she felt strangely drowsy and indifferent. Their dream was near the waking, this dream in which she and Dick had lived, and moved, and had their being, for the last month. Now they were coming back to daylight, actualities, and convention, but she was too tired in mind and body to care what happened. The last moment in which she felt anything was when she waited for Dick in the mango grove, and wondered whether he would ever come back. Now she only desired to lie still and rest. At last, when she was nearly asleep, she was startled by Richard's voice. He had raised up the right-hand curtain of the palanquin and was walking beside her, with his horse's reins across his arm.

"Helen, I want to speak to you," he was saying, and she roused herself to listen.

"Yes," she said.

"We can't be any distance from the camp now. I expect to be challenged every moment. There is something I want to say."

"Yes," said Helen, again.

He paused, made a perceptible effort, and spoke.

"I want to tell you what to say."

"Yes."

"Every one will ask questions, of course. They will want to know every detail, and some of the details—well, they are unnecessary."

Helen had a perfectly detached vision of herself telling a row of men in uniform about that moment under the dhak tree when she and Richard kissed, and he remembered. The vision stirred her sense of humour. Was this what Richard meant by an unnecessary detail?

"Yes," she said. "What shall I say?"

Richard was frowning in the dark. He hated this task more than he had ever hated anything in his whole life. It seemed to degrade him—and her. He hurried over the words.

"Say that I was wounded—badly wounded on the head, and wandered away in a delirious state. You followed me. I was very ill. You nursed me, and as soon as we heard of the relief having come up, we made our way here across country. It will be better not to say that I lost my memory for a time."

The last sentence was the most difficult, and the most essential part of what he had nerved himself to say. He had imagination, and could divine what might have been whispered, not now, but later on. Even as it was——

"Yes," repeated Helen. She wondered how many more times she would say it. It seemed quite impossible to say anything else.

There was a pause. Then Richard said:

"I shall join Havelock's force as a volunteer, if they will have me. They will send you in to Cawnpore at once, and then down to Allahabad, if they've got their communications open. One can't make any plans, but you will be quite safe now. If all goes well you could get a passage home in the autumn."

This was the waking indeed.

The dawn light was very chill and grey as it struck upon Helen's heart. Something colder and more dreadful than tragedy touched her, and pointed to the future. She looked where the finger pointed, and saw a monotonous life, in which she earned enough to keep her body alive, whilst her heart starved slowly without love, without Dick.

"Yes," she said once more. Then her tongue was loosened. "I thought—if I could teach," she faltered. "I am very fond of children. That would be the best. I must do something. Perhaps at Allahabad I might find something to do."

Richard bent his head as if to look at her, but it was too dark to see anything inside the palanquin. He seemed about to speak, but instead he turned quickly away, and mounted. Ten minutes later a challenge came sharply out of the dark: "Who goes there?" and at the sound of the English voice Helen, to her own unbounded surprise, burst suddenly into tears. The best comfort that she took with her into Cawnpore next day was a bruised hand. Captain Morton had bruised it when he said good-bye.

CHAPTER XXVI

Dream-shod I wandered forth,
    Where all ways meet,
But, oh, the ways of the world,
    They bruise my feet.
The dream wherewith I was shod
    Forsakes my need,
Barefoot I wander now,
    And my feet bleed.

HELEN WILMOT was sent down to Allahabad on the first opportunity that offered and there she spent the winter months. In mid-September Delhi fell, and on the 25th, Outram and Havelock entered Lucknow, but that cold weather was one of incessant campaigning.

Lucknow was relieved a second time by Colin Campbell, but he was unable to hold the position, and fell back upon Cawnpore, bringing with him the remnant of the heroic garrison.

It was not until the end of March that the campaigns in Oude came to an end with the final fall of Lucknow. The great wind was failing, slackening, dying. Only here and there it eddied back upon its course, and blew the leaves about. They rustled from the trees, and were crushed

364

into silence beneath the feet of many marching
men. Slower, colder, fainter came the breath
of the conflict. Then it ceased upon the still
air, and there was a great calm. Men fell to
counting up the missing and the lost. In the
roll of the regiments, how many regiments gone!
In the ranks, what gaps! At mess how many
missed and seen no more, how many remembered
but called no more familiarly by name! In the
homes of the English, what desolation of mother,
husband, wife, who often did not know what
grave, if any, held their dead!

And up and down the villages of Oude—vacant
places everywhere—sons, fathers, and husbands,
who were wept and prayed for by the dark, patient women, who neither knew nor cared who
ruled them, but cared sorely, with grieving
loving hearts, because they must miss their
men-folk.

The wind had left much desolation behind it.

Captain Morton remained with Havelock's
force. Occasionally Helen had a short note
from him. He wrote once that he had been
wounded in the arm, but that it was nothing.
It was from the newspapers that she learned
that he had been recommended for the V. C.

Once he inquired whether she wished to go to
England, and when she replied that she was
teaching the children of a Mrs. Montgomery,
and did not wish to make any change for the
present, he offered no comment. About a month

later, however, Helen received a letter from Floss
Monteith, who wrote from Mian Mir:

"Dick says you don't want to go home, and
that you are teaching that horrid Montgomery
woman's children. If you don't come and join
me as soon as ever you can, I will never speak
to you again—never! Don't tell me you can
possibly *like* those children, or want to stay with
them, snub-nosed creatures with freckles and
pigtails—dreadful. And I can offer you Jack
with his beautiful Roman nose (it really *is*,
Helen) and Megsie Lizzie. Did I tell you that
I was keeping her? There are very few relations, and none of them absolutely *yearn* to have
the darling, so I told John it was the most delightfully easy way of acquiring a daughter that
I had ever *heard* of, and after he had said ' Now,
Floss!' about seven hundred times, he gave in,
and we are going to adopt her properly. So
there, Miss Helen, there's a bait for you. I
know you don't want to see *me*. I do wish all
this muddling sort of fighting would stop. I'm
so deadly sick of it all."

Helen wrote a grateful acceptance, but it was
not until the end of April that she was able to
join Mrs. Monteith, and proceed with her and
the children to Simla.

Megsie Lizzie was very much pleased to see
her.

"My papa and my mamma went to Heaven,"
she informed Helen. "I went to Simla. I like

Simla, and I love Mamsie. I am to live with
Mamsie now, and be her little girl. When I am
quite grown up, I shall marry Jack, because I
do hate sums. Jack does sums as easy as easy.
When I marry him, he shall do them all, and
my children sha'n't learn any 'rithmetic, except
only the boys, because they have to, and they
can take after Jack, so as it won't be any trouble
to them."

One day in July, Helen was sitting with the
children in a room that looked across a wide
valley to a brown and stony hill that was sometimes just brown and covered with stones, and
sometimes put on a blue garment of mystery.

The children were supposed to be doing lessons, and Megsie Lizzie's air of detached good
temper contrasted strongly with the cross but
determined attention with which Jack was at-
tacking a column of figures.

"Megsie Lizzie, you are really not attending
at all," said Helen for the twentieth time.

"No," said Megsie Lizzie with an indulgent
smile.

Mrs. Monteith, sitting in a corner with some
needlework, giggled audibly, and Helen looked
preternaturally grave.

"But why don't you attend, Meg?" she asked,
and Megsie Lizzie nodded wisely.

"Because I 've got something *much,* much
more int'resting to think about. Much, much
more int'resting, Helen, darling. I am think-

ing about my dear Captain Dick. Don't you
think he is much, much more int'resting than
sums? Don't you ever think about him, Helen,
darling?"

Mrs. Monteith stopped with her needle in the
air, and looked wickedly at Helen.

"He is a very interesting person, is n't he,
Meg?" she said in a charitable voice that made
Helen long to shake her.

"Oh, yes, he *is*," said Megsie Lizzie with conviction. "When is he coming to see us, darling,
darling Helen?"

"You had better ask Mamsie," said Helen
with composure.

"Oh, I expect Helen knows more about it
than I do," said Mrs. Monteith, who had no
sense of responsibility—no sense of decency, her
husband told her afterwards, when she was relating what had passed. Then she caught up
her work and fled, leaving Helen very angry indeed. Even Megsie Lizzie recognised that she
had better stop thinking about Captain Dick
and attend to her sum for a time. About a
week later, Richard Morton, who was back at
Urzeepore, setting his district to rights, received
a letter from his "affectionate cousin, Floss
Monteith."

"My dear Richard, when are you coming to
see us?" she wrote. "I have n't asked you before, I know, but I never expected that to be any

obstacle. Perhaps you thought Helen would n't'
be glad to see you! Now I am going to be fright-
fully indiscreet, and ask you point blank, are
you going to marry Helen Wilmot, or are you
not? Of course Helen has never said *one* word,
and I don't insult you by imagining you would
insult her—no, I 've got that into a muddle, but
I am sure you know what I mean.

"If you don't want to marry her, there 's a
delightful Mr. Humphreys up here whom I have
been keeping at arm's length, for three months,
simply and solely on your account. He 's really
much nicer than you, and he *is* in love with
Helen. I am simply the most unselfish saint
that ever breathed, for what I shall do without
her, I can't imagine, but I am not going to have
her spending her one and only life in teaching
other people's children, even if they are such
darlings as Jack and Meg. Did you ever see
Helen with a child cuddled up in her arms? It
always makes me want to cry."

Of course there was a postscript—and an important one.

"*P.S.*—People have begun to talk. I always
said they would when they had had a little
time to forget the horrors, and really it 's no
use your being like John and swearing and saying things about people's indecent minds. That
is the sort of minds they 've got, so it is no good

24

being angry about it that I can see. One can't
live on a desert island, and personally I don't
want to. A cat of a woman who came to tea
yesterday began discoursing to Helen on what a
delightfully romantic time she must have had,
lost in the jungle with that fascinating Captain
Morton. (When did you fascinate Bella Mowbray, Dick? Dreadful person.) Helen was
quite equal to the occasion, of course. I saw
her gaze earnestly at the viper, and then she
said, ' Oh, but it is so difficult to feel properly
romantic when you are always hungry, and I
am sure you would n't have thought Richard at
all fascinating in a beard.' So you see, Dick,
that people *are* talking. I must go and dress
for dinner.

"*P.P.S.*—Helen may say what she likes about
the beard, but I think I do agree with the viper
in a way. Don't be angry."

Richard Morton was very angry indeed. He
wrote a letter full of polite fury to Mrs. Monteith, who laughed till she cried over it. Its
general tenor may be deduced from her reply,
which is short enough to be given in full.

"O Richard, *O mon roi!* What a *crushing*
letter. I should be sorry to be a disappointment, but did you really expect me to be
crushed? If you did, you must have forgotten
what I am like quite dreadfully, and the sooner

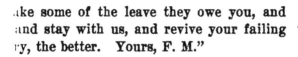

ıke some of the leave they owe you, and
ınd stay with us, and revive your failing
ry, the better. Yours, F. M."

ʼ time there were three postscripts.

ʻ.S.—Mr. Humphreys dined here last night.
a dear.
ʼ.P.S.—I am writing to take Helen's passage
ours in October. Mr. H. is also taking
ʼugh. He will probably sail on the same

.\'.B.—Megsie Lizzie sends her love, but if
want any one else's you will have to come
ask for it."

ıchard frowned, laughed in spite of himself,
. frowned again. Then he opened a telegram
:h informed him that his application for
. t leave had been granted, and finally he
ʼd for Imam Bux, and told him to pack his
ʼıes.

CHAPTER XXVII

HOW RICHARD MORTON REPEATED A LESSON

Turn, and return again,
O return again.
Wind-hush and Sun-burst
Follow after rain.
Every drop on every leaf,
All along the lane,
Has a rainbow of its own
To make the promise plain.
O have done with weeping now,
O have done with pain,
Turn, and turn again, my Heart,
O return again.

AT the end of the first week in August, Helen Wilmot was sitting in the small verandah that ran along the western side of the Monteiths' house in Simla. The cliff dropped very sharply, and the verandah was built out over its edge, and supported underneath by rough wooden posts, which were really the trunks of pine trees with the bark left on.

Helen was alone, for the children had gone out with the ayah and bearer, and the Monteiths to tea, a purely duty tea, and sure to be dreadfully dull, as Mrs. Floss had explained with a groan.

Sitting here alone in the afternoon stillness, Helen looked down upon the tops of the tall dark trees that rose below, and across a clear wide stretch of valley to the near and the far-off hills. It had rained until noon, but now there was sunshine everywhere, and the warm air was full of the scent of the pines. Two miles away a huge dark vulture hung motionless, with the sun on his open wings, floating upon the air, as a swimmer floats on the sea.

Helen's eyes had been fixed upon him for ten full minutes, before she saw him stir so much as a feather. Then he turned with an indescribable sliding movement that sent him drifting, without beat of wing, a mile and more down the invisible slopes of the air.

Helen had a book in her lap, but she did not look at it. The day was too beautiful, the book of the colours too radiantly open before her. And the uppermost colour was blue, a still, fine blue that was like an enfolding garment of peace.

The shadows between pine and pine were a very pure deep indigo; the hills were hyacinth-coloured with hollows in them that held a violet mist. Across the farthest, bluest hill of all, a wreath of vapour hung like an opal-tinted garland. Helen watched it rise and change, break into an exquisite winglike shape, and warm slowly from white to ivory, from ivory to gold, and from gold to a deep and burning rose, as the sun sank, and every cloud and mist-wreath glowed in the slanting rays.

The warm light poured into the verandah. It fell full on Helen, and she lifted her head, and gazed with wide, delighted eyes upon the changing beauty of the hills.

Richard Morton, coming quietly through the house, stood at the open door and looked at her with something of the same expression. It was more than a year since he had seen her, and then she had been worn and weary, and she had walked beside him in rags, with her hair in a rough braid, and a coarse, stained sheet about her tired body.

To-day she wore a dress of white muslin, delicately fresh and spotless. There was a forget-me-not coloured ribbon at her waist, and her black hair was plaited into a crown about her head. Richard remembered suddenly that he had never seen her in colours before; it had always been black or grey. Now he took the blue as a good omen, and he thought that it became her as it never becomes the fair women who invariably affect it.

He stepped out on to the verandah, and as the rough flooring creaked under his tread, Helen said in a startled tone:

" Is it you, Colonel Monteith? "

Richard watched to see if she would turn her head, but instead she leaned her arm upon the railing before her, and he saw it tremble a little as the wide muslin sleeve fell away.

"Did you think it was?" he asked at last in a quiet voice, and still without turning Helen whispered: "No."

He came forward and sat down in the empty chair on her right. By the time he had settled himself, Helen had moved, and was looking at him. He had changed too. The beard was gone, and the firm lines of chin and lip were visible.

"You startled me so," she explained. "Floss did n't say——"

"Floss did n't know. That is to say, she asked me to come whenever I could, and I happened to get some leave, and—well, I thought I would just come."

There was a pause. One of those pauses that are so hard to fill—they occur when there is at once too much or too little to say. Helen began to feel as if she would give the world to be able to run away. She longed for an earthquake, or Floss and the children. Suddenly Richard Morton leaned forward and laid his right hand, palm uppermost, upon her knee.

"Well, Helen," he said quietly.

Her startled glance went to his face, and found it set and earnest.

"Well, my dear," he said again, and Helen took a little quick breath and put her hand in his.

He let it lie there, and felt it quiver, but he did not close his own.

"Have you thought it well over?" he asked. "Floss said there was some one else. That was why I came up. You might do better with a better fellow. I made a bad failure, Helen. If I had been a different sort of man——"

Helen lifted beseeching eyes. She could neither speak to accuse Adela, nor bear to listen whilst he accused himself.

Richard Morton smiled a little bitterly in answer to her look.

"I 've got to say it—this once at least," he said. "You must face it, Helen. I was a bad ·nsband—jealous, impatient. I expected her ..lways to think as I did, see things as I did. I forgot how young she was. I want you to realise it."

Helen looked down at her hand lying in his.

"Please—please," she said very low; "I can't say anything. You know I can't, but when you say those things to me, you break my heart— you do indeed."

"Do I?"

His eyes dwelt on her.

"You know that you do."

"You would do better to give the heart to some one who would not break it, Helen," he said.

Helen flung up her head, and looked at him, an infinite pride behind the blinding tears.

"It is yours; you know that it is yours. If you want to break it. It is for you, not for any one else."

His hand closed hard on hers.

"Do you love me like that?"

"Just like that."

"And how do I love you?"

"I don't know."

"Don't you?"

Helen's eyes fell, her lips trembled into a smile.

"You have n't said that you love me at all. You only said that you were going to break my heart. I don't quite know why, or whether you thought that was a sort of—of equivalent for the things that people generally say."

Richard Morton leaned a little nearer.

She could see that his lips were not quite steady.

"What must I say? What do—people—generally say?"

"They say—'I love you.'"

"That is not very hard, Helen. I love you."

"Very—much—indeed."

Her voice shook more and more.

Something was coming closer, something that she was afraid of.

"Yes—dear."

"Dick!"

She threw him a misty, imploring look, and suddenly he let go her hand, and put both his arms about her.

ing about my dear Captain Dick. Don't you think he is much, much more int'resting than sums? Don't you ever think about him, Helen, darling?"

Mrs. Monteith stopped with her needle in the air, and looked wickedly at Helen.

"He is a very interesting person, is n't he, Meg?" she said in a charitable voice that made Helen long to shake her.

"Oh, yes, he *is*," said Megsie Lizzie with conviction. "When is he coming to see us, darling, darling Helen?"

"You had better ask Mamsie," said Helen with composure.

"Oh, I expect Helen knows more about it than I do," said Mrs. Monteith, who had no sense of responsibility—no sense of decency, her husband told her afterwards, when she was relating what had passed. Then she caught up her work and fled, leaving Helen very angry indeed. Even Megsie Lizzie recognised that she had better stop thinking about Captain Dick and attend to her sum for a time. About a week later, Richard Morton, who was back at Urzeepore, setting his district to rights, received a letter from his "affectionate cousin, Floss Monteith."

"My dear Richard, when are you coming to see us?" she wrote. "I have n't asked you before, I know, but I never expected that to be any

obstacle. Perhaps you thought Helen would n't'
be glad to see you! Now I am going to be fright-
fully indiscreet, and ask you point blank, are
you going to marry Helen Wilmot, or are you
not? Of course Helen has never said *one* word,
and I don't insult you by imagining you would
insult her—no, I 've got that into a muddle, but
I am sure you know what I mean.

" If you don't want to marry her, there 's a
delightful Mr. Humphreys up here whom I have
been keeping at arm's length, for three months,
simply and solely on your account. He 's really
much nicer than you, and he *is* in love with
Helen. I am simply the most unselfish saint
that ever breathed, for what I shall do without
her, I can't imagine, but I am not going to have
her spending her one and only life in teaching
other people's children, even if they are such
darlings as Jack and Meg. Did you ever see
Helen with a child cuddled up in her arms? It
always makes me want to cry."

Of course there was a postscript—and an important one.

" *P.S.*—People have begun to talk. I always
said they would when they had had a little
time to forget the horrors, and really it 's no
use your being like John and swearing and saying things about people's indecent minds. That
is the sort of minds they 've got, so it is no good

24

CHAPTER XXVIII

THE SHADOW

My Love, he took me by the hand, and kissed my soul
   away,
   We two will love past Death and Fate, past Life and
     Time, he swore.
I gave him all I had to give for ever and a day;
   We did not hear the foot of Change that halted at the
     door,
   We did not see the shadows fall across the shining floor.

We had sweet laughter in our ears, sweet music on our
   tongue,
   How should we hear the footfall, or see the shadow
     rise?
We could not hear the foot of Change with half our songs
   unsung,
   We could not see the shadow for the sunlight in our eyes,
   We were too strong to be afraid, too merry to be wise.

ONE day in December Helen Morton was
reading her English mail which had just
come in. She sat on the arm of her husband's
office-chair to do so, and strewed odd sheets of
paper here and there upon his office-table. The
long, full skirt of her dark green riding-habit
swept the floor, and a wide dark green hat hung
from the corner of the bookcase against the wall.

Richard was trying to write. Every now and then he observed patiently:

"My dear child, how can I work?"

"I don't want you to work," said Helen in reply.

"Women have no conscience—absolutely none —about a man's work. It's queer too, for they allow it to become a perfect disease over other much less important things. Helen, do be quiet. I do not want to hear what your Aunt Harriet says."

"It's all about Hetty's new baby," said Helen, gurgling with laughter. "It is very improving indeed, Dick, and I think it will be so good for you. Aunt Harriet is a most improving person, and so is Hetty, and so is Hetty's boy, and so is Hetty's baby. They simply overflow with moral instruction. This new baby is a pattern for infants. So is little Alfred a model for all children of eighteen months. Aunt Harriet says so much about their virtues that I am sure they must be distressingly plain. Dick, you shall listen. I always have to read Aunt Harriet's letters right through in case a crumb of real news should have got in by accident amongst the moral maxims, and I simply won't suffer alone—you have got to attend. Listen to this. ' If all Mothers ' (with a capital M) ' were as wise as Hetty, we should hear less about wakeful nights with teething infants. Hetty has *always* ' (underlined)—where was I? Oh!—' Hetty has *always* made a point of—' Dick, you are not listening."

" No, darling," said Richard, grinning.

Helen rumpled his hair.

" Alfred has six teeth," she said, bubbling over. " He grows more like his father every day, and he has hair that inclines to be auburn. Oh, dear, oh, dear, I think I will save up the other two sheets until bedtime. I shall make you attend then, and there are some perfectly thrilling pieces about Hetty's management of the baby."

" Really," murmured Richard.

Helen laid Mrs. Middleton's letter down on the top of an official blue-book, and opened another.

" The lamb," she exclaimed, after a moment, in a tender, laughing voice, and Richard groaned, put his arm about her waist, and kissed her with the air of a martyr.

" Are you calling me these nice names, wretch," he inquired.

" Not this time, darling. Oh, Dick, don't be so foolish. You are much, much more like a bear than a lamb. It is Megsie Lizzie who is a lamb. Just listen to her letter. She is so proud of being able to write better than Jack, though he does beat her at sums. Now listen.

" ' Darlingest, Belovedest, Angelest, and most Beautifulest, And most Precious Helen Lady,—

" ' I love you so that I can hardly bare to lose sight of you, And you are so " Precious," And

you are so "Tender" that even a "Fly" I will
not allow settle itself down on you. And all the
toys, And all the "Dollies" even down to the
books send their love.

" ' From

" ' Megsie Lizzie.' "

"Good heavens!" said Dick, laughing. "How
on earth am I to compete with remarks of this
impassioned nature?"

"Isn't she sweet?"

Helen gave a little sigh.

"You dear," said Richard. He leaned his
head against her, and looked up half-mis-
chievously.

"What was that sigh for? Do you covet
Megsie Lizzie? I believe you do? I believe I
should be jealous. Don't use up all your love
upon other people's children, Helen lady. Keep
a little for—ours. Shall we call her Meg, if
she is a girl. I believe you want a girl."

Helen put her hand quickly over her eyes. It
was the instinctive action of one who sees so
bright a light that it is almost unbearable.

"Don't, Dick," she said in a very shaky voice.
"It is too much—too much—happiness. I am
afraid of it. We are too happy."

He put his arms round her and held her tight.

"Dear goose," he said, "shall I beat you, or
make love to some one else? Would that make
you more comfortable in your darling, foolish

mind? This is the 'happy ever after' part of the story. What are you afraid of?"

"I don't know," said Helen, laughing. "Oh, Dick, my hair—I shall have to do it again. Captain Carlton is such a perfectly neat and proper person, that I could n't possibly go out riding with him unless I were perfectly neat and proper too, and the horses will be round in a minute. Are you ready?"

"Have you given me a chance?" said Richard. "No, seriously, you will have to go without me to-day, I can't spare the time. Look at this pile of papers. The people at headquarters are possessed by a positively indecent spirit of curiosity at present. They want to know everything that has happened in the Urzeepore district, from the Flood downwards, and by the time I have collected information as to the grandfathers and grandmothers of all my villagers, I shall get back an official request for the names, ages, sexes, and pedigrees of the grandmothers' cats. And if I don't answer all the questions very nicely, they won't make me a Commissioner."

"Oh, Dick, have you heard anything?"

"A line from Hazelton—private, of course. He says they will give me the next district that is going. Shall you like to be Mrs. Commissioner and Lady Morton by and by?"

"I 'd like you to be Sir Richard," said Helen, and her eyes shone. Then she put one arm round his neck and whispered:

"Don't be too ambitious, Dick."

"Why not, child? It is all for you."

"And I don't care—not a bit, except for you. I should be just as happy, and just as proud of you, if you were a stone-breaker, and I had to bring you your dinner in a red-spotted cotton handkerchief every day at twelve o'clock, and you beat me on Saturday nights when you brought the wages home."

"Or you beat me, when I did n't bring 'em —eh? Undiscriminating young female. I 'd much rather not break stones if you don't mind. Do go away, Helen. I shall never get done."

"You are sure you can't come out?"

"Quite sure, my child. Run away, and tidy yourself and have a nice ride!"

"Really, Dick, I 'm not ten years old!"

"Then you should n't have your hair hanging down. It misleads people. Give me a kiss and fly."

She bent over to kiss him, and her eye was caught by a line in the letter he had been writing.

"Dick, I could n't help seeing," she said in a startled voice.

"What?"

"Your letter. Why do you say—'I have received no reliable intelligence of the presence of any white woman in this district'?"

Richard hesitated.

"I am sorry you saw it, dear," he said. "They have got an idea. There have been rumours—

you know they have never stopped trying to trace Miss Wheeler."

"Dick, I thought she was dead. I thought they were sure of it now."

Helen's voice was low and horrified.

"No, they are not sure," said Richard Morton.

"Oh, Dick—how—how dreadful!"

He put his arm round her.

"All this time," said Helen faintly.

Then after a pause she asked:

"Have they heard of her, of any one, near here?"

"There have been continual rumours, first from one part of Oude, then from another. Child, don't look like that. I don't believe in the tales myself, and—even if they were true, in the present state of the country, no one would dare to keep her against her will."

Helen exclaimed sharply:

"She could n't! Oh, Dick!"

Richard Morton spoke in a hard, unwilling voice.

"Helen, you must realise there was only one condition under which any woman could have saved herself from the Cawnpore Massacre. If she had accepted a native husband—if there were a child—what would she, what could she ask, but to be left alone, to be thought dead? What could be more horribly cruel than to drag her back to publicity—gossip—all the newspapers ringing with her story?"

He broke off in strong distaste, and Helen shuddered.

"If it had been I—" she whispered against his cheek, and felt his grasp tighten until it hurt her.

"Don't talk nonsense," he commanded roughly. "It could never have been you. There was always a choice—always death." After a moment he got up, and pulled her to her feet.

"Helen, you are a morbid goose," he said resolutely. "Go and tidy yourself. Freddy would n't be seen with you as you are. Be off, and please don't come back until I have got through with this pile of papers. There. Are you good?"

"Moderately," said Helen with a shaky smile. Then she ran away to her room.

When she came out upon the verandah in five minutes' time, Freddy Carlton was waiting for her, very spick and span. He had not altered at all since he and Richard had talked together on the night of Hetty Lavington's ball. He had kept his air of cheerful irresponsibility, just as he had kept his freckles, his sandy hair, and his affection for Richard Morton. Now he found himself extending this affection to Richard's wife.

They rode away, and Helen exclaimed at the sharpness of the air. Urzeepore in December could be cold, and she was glad of her thick cloth habit. They cantered, to warm themselves, and presently, when they drew rein again, Freddy's talk was of Dick and the good times they had had together.

Helen found this very pleasant. Her heart warmed to dapper little Freddy, and she beamed on him in a sisterly manner which he thought highly agreeable.

After they had skirted the cantonment, they turned back, and followed the high-road which ran past the native city.

The road was bordered by dark tamarisk trees and straggling mimosa bushes, bloomless now. In another month or six weeks, the highways and the crossways would be full of the clinging scent of the clustered yellow blossoms.

To and fro in the dust went the country people, and Helen stopped talking to watch them as they passed—men with dark blankets over their heads, and women lightly veiled, with a barefoot child at their swinging skirts.

A group of very brightly-dressed women went by chattering. They were bold and handsome of face, and not too closely veiled for the fact to be evident. They wore tight bodices and embroidered jackets and gowns of red and green kharua cloth. One or two had a very high wooden horn on the head, over which the cloth veil fell down in heavy, graceful folds. All were festooned with innumerable beads, cowries, tassels, and brightly-coloured cords, and their

arms were covered with bangles made of horn or
brass. Every brown finger had its ring of silver,
brass, or lead.

"Who are these?" asked Helen.

Freddy Carlton settled his glass into his eye,
peered at them, and answered:

"Banjaras; sort of gipsies. Fine, big, up-
standing women, are n't they, Mrs. Morton?
They beat their husbands, I 'm told. Regular
amazons according to Smith-Bullton, who is my
authority."

Behind the Banjara women a palanquin was
jogging along very slowly. There was a little
wind abroad, and it stirred up the dust, and
blew it about. Freddy Carlton contemplated it
with disfavour.

"We can strike off here, and get out of the
crowd," he said, and turned his horse, Helen
following him.

Just as she passed the palanquin, a sudden
gust blew out the faded curtains and a hand
came from between their folds and caught at
them to pull them in. Helen rode on for about
fifty yards. Then she turned to Captain Carlton,
and said abruptly:

"I must go back."

"But I think this is really our shortest way,
Mrs. Morton."

"No—I don't mean home. I want to go back.
I must see where that janpan goes to."

Freddy stared.

" What, that one we passed just now? What
is it, Mrs. Morton? "

Helen was rather pale. Her eyes had a frightened look.

" Captain Carlton—you 'll think me very foolish, I 'm afraid, but just now when the wind
blew the curtains of the palanquin——"

" Yes? "

" The woman inside put up her hand to hold
them together. I only saw part of it—three
fingers—but—they were white."

They looked at each other. Then Freddy tried
to laugh.

" Oh, come, Mrs. Morton," he said; but Helen
insisted.

" Did n't Dick tell you? They really do think
that there is a white woman somewhere about
here. Dick had a letter to-day—he was answering it when I came out. We must go back. I
shall never forget it, if we don't."

Freddy began to feel distinctly uncomfortable.

" It was probably a Kashmiri woman. They
are very fair. But if you feel disturbed, let us
make for home, and you can tell Richard, and
then let him see about it."

" It was n't a Kashmiri," said Helen, with a
shrinking look. " It was n't really, I must go
back. It will be too late if we wait, and I can't
let you go alone either. I am coming. I must
come."

They rode back in silence.

There was no sign of the palanquin upon the road before them. They rode towards the city, and presently Freddy stopped a native and questioned him.

"It has gone down there, to the native serai," he said. "Really, Mrs. Morton, you can't go there after it. I could n't let you. It's not a fit place. Dick would n't like it. Do go home, and let him make the proper inquiries."

Helen shook her head.

"I can't," she said. "Please don't think me very obstinate," and she tried to smile. "Please don't, Captain Carlton, but I just can't go home without seeing the woman for myself."

They turned into a narrow, dirty lane, between two rows of rickety houses with little gimcrack balconies that leaned together and seemed about to fall. At the far end, the courtyard of the serai opened. A small crowd of gaping loafers who were collected about the gate stared widely at the unwonted sight of a sahib and memsahib drawing up before the native rest house.

Again did Captain Carlton question, and receive voluble answers.

"Oh, yes, a palanquin had arrived. There was a woman in it. She had gone in there"— half a dozen hands pointed to one of the ramshackle doors that opened upon the courtyard. No, nobody knew where she came from. No, she had had no servant, and her palanquin bearers were not here. They had run away at once, as

if they were frightened. God knew what had
frightened them. Nobody else knew anything.
The bearers said they knew nothing about the
woman, they had only brought her one stage,
from Ghara. Then they ran away as if the devil
were at their heels. Who knows why they ran?

Helen slipped from her saddle. She was behind Captain Carlton's back, and he did not
see her. He was leaning over and talking to
the men. She had heard enough. She left the
reins hanging, and ran on tingling feet across
the trodden mud of the yard, and before Freddy
Carlton realised what she meant to do, she had
disappeared behind the door to which the natives
had pointed.

CHAPTER XXIX

MRS. MORTON

Where have you been this long, long time?
   I have been dead,
With the stone of forgetfulness at my feet,
   And the naming stone at my head.

Why did you come from the grave again?
   Our tears were shed.
You should have slept till the Judgment Day,
   You who are dead.

HELEN shut the door behind her quickly because she did not wish Freddy Carlton to follow her, and at first the place was so dark that she could see nothing.

Six feet up in the wall beside the door there was a small square window with no glass in it. A little light came in through this, and as Helen's eyes grew accustomed to the dusk, she made out the opposite wall of the room, a native string bed pushed against it, and a white form huddled upon the bed in a crouching position. Little by little, details began to emerge from the gloom. The form was a woman's form, and it was covered from head to foot with a coarse white sheet. One fold of the sheet was shaking, as if it were being held together by a shaking hand.

Helen took her hand off the latch, and moved away from the door. As she did so, the light from the window fell on her, and she saw the woman on the bed lift the corner of the sheet that shook, and look from under it. There was a gasping sound. Then Helen forced herself to speak. It was too dreadful. She must get it over.

"I came—I saw your hand—who—who are you?"

Helen was never quite sure if she heard her own name or not. She never could quite recollect anything, except that her heart began to throb loudly and painfully, and that the woman began to fumble with the sheet that covered her. Her hands were very hesitating and feeble. Helen's only clear impression was the horrible one that this was a corpse struggling to release itself from a shroud. Her own flesh chilled momentarily. Then the sheet fell back, and it was dead Adela whom she saw only two yards away from her in the dusk.

The shock was so great, so sudden, so overwhelming, that Helen could feel nothing at all. She leaned against the mud wall behind her, and felt the ground waver, waver beneath her feet. Her eyes looked at Adela, and saw thin, hectic cheeks, hollow eyes, and a head shorn of all its chestnut curls. Adela's lips were moving piteously, but the noise in Helen's ears was too loud to let her hear.

Suddenly it ceased, and a chill, deadly quiet came instead. From beating violently, her heart seemed to have stopped beating altogether. From a state of wild confusion her brain passed to one of clear and cold decision.

"Adela," she said in a quiet, intense voice; and Adela shuddered into a sob.

"Oh, Helen!" she said. "Helen—don't look at me like that. Helen, don't!"

"Hush!" said Helen sharply.

Both women heard a man's footsteps; it came close to the door, and Freddy Carlton called aloud:

"Mrs. Morton."

Adela made a shrinking movement, and reached for her veil, but Helen went quickly to the door. She opened it a little, and stood in the gap.

"Will you wait, please," she said in a low voice.

Freddy peered at her, glass in eye. He looked much disturbed.

"What is it? Good heavens!"

"Please." Helen put out her hand. "I have had—a shock. It is some one—I used—to know. Will you get bearers for the palanquin? I must take her away from here."

"Who is it?" asked Captain Carlton in an agitated whisper, singularly unlike his usual placid tones.

"I think I had better not say yet."

Helen spoke very slowly. It mattered so intensely what she said, what she did. For Dick's sake—for Dick's sake. Her brain was working all the time, but she had not begun to feel. It was as if some one had struck her heart a very heavy blow, and stunned it. There was no feeling there. Only when Dick's name passed through her mind, the numbness yielded, and was shot with little quivering pains. No, she must not begin to think of Dick. Not yet. She looked so ghastly that Captain Carlton blurted out:

"Are you going to faint?"

"Oh, no."

Helen actually smiled. Then she turned and went back, shutting the door behind her.

"Helen, aren't you glad—to see me?" said Adela. It was quite her old fretful voice, but so weak.

Helen looked at her in silence.

She had gathered the veil about her again, and with her shorn head covered, she looked less horribly unlike the Adela of the old days. There was a high flush on her cheeks, and her eyes were brilliant under the beautiful arched brows.

"Tell me," said Helen, standing against the wall. Her long green habit fell about her feet. Her hat had fallen back. Her face showed pale and stern against it.

"What do you mean? Oh, Helen, how unkind you are. If you knew what I have been through. *Any* one would be sorry for me."

Helen's lips moved stiffly as if they were going to smile. Very stiffly she closed them again.

"You have n't changed, Adie," she said in a queer voice.

"My hair must make a great difference," said Adela feebly. "And I am very ill. My heart is bad—I faint—often; and I have had dysentery for weeks and weeks. That is why I am so thin. And they did n't give me enough to eat after the baby died. Anunda—she was the only one who was friendly—she said they wanted me to die too. I should n't wonder. I should n't wonder if they had put powdered glass in my food, so as to give me dysentery. They do do things like that, you know. I did n't know before, but now I do."

Helen put one hand over the other and dug her nails deep into the palm.

"Who were—they—Adela?" she managed to say.

"Frank's mother—and her relations. I think she is half mad. She only thinks about her prayers. Oh, you don't know what it has been."

"Frank?"

"Frank Manners. You must remember him, Helen, and how much in love with me he always was. He saved my life that awful day at the ghaut. Helen, don't look so—when Richard was dead, and every one, what could I do except marry him? He was always very devoted to me."

Helen repeated four words mechanically: "When Richard was dead."

Adela bridled.

"Of course under other circumstances I should have waited a year. *At least* a year. I have always said a year was the least. You remember, Helen, I said so to you often in Cawnpore, when we thought that Richard was dead. I said I should *insist* on waiting eighteen months, though poor Richard and I—well, you know that he never really understood me, though I think he meant to be kind."

The tears came up in Adela's eyes, flooding their brilliance. Her voice faltered.

"As things were—I had no choice. Helen, you do see it—I could n't help doing it. Helen!"

"You married Francis Manners," said Helen very slowly.

"I—I had to," whispered Adela.

"And then?"

"He took me to his mother—a dreadful old woman—quite mad, and Frank was mad too, I think. He was n't at all like he used to be. He took opium, and talked in such a wild way, and he must have been mad because—oh, Helen, . at last he killed himself."

Helen said nothing. She only leaned against the wall, and Adela went on, shuddering:

"He came in one morning, and he said, 'It is all over,' and then he kissed me quite wildly,

and went away, and shot himself, and his mother
came in and cursed me. It was dreadful. And
Anunda said that all the English women had
been murdered, and thrown down the well
near the Bibi Kotee. She cried, and said that
that was why Frank shot himself—because he
could n't bear it—and they all seemed to think
that it was my fault somehow. And how could
it be? "

Adela broke off, shivering under her light
clothing.

" Helen, why don't you say something? "

" Go on," said Helen.

" They took me away in the night. They
would have left me behind to be killed, but I
told them that I thought I was going to have
a baby. Anunda put it into my head, and said
Frank's mother would not let me be killed if
she thought that, and after all it was true,
though I was not sure then. They took me to
Lucknow."

" Go on," said Helen again.

" I don't know where we went to after Lucknow. We kept on moving, and I never saw any
one except those dreadful native women, and
they only cared for the baby. They would have
been very glad for me to die. But I did n't die.
The baby was born in April. I don't know
where we were. I never saw anything but the
one room they kept me in."

" Yes—go on."

Adela caught her breath as if she were in pain.

"Six weeks ago, the baby died. It was always sickly. Then it got fever and died. Then I began to be ill. At last they turned me out. I think they were afraid to keep me. Anunda said so. They put me in a janpan and sent me away, and after two stages the bearers ran off, and I had to get others. I thought I would come here. It was n't any farther than going anywhere else."

There was a pause, and then Helen said:

"Dick is alive."

Adela cried out sharply, and at the same moment Freddy Carlton knocked on the crazy door; they heard his voice and the creak of the hinge.

"Mrs. Morton! Are you ready? The bearers are here."

Adela crouched down, trembling in every limb.

"Helen, how does he know? How does that man know? You did n't tell him. I heard what you said. How does he know?"

Helen's throat contracted.

"He does n't know," she said.

"But he does. He called my name. Oh, don't let him come, don't let any one see me."

"Mrs. Morton."

Freddy's voice was urgent. A crowd was collecting, and he was on thorns until the two women had been got away.

Helen went to the door.

" In one moment," she said.

Then she turned to meet Adela's eyes, brilliant with fear and suspicion.

" Helen—was he calling—you? "

" Yes—he was calling me."

" You are married? "

Helen pulled the glove from her left hand and let it fall upon the floor.   Then she stretched out her hand towards Adela.   There was only one ring on it—a small narrow ring.

Adela looked and felt the breath flutter in her throat.

" Who is your husband? " she said faintly, and then her voice sharpened, and she repeated louder, " Helen, who is your husband? "

Helen looked at her.

Adela's colour wavered.   The high bright flush went out like a blown flame.   Then it leaped again higher than before.

" Not—Richard? " she said in a quick, flurried way.   " No, no, oh, no, no, no!   Not Richard? "

Helen bent her head.   Her shoulders felt as if they supported some intolerable weight.   She needed all her strength to raise her head again.

" Nellie—Nellie! "

Adela began to pant like a tired animal.   A look of terror came into her eyes.

" I 'm—going to—faint! " she gasped, and suddenly she fell forwards, all in a heap amongst the folds of her widow's sheet.

26

CHAPTER XXX

A DAY OF JUDGMENT

Look in my eyes, O you whom I love,
    Look in my eyes and see,
Here is my soul, like a naked thing,
    Naked to you and me.
If there be spot on the naked soul,
    If there be stain of mire,
Look on it now, O you whom I love,
    Look and search it with fire.

RICHARD MORTON looked up from his writing as his wife came into the room. The lamps had been brought in an hour before. One stood upon the table, and the light beat down upon the white papers, leaving the upper part of the room in shadow.

"You *are* late," he exclaimed. "Where have you been?"

Helen did not answer. She came and stood by the table, leaning on it with one ungloved hand. With the other she took off her hat, and let it fall upon the matting.

"Tired?" said Captain Morton.

He pushed his chair a little farther from the table and swung round in it.

Helen lifted her head with a sudden movement. Words that she had heard once flamed in the darkness of her mind.

"Lead me, O Zeus and Destiny "—the words were blurred. She thought that they went on: " But if there be no leading, I needs must follow still."

" I needs must follow "—the coward as well as the brave. Only it was easier to be brave.

" Helen," said Richard uneasily, and she slipped upon her knees and leaned forward against his breast. In a moment his arms were about her, holding her.

" Dick, do you love me? " she said at last.

" Don't you know? "

" Say it."

" I love you."

He spoke very slowly. At the last word she turned her lips to his, and they kissed, a long, long kiss.

" How much? " whispered Helen, with her face against his.

" As much as I know how to. More than I knew how to yesterday. More every day."

" And if I changed—if I grew ill, or died? When we grow old—when trouble comes—or death——"

" I love you. There is no past or future, it is all love."

" When trouble comes——"

" We shall be together."

" If we were not? "

He was silent, holding her close.

" Dick, if we were not? "

" Darling, what could separate us? Foolish heart."

" Dick, kiss me again."

He kissed her. Her lips were very cold. Richard Morton began to be afraid, very much afraid.

With a movement that was almost rough, he put his right hand under Helen's chin, and turned her face to the light. She yielded at once to his touch, and he saw her, all white in the yellow glow. There were lines upon her face that no one should have seen there for ten more years at least. Every feature seemed finer, as if the fulness of youth were gone. She stared into the flame of the lamp, and then turned a little and looked at her husband. He saw her eyes, darkly passionate, and her lips set in a strange smile.

" Helen, what is it? " he exclaimed sharply.

She spoke in a quiet voice.

" It is trouble, Dick."

" You are not ill? "

" No. That would be easy. I am not at all ill."

He laughed in his relief.

" Then it is nothing very bad. Tell me. Tell me at once—you look as if the world had fallen to pieces."

" I think it has," said Helen.

Then she looked at him and said very simply:
"Adela is alive, Dick."

Richard Morton knew then what he had been
afraid of. That look on Helen's face. He had
heard of women whose minds became unhinged
when a child was coming to them. He put his
arms about her, and spoke soothingly.

"Darling, you are not well."

Helen smiled at him in a heart-breaking
way.

"I'm not mad, Dick—I don't know why I'm
not, but I'm not. It is true. The woman, the
woman we were speaking of. It was Adela. I
have seen her."

"You've—seen—her?"

"Yes, darling. There was a palanquin, and
the wind blew out the curtains. I saw the hand
that pulled the curtains in. It was white. I
made Captain Carlton follow to the serai. Then
I went in, and the woman was Adela."

She spoke reasonably, calmly.

Richard Morton took her by the arm with a
grip that left a bruise there.

"Do you know—do you realise what you are
saying? For God's sake, Helen——"

Her eyes rested on his for a moment. The
desperate wounded passion in them answered
for her. To hurt the thing you love best in
the world—to hurt the soul that is more to you
than your own—Helen realised it, and her eyes
made the answer.

" It is impossible." Richard's voice was quick with protest.

" Dick, it is true," she said; " it is quite true, Dick. I brought her away. She is here."

" Here! "

" How could I leave her? She is ill. I think she is very ill indeed. She fainted."

" It is impossible," said Richard Morton again, but his voice had fallen.

" It is true," repeated Helen. " She thought that you were dead. She married! "

Richard flung out his hand with an oath.

Helen put both her hands over it, and went on speaking in the same steady and yet hesitating manner :

" It was the Nana's nephew, Francis Manners, whom she used to know in England. She thought you were dead. You must remember that, Dick; and he saved her life, and she had known him before. Then he died—he killed himself. He was weak, not wicked, and he could n't stand it all; so he killed himself. His mother protected Adela because of the child. There was a baby. It died too. Then they turned her out. Poor Adie. She is so ill—she has suffered so dreadfully."

Helen's voice had dropped to a languid, half-conscious murmur. She began to understand how it was that Adela had been able to tell her tale so calmly. When you have thought of

dreadful things for long enough, they hardly
seem dreadful after all.

Richard's grip upon her arm roused her.

" Helen! Is this true? "

" Yes, Dick. It is true."

He turned from her, throwing out his arms
across the table, and letting his head fall upon
them :

" My God—Helen, what have I done to you? "

Helen started. She had not begun to think
of herself. It was Dick, the separation, not
herself at all.

The agony of Richard Morton's voice struck
through her defences. She saw herself suddenly
as he saw her—stripped of her wifehood, defenceless to the world, mother of a nameless child.
This was what was hurting him so—this.

She pressed against him as she knelt, lifting
his head, drawing it to her heart, holding him
to her with all her strength.

" Dick, love — love — don't think it — never
think it. I am proud—I am proud—" The
force of her feeling broke the words, her voice
trembled on them. Her eyes were shining.

" You — don't — realise," groaned Richard
Morton.

Helen put her soft cheek against his.

" I do—I do really—but it does n't matter.
This is—too big a thing for it to matter at all.
Dick, listen—won't you listen to me? Oh, do
you think I could ever be anything but proud—

so proud, because I was your wife? Do you
think I should ever be ashamed? I shall thank
God every day."

Richard's arms closed hard about her.

" My wife—my wife," he said, and they clung
together.

Then Helen lifted her head and smiled at him.

" Don't you understand now? " she said.
" Oh, Dick, I think you do—I think you must.
How many women have never had—this at
all. How can I help being proud and thankful? "

After a while he loosed her and leaned his
head on his hand, half turned towards the table
again.

" You say she is here? "

" Yes, I put her to bed. The doctor is coming."

" Does Carlton know? "

" No. I said it was some one I had known.
He was so very kind. He asked no questions."

There was a pause. Then Helen said:

" Dick, I must go back to her. She isn't fit
to be left. The ayah is there now, but I can't
leave her. She is so ill."

It was almost a relief when she was gone.
Pain should be a secret thing. It is not decent
that any one should look upon great agony, least
of all one who, seeing, must share it. A man
upon the rack does not ask that his wife should
stand beside him to watch the straining of his
self-control, or to see the sweat rise cold as death

upon his brow. Richard Morton was glad to be
alone, and as soon as the bewilderment of anguish had passed a little, he began to think, and
to plan, for he was before all things a man of
action.

When Helen returned, she found him walking
up and down the room, with great impatient
strides. His manner had altered completely.
All the emotion had gone out of it. It was
short, dry, businesslike, and he frowned as he
walked, drawing his brows together till they
made a thin, straight line of black above the
hard blue of his eyes. No eyes can look so hard
as the blue eyes which are merry when a man
laughs.

"Helen, come here," he said; and when she
came to him, he put his hand on her shoulder.

"Look here, we have got to keep our heads,"
he said. "When Renshaw comes, you are not
to let him suspect. Tell—her. She can't
wish—" He broke off, frowned more deeply
still, and went on: "It's got to be hushed up,
at any rate until we can get out of the country.
Ultimately, I suppose, every one will know. We
sha'n't hear what they say, so it won't affect
us much. I can manage to get leave at once,
I think. Then we will go to America. That
will be best."

Helen looked at him in a dazed, frightened
fashion.

"Dick, what do you mean?"

" Was I obscure?   I shall take you to America.
It will mean sending in my papers as soon as
we get clear of India."

" And your career? " said Helen; but as she
said it her pride leapt up, because she knew very
well what he would say.

He said it with no emotion at all, as a man
states a plain fact—briefly.

" You come first."

Helen put out her hand and touched him on
the wrist.

" Dick, we can't."

A sudden passion leapt into his voice.

" Did you think that I would let you go? "

" You—Dick—you must."

She would have leaned against him, but his
hand was on her arm, and he kept her off.

" Do you dream that I will ever let you go? "

Helen lifted her eyes to his.

" Dick, don't hold me away.   Let me come to
you.   Now look at me.   Yes, I want to kiss you.
Oh, Dick, you know that we can't do it."

" You are mine."

" It is because of that."   Helen's voice fell
low, and broke on a sob.   " If we cared less—
if it meant less.   We can't spoil a perfect thing.
We can't destroy our strength.   It would be
running away.   We are strong.   We have so
much.   We can't run away.   And there is Adie
—poor, poor Adie.   Dick, if you saw her—oh,
Dick, it is harder for you——"

Richard Morton threw back his head with a jerk.

"Sentiment," he said roughly, "fine words, Helen. But you are mine, and I will never let you go. Before God I won't. Shake off this folly. Rouse yourself—do you realise your position? Have you forgotten the child—our child —yours and mine? What is any tie to that?"

Helen raised her face to his.

"No, Dick, I had n't—forgotten. That was why I said it was harder for you; I shall have the child."

He turned from her abruptly.

"What are you made of? My God, Helen, you can't—you can't do it."

A clatter of hoofs came along the drive. A horse drew up at the verandah steps.

"Any one there?" shouted Dr. Renshaw.

CHAPTER XXXI

THE END

Æon on æon, age on endless age,
  The Watcher of the Universe is set.
His garment stirs the waters, and they live.
  Lord, what is man that Thou art mindful yet?

Lord, what is man? The tide that we call Life
  Ebbs deep, and draws us down in Time's dark Sea;
But when Death's breaking wave has turned the flood,
  Shall it not bear us back again to Thee?

DR. RENSHAW latched the door of the sick-room behind him, and came out into the middle of the dining-room.

He was a small stout man, who was quiet at a patient's bedside and fussily noisy everywhere else. He took out a pocket-handkerchief that crackled with starch, chafed his forehead with it, blew out his short grey moustache and beard, and rammed the handkerchief back into his pocket again with a force that threatened to burst the lining.

"What's the good of talking?" he burst out, although Helen had said nothing. She leaned on the table and waited, and he took a short turn to the window, and then came back.

412

"Who is she? I suppose you won't tell me. Want to hush it up. No wonder. But I shall have to put a name on the certificate."

"The certificate?" said Helen faintly.

"Why, yes—dying—of course she's dying. Dysentery for weeks, and a heart like that— what can I, or any one else, do with a bit of worn-out mechanism? It's worn out—worn to a standstill; nobody can do anything. Just as well, perhaps, poor unfortunate creature—but that's not my business. I'll send you some drops. They may keep her going till the morning."

"You are not going——"

"My dear lady, fifty doctors wouldn't do her any good by staying. All the same, I'd stay if I could, but I've come from the Jamesons' now. She's bad, very bad, and he's tearing his hair out, poor boy, and looking down the road to see if I'm in sight. Oh, she's not going to die; but he's nervous, and she's quite bad enough. I shall be there all night."

Helen opened her lips again.

"What can I do?"

"Make her comfortable; be nice to her. Talk? No, it won't make any difference, if she wants to. It's just a sputter before the flame goes out. I suppose she does want to talk to another woman, after all those months——"

And Dr. Renshaw swore under his breath, apologised to Helen for having done so, and stumbled out upon the verandah, catching his heel in the matting as he went.

Helen followed him, obtained a few more instructions, and then stood still, and heard him ride away.

When he was gone she came very slowly back into the room where Adela was lying. The numbness that had deadened feeling, had passed an hour ago. In Dick's arms it had merged into an exaltation that partook at the same time of the intensest pain and the most exquisite joy.

Every fresh realisation, every new revelation of love, is joy. Even the sharp dividing sword of death, or deathlike parting, cannot alter that truth. The joy and pain do not mix. They lie apart, with the sword between, and every pulse, and every feeling, quivers to the double passion.

Now the exaltation which had possessed and sustained Helen fluttered, dropped, passed in its turn into a purely human feeling of pity.

Suddenly as she crossed the lamp-lit room, there were tears at her heart. She came up close to the bed, and saw that Adela was weeping, in a weak and desolate way, that brought the tears in a stinging rush from her heart to her eyes.

"Adie—don't—what is it?" she whispered, and she knelt by the bed, and put her arm across the heaving breast.

Adela made a small, vexed movement.

"You might have made me fit to be seen," she

said feebly. " You just brought him in—that
horrid man—it was most unkind."

" But you are quite, quite tidy," said Helen
soothingly. " There, Adie, don't. It is so bad
for you."

" What did he say? "

" He said that you must rest. He is sending
you some medicine."

Adela caught at her cousin's wrist, and
held it tight. Her fingers were very thin and
dry.

" Nellie," she whispered, " am I very ill?
Sometimes I feel so—frightened. Nellie, don't
let him come again—that man."

" He is very kind," began Helen, but the
fingers at her wrist became rigid.

" Doctors come—when you die," said Adela.
Her teeth chattered. For a moment she looked
ghastly.

A panic seized Helen.

" Adie," she said, forcing her voice, " would
you like — to see — Dick? " She kneeled up
straight beside the bed as she spoke. Adela
started; she turned her eyes on Helen's face.
They were frightened and brilliant.

" No—oh, no," she half sobbed. " Don't let
him—don't let him come—see me—like this."

With her free hand she drew the sheet up
close. The other burned on Helen's.

There was a knock on the door and Helen
released herself, and took a medicine bottle from

the waiting servant, who averted his eyes respect-
fully from the half-opened door.

Standing by the lamp, Helen measured out
the prescribed dose, and then came back to her
old place.

When Adela had drunk the medicine she lay
quite still for ten minutes. Then she said in
a languid voice:

"Give me your handglass, Helen."

Helen looked startled.

"Yes, I want it. Get it for me."

Helen got up, but she went first to a box that
stood in the corner of the room. She bent over
it for a moment, and then came back with a
light scarf of Honiton lace in her hand.

Adela reached out her shaking fingers for it
with a pleased look.

"How pretty! Where did you get it?"

"It was a present," said Helen in a low
voice.

It had been Floss Monteith's wedding present.
She remembered how she and Dick had unfastened the parcel together. As she answered, she
stooped and arranged the scarf lightly about
Adela's head and shoulders, as she lay high upon
the pillows. The lace folds, with the pattern
of field flowers and butterflies, came down on
either side of the thin cheeks and hid the hollows
in them. The light, close tracery disguised the
lack of those pretty curls which had been Adela's
pride.

When Helen held up the glass, Adela smiled in a vague, pleased manner.

" I look—nice," she said, " quite nice—but it wants colour. Have you anything pink? I do love pink—and "—with one of her old inconsequent tones—" I 'm not really a widow, you see, am I? The pink won't matter."

She accentuated the last word, and an inward spasm of a laughter more tragic than tears shook Helen, and made composure very hard.

" No, it won't matter," she said gently, and fetched a strand of rose-coloured velvet, knotting it in the lace at 'Adela's breast. Nothing mattered except to give a little relief, a little pleasure where there had been so much pain.

Adela lay there smiling at her own image. She would not let Helen take the glass away. Sometimes she shut her eyes, and then again she would open them upon a startled, questioning look. Then when she saw Helen and her own reflection she would smile once more.

Once the smile went suddenly, and she put out her hand and touched Helen. Her fingers fluttered.

" Nellie," she whispered.

" What is it? " asked Helen.

" Come a little nearer. Bend down. Put your head here on the pillow, like you used to do—long ago. Nellie—it was a dear little baby. It was only a little bit dark, and its eyes were very like mine. I wish you had seen it. I

27

did n't like babies before, but it had such a little soft round head. I cried—all day—when it died."

Helen drew in her breath sharply, but Adela's hand strayed from hers, and fidgeted aimlessly with the hem of the sheet. After some time she said in a faint voice:

"Is—Richard—angry?"

"Oh, no one is angry, Adie—Adie dear," said Helen.

"I could n't—help it."

After a pause she said again:

"Where is Richard?"

"Do you want him?"

"Yes—I think so—if he is n't cross. His hands are so warm; I 'm cold."

Helen went through the silent house to Richard Morton's study, and found him sitting at his table writing. His pen drove hard across the sheet of paper before him. He threw her a fierce, almost antagonistic glance as she came in, and she divined the anger, the jealous passion which would hold her against herself, against the world.

She stood by him for a moment, putting her hand on his, drawing him gently. Then she said in a low voice:

"Dick, she wants you."

He turned on her; his face was hard.

"Helen, you *must* understand me. I will not see her. She has no claim—not a shadow. I will provide for her, but I will not see her. What you are made of, God knows. It's not decent. For Heaven's sake get her out of this house, or come out of it with me. Can't you see it is impossible—outrageous—that we should be under the same roof?"

"She is dying, Dick," said Helen in her low, even tones.

He pushed back his chair and stared at her.

"What did you say?"

"She is dying—Adela is dying."

"How?"

His tone was incredulous and angry. He had had no time to adjust it to this new shock.

Helen looked away, because his eyes hurt her so.

"She has had dysentery," she said quickly. "She has had it for weeks. Now her heart is failing. You know it was never very strong, and Aunt Lucy—she died of heart trouble. Dr. Renshaw says that nothing can be done. He says that she won't suffer. And—Dick, she wants you."

Richard Morton got up. His face was quite grey. To the end, to the very end, he must play his part in this intolerable tragedy. He must go to this dying woman who was Adela, who had been his wife and his beloved, and he must take her hand, and go down with her amongst the shadows.

At the door Helen stopped him.

"She doesn't know she is dying," she whispered; "and, Dick, I think she doesn't realise —anything. It is so pitiful."

A yard inside the lamp-lit room, Helen's feet faltered. Adela had turned a little upon the pillows. Her eyes were very bright, but they had an unseeing look. The colour in her cheeks flickered.

"Richard," she called; and as Richard Morton went forward and sat down beside the bed Helen drew back, and shut the door upon them. Then she groped for a chair, and sat down upon it, whilst the room spun about her, and a long, long time went by. Every now and then one of the servants came and asked for an order. Helen answered composedly.

Food was to be left on the table. No, there would be no dinner that night. The memsahib was too ill. Imam Bux must stay in the sahib's office, within call. Milk must be boiled, and brought here.

Helen arranged everything with method. Then she sent even the ayah away into her dressing-room, bidding her sleep, and sat down for the night's vigil.

It was a very long night.

The shaded lamp stood in a corner. Just beneath it was a circle of golden light. Outside this circle, the room was full of shadows that grew deeper and softer as they stretched away from the lamplight.

One very black shadow lay like a pool of deep, still water across the threshold of that closed door. Long, long afterwards, when people spoke of haunted houses, Helen's heart went back to that room, the room where Richard and Adela were. If one poor, disembodied soul may have a power of terror upon men, what dreadful power may not the embodied soul exert upon itself? The ghosts that haunt men's lives are the ghosts they have raised themselves. The most terrible spirit of all is the spirit of love profaned.

In the room with the closed doors, where Adela was dying, death was the least fearful thing. It had ceased even to terrify Adela, as she lay with its rising mists about her, deadening thought and fear before they stopped the failing, faltering heart. She lay in peace, and became less and less aware of the warmth of Richard's hand that held her own.

And Richard Morton?

At the first touch of that thin, fluttering hand the anger went out of him, and a quick wave of pity rose until it took his very breath. So frail —so weak—so broken—and those brilliant eyes, large and startled as they met his. He in his strength to enter into judgment? Was he the Almighty who had made this frailty? Who but the Almighty and the All-Merciful could mete out judgment and pity to His creature?

There was no sound in the room, except the

soft sound of their breathing and a little crackling rustle from the dry wood that burned upon
the open hearth. The firelight reached out into
the dusk and warmed it. The lamp burned
steadily in a distant corner. The room was very
still.

And Richard Morton began to remember.
Quick memories stabbed his heart. The firelight, and the darkness, and that small hand
in his. The past came up about him as he sat
and held his vigil. Once the door opened, and
Helen came in. Richard did not move. He saw
her touch first the wall and then a chair as she
came. Her black hair had fallen low upon her
neck. She leaned a while against the dressing-
table, then steadied her hand to pour another
dose of the medicine, and brought it to the bedside, moving very slowly.

But Adela turned her head aside with a little
moaning sound. Helen knelt down, and tried
again, and yet again.

Then she shook her head, rose to her feet, and
went out, holding to the doorpost as she went.

Once more the door was shut.

Helen waited alone, leaning back, her head
against the wooden rail of the chair, her arms
stretched out on either side, her hands open and
relaxed. She looked past the fluttering lamp,
into the darkness that hid the corners of the
room, and into the black pool-like shadow that
lay across the threshold which she had just

crossed. The door was shut now between her and Dick. The door was shut and fastened. Dick was behind it, not with Adela who was dying, who might even now be dead, but with his memories of Adela. Memories never die. They sleep. We think them dead, then they rise up, and the face of the sun is darkened with them in the full midday of love.

They never die.

To Adela, Richard Morton had given his youth, his aspirations, and his love. That she had not been able to receive them mattered very little. They were given, and given with both hands, the gifts of an ardent heart.

Dick was in there with his gifts, and dead gifts have ghastly faces. Helen had her gifts too, but she and they were shut out. She had neither part nor lot. In that hour she knew the meaning of the outer darkness. It closed upon her, her being was alone in it. Somewhere beyond it Dick called with a voice of pain.

Once before he had called and she had followed through the deep waters. Now she could not rise and go to him because it was not she to whom he called. He called to that which had no longer the breath of life. She could not go to him. She could not help him.

Love does not ask for gifts, it asks to give. When it can give no longer, it turns to anguish. Helen's suffering became very great. She bore with Adela the burden of dying, and with Dick the burden of remembrance.

And she too remembered. Every kiss, every touch, every word.

The hours of the night went by. When at last Helen moved, and rose from her chair, she stood by the door for a long time listening, her feet in the black shadow, her head bowed forward in the dusk that was mingled of the lamplight and the first beginnings of the day.

When she had stood listening for a long while, a bird chirped at one of the high windows. Helen trembled a little, then pushed the door and passed the threshold.

A greyish dimness came in through the small window that was under the roof. It looked like a mist, as it mixed with the shadows that clung about the raftered ceiling. The lamp on the dressing-table burned with a garish yellow flame. Its light reached across to the bed, but fell short of Adela's face.

Helen came near, kneeled down, and put her hand on Dick's, which had lost its warmth, and upon Adela's, which was cold.

After a breathless moment she hid her face and prayed.

She prayed for them all. For Adela—poor Adie—not her fault. How could it be her fault when she was made like that?—and we loved her —we did love her—poor, poor Adie. For Dick— he has been so hurt, don't hurt him any more

—please, please don't hurt him any more. For herself—that I may comfort—that I may help.

She prayed these childish phrases over and over. Not her fault—don't hurt him—let me comfort. O God—God—God——

All form was gone. Only the power that is within, the spirit which is man, beat at the immortal doors, cried to the Immortal Love.

And in the end there was light—something that shone—that answered,—an inflowing of life.

Helen leaned upon the bed, and rose unsteadily to her feet.

"Dick," she said very low, and he moved, showing her a face she scarcely knew.

"She is—gone," Helen said in a quivering voice. She put out her hand, and touched Adela upon the brow. The cold of death was there, but Helen's hand lingered in a sort of trembling tenderness, before she drew the sheet up high and smooth above the pillow and above Adela's dead face of peace. When it was done she turned towards Richard Morton, swaying.

"Dick," she said again, and her shaking hand found his, and drew him, until he came stiffly to his feet, and stood beside her. Her touch clung rather than compelled, and he obeyed its tremulous weakness. They passed the threshold; and the door was shut.

In the farther room the lamp was living upon the very last of its spent oil. It flickered, and the shadows leapt, it died, and they crowded in

upon the dying glow. Helen put out her hand
and turned the wick down.

For a moment the dark was all. Then she
went to the window, drew back the curtain that
hung there, unlatched the long glass door, and
flung it wide to the cold morning air.

Richard Morton moved past her as she drew
back. Without turning his head he went out
upon the verandah, and Helen followed. It
was dusk still, and there were no stars, but
it was not the darkness of the closely curtained
room. There was a greyness mixed with it, and
a faint shining light that awoke far off in the
east.

Helen watched the sky where the stars had
faded, and words from the gospel of Saint John
rose up in her mind. She saw them there like
slowly floating birds with tender, dawn-flushed
wings. " The light shineth in the darkness, and
the darkness comprehended it not."

" When you understand, it grows light," she
said under her breath.

She looked at Richard Morton, and her heart
yearned over him. If he were her child, she
could comfort him now. Was there no comfort
for the father of her child? The greyness increased, until the dark was gone. She saw his
haggard face, and the strained endurance with
which he met the day. In that moment her love
for him became pure agony. The need to speak,
to touch him, burned in her; but there were no

words to vex this stillness of the dawn. She took his hand, still chilly from Adela's touch, lifted it to her bosom, and held it there. Her heart beat against it. It grew warm, and closed on hers in a strong grip that hurt, and healed.

The light brightened in the east. They stood together and waited for the sun to rise.

THE END

CPSIA information can be obtained at www.ICGtesting.com
Printed in the USA
BVOW08*1817290716

457107BV00004B/15/P